Science and Apocalypse in Bertrand Russell

Science and Apocalypse in Bertrand Russell

A Cultural Sociology

Javier Pérez-Jara and Lino Camprubí

LEXINGTON BOOKS
Lanham • Boulder • New York • London

Published by Lexington Books
An imprint of The Rowman & Littlefield Publishing Group, Inc.
4501 Forbes Boulevard, Suite 200, Lanham, Maryland 20706
www.rowman.com

86-90 Paul Street, London EC2A 4NE

Copyright © 2022 by The Rowman & Littlefield Publishing Group, Inc.

All rights reserved. No part of this book may be reproduced in any form or by any electronic or mechanical means, including information storage and retrieval systems, without written permission from the publisher, except by a reviewer who may quote passages in a review.

British Library Cataloguing in Publication Information Available

Library of Congress Cataloging-in-Publication Data

Names: Pérez-Jara, Javier, author. | Camprubí, Lino, 1981– author.
Title: Science and apocalypse in Bertrand Russell : a cultural sociology / Javier Pérez-Jara and Lino Camprubí.
Description: Lanham : Lexington Books, [2022] | Includes bibliographical references and index.
Identifiers: LCCN 2022014210 (print) | LCCN 2022014211 (ebook) | ISBN 9781793618474 (cloth) | ISBN 9781793618498 (paper) | ISBN 9781793618481 (ebook)
Subjects: LCSH: Russell, Bertrand, 1872–1970.
Classification: LCC B1649.R94 P47 2022 (print) | LCC B1649.R94 (ebook) | DDC 192—dc23/eng/20220519
LC record available at https://lccn.loc.gov/2022014210
LC ebook record available at https://lccn.loc.gov/2022014211

About the Authors

Javier Pérez-Jara is a Faculty Fellow at Yale University's Center for Cultural Sociology and an Assistant Professor of Philosophy and Sociology at Beijing Foreign Studies University. He has held visiting teaching and research positions across the world, including the University of Cambridge, Stanford University, Yale University, Kyoto University, Kyoto Sangyo University, the University of Seville, the Aristotle University of Thessaloniki, the Taiwanese Fu Jen Catholic University, and Minzu University of China.

Among other publications, he is co-editor (with Gustavo Romero and Lino Camprubí) of *Contemporary Materialism: Its Ontology and Epistemology* (2022). His current teaching and research explore the theoretical and practical bridges between cultural sociology and philosophy.

Lino Camprubí is a Ramón y Cajal Researcher at the Universidad de Sevilla and PI of ERC-CoG DEEPMED. After graduate studies in Cornell, he obtained his PhD in UCLA in 2011. He has worked as a researcher at the UABarcelona and the MPIWG in Berlin, as a visiting lecturer at UChicago, and as a visiting researcher at IMERA in Marseille. He is co-PI of the research project IBEROT@C and PI of the ERC-CoG DEEPMED.

Camprubí is the author of *Engineers and the Making of the Francoist Regime* (2014) and *Los ingenieros de Franco* (2017), recipient of the ICOHTEC 2018 Book Prize. He has also co-edited *Technology and Globalization* (2018), *De la Guerra Fría al calentamiento global* (2018) and the special issue "Experiencing the Global Environment" (*SHPS,* 2018). He has co-edited an interdisciplinary book on the coronacrisis (*Sociedad entre pandemias,* 2021) and, together with Gustavo Romero and Javier Pérez-Jara, *Contemporary Materialism: Its Ontology and Epistemology* (2022).

To Leo & Adriano

Contents

Acknowledgments	ix
Introduction: The Wings of Icarus	1
1 The Dying Sacred Fire of Mathematics and Logic	27
2 World War I and the Dethronement of Science	65
3 The Tortuous Mazes of Mind and Matter	89
4 Lights and Shadows of Nuclear Death	119
5 The Vietnam War and the Judgment Day	165
Conclusion: The History of Humankind and the Rashomon Effect	185
Bibliography	201
Index	219
About the Authors	245

Acknowledgments

Writing a book is a convoluted way of getting into unpayable debts. A four-handed book doubles the personal debits acquired with loved ones who have endured and supported the process, as well as with friends and colleagues who have discussed ideas with each of the authors.

The introductory chapter and the chapter on nuclear weapons benefited immensely by Javier's discussion of previous drafts at Yale University's Center for Cultural Sociology during his visiting stay in the Fall Semester 2021–2022. He would like to thank all the Yale CCS's Fellows that gave him insightful feedback. And, in particular, we would like to thank Jeffrey Alexander for his encouragement and helpful feedback. Alexander's "strong program" in cultural sociology is one of the main intellectual pillars of this book.

Javier also discussed previous versions of the chapter on the Vietnam War at the University of Cambridge's Department of Sociology and the Centre of Governance and Human Rights in 2014 and 2015. A very early version was published at the Cambridge Centre of Governance and Human Rights's Working Paper Series. The chapter on the Great War was also presented at the University of London's Institute of Historical Research in 2015. Javier would like to express his most sincere gratitude to Patrick Baert (Cambridge University). Baert's generous guidance introduced Javier to the sociology of intellectuals several years ago, and without him, this book would never have seen the light. The chapters on the Great War and the Vietnam War have changed a lot since then, not the least thanks to very fruitful discussions in talks and conferences during his visiting research stays at Kyoto University (Summer 2017 and Winter 2018) and Kyoto Sangyo University (Fall Semester 2019–2020). He would like to thank Mizutani Masahiko and Kodama Satoshi (Kyoto University), and Fujino Atsuko, Ito Kimio, Piya Tom, and

Nohara Jun (Kyoto Sangyo University) for all their hospitality, encouragement, and wise comments.

The mind and matter chapter revisits some of the ideas of Javier's first book on Bertrand Russell (2014). The encouragement and inspiration of philosopher Gustavo Bueno, who passed away in 2016, still permeates that chapter and the rest of the book. This chapter was also presented at special seminars at Tokyo University (2017) and Hong Kong University (2018).

We presented the book's introduction and the chapter on mathematics at two different meetings at the Faculty of Philosophy of the Universidad de Sevilla in the spring of 2020. We thank specially José Ferreirós's help with some technical passages as well as with the general cultural perception of mathematics in the turn of the 20th century.

We would like to give a special thanks to Lexington's staff, particularly Jana Hodges-Kluck, who was always encouraging about this book, and led us through a review process which has improved and strengthened the final result in very important ways.

Introduction
The Wings of Icarus

This book provides a cultural-sociological analysis of the general themes of science, technology, utopia, and apocalypse through one of the most indisputable public intellectuals of the 20th century: Lord Bertrand Russell (1872–1970). The century through which Russell lived was a rather intense one. The world underwent rapid and profound changes. The scientific, political, economic, and moral landscape of Russell's late years hardly resembled that of his childhood. And Russell was not a passive witness. He intervened in some of these changes and their interpretations through innumerable writings, speeches, and social performances.

Aside of his undisputed contributions to analytic philosophy and philosophical logic, Russell commented on revolutionary developments happening in sciences as diverse as mathematics, physics, biology, and psychology. He was no less vocal on political and moral issues. Russell's image became associated with progressive political engagement. This brought him both fame and trouble, including ending up in jail twice, the last time as an aging man. In his crusade to transform public opinion, Russell fought for decriminalizing homosexuality, transforming education, women's suffrage, and sexual liberation. But perhaps his most renowned activist engagement was his militant pacifism during World War I and the Cold War. World War I consolidated Russell's fame. The Cold War internationalized it. The Einstein-Russell manifesto and his self-invested role as a pacifist mediator during the Cuban Missile Crisis made world news. From 1963 onwards, the Bertrand Russell Peace Foundation proclaimed as its objective no less than enforcing human rights and peace on a global scale. As part of that endeavor, in the so-called Russell Tribunal aimed to judge and condemn the war crimes committed by the United States and its allies in the Vietnam War.

Is there something new to say about Russell's life and work? As a leading philosophical and public figure, Russell's thought has received significant attention both during his life and after it. Most of this work deals with certain aspects or periods of Russell's thought. In the chapters that follow we engage with a vast literature specializing on Russellian topoi as diverse as logical atomism, logicism, theory of knowledge, atheism, views on education, psychology, anthropology, and nuclear war, among many others. But what we are after cuts across these bodies of literature. Our aim is to analyze Russell's changing valuations of the place of science and technology in society. This question, despite its profound implications in the developments of some of Russell's key ideas on politics, epistemology and ontology, has largely been missed by many Russell commentators. The reason is disciplinary. Analytic philosophers have usually accepted Russell's own categorization of his ethical and political writings as lying outside the field of strict philosophy. Focusing instead on Russell's ontological and epistemological works, these scholars have tended to disregard Russell's "humanistic" writings. On the other hand, moral philosophers, social scientists, and human-rights activists have tended to focus on Russell's ethical and political writings, often overlooking Russell's ontological and epistemological statements. Ironically, Russell himself contributed to the division of his interpreters. He did so not only through his own autobiographical reconstructions but also by digging the analytic-continental philosophy gap. After the abandonment of his idealist stage, Russell presented his ontology and epistemology as essentially supported on mathematical logic, physiology, physics, and psychology. In contrast, he famously dismissed a significant share of continental philosophy as arbitrary and lacking of scientific rigor. Sharing this view, some of Russell's interpreters have come to dismiss much of his own humanistic writings on politics and moral.

This specialization, while productive, risks missing substantive connections. One thinks of the Indian legend of the elephant and the blind: the authors who have only studied the philosophy of language or Russell's ethics would act, for example, like the blind man who clung to the trunk of the elephant, thinking, without knowing the other parts, that it was a snake. But the analogy is limited. The elephant in Russell's philosophy is a Lamarckian one, constantly mutating while preserving certain recognizable morphologies. We claim that something is gained when looking at Russell's thought as a changing system of ideas.

A few works do offer a larger picture. As in a multicursal maze, a variety of Ariadne's threads are available as guides through Russell's intellectual biography. Russell himself offered three main threads in the opening of his *Autobiography*: "Three passions, simple but overwhelmingly strong, have governed my life: the longing for love, the search for knowledge, and unbearable pity for the suffering of mankind." Two of Russell's biographers, Ronald Clark (1975) and Caroline Moorehead (1992), mainly focus on Russell's turbulent pursuits of his first and third passions, largely forgetting about the second.

On the other hand, analytic philosophers' insightful approaches to Russell often epitomize the focus on Russell's second passion. Anything outside epistemology and ontology is for them, as was for Russell himself, hardly worth philosophical attention. Introductory accounts of Russell's philosophy tend to be written by experts in analytic philosophy, and focus on Russell's "strict philosophy" (his second passion), including perhaps some rather uncritical excursions into his politics (two valuable examples, one a classic and one more recent, are Ayer 1971 and Broncano 2015). Ryan Allan's book on Russell (1988) is explicitly not a biography, but it does discuss Russell's ideas as they changed through the years. His focus, however, is decidedly on political and moral ideas, Russell's third passion.

To our knowledge, the main work that can successfully claim to have followed all of the three Ariadne's threads offered by Russell is the magnificent two-volume biography written by philosopher and biographer Ray Monk (1996 and 2001). Monk skillfully waves together an impressive array of sources into an insightful narrative which enables him to turn Russell's *Autobiography* upside down, revealing aspects of Russell's philosophical and personal life which were not obvious for Russell himself. As Monk admits and others have pointed out, however, his second volume, devoted to post-1920 Russell, goes a little too far in the way of a critique. At times, it gets closer to a "pathography" than would be desirable to understand some of the relevant events (Madigan 2003). Let us be clear, we completely agree with Monk in that Russell's thought and personal behavior was often fraught with internal contradictions. Many of Russell's friends and rivals noted during and after Russell's life that the great master of mathematical philosophy often abandoned all sense of rigor when discussing other philosophical and political topics. But reading Monk is hard to understand Russell's popular success in the second part of his life.

Russell contributed to the popularization of philosophy itself and of the persona of the philosopher. And this was an internal part of Russell's own conception of the duty of the philosopher. It is also one of the main concerns of the present book. Our book is not a biography. It attempts, however, to gauge Russell's throughout time and in a comprehensive way. Because we focus on Russell's ideas, we mention Russell's passionate private life only when it is relevant to understand his thought or the context of his public interventions. To put it more strongly: we are more interested in the many lives of Russell's ideas than we are in the life of Bertrand Russell. Nevertheless, we think that individuals' performances and their positionings play crucial roles in the diffusion of intellectual products (Baert 2011a, 2011b, 2012; Baert & Morgan 2017). Our object of study is Russell as a public intellectual. We do follow the chronological order of Russell's life to track his engagements with some of the main issues of the turbulent times he lived through and participated in. But, on occasions, we are comfortable with seeing ideas and the sociocultural factors that inform their mutual relationships as governing Russell's public utterances rather than the opposite. This is why we rely more on public discourse than on private correspondence—which we nevertheless use when relevant to our goals.

These demarcations still leave us with a vast array of materials and topics to navigate through. Of course, we do not claim to cover all of Russell's ideas and public engagements. The Ariadne's thread that guides our excursion onto Russell's labyrinthine intellectual pathway is formed by the mutual relationships between the ideas of science and technology, on the one hand, and utopia and apocalypse on the other. This thread enables us to discuss Russell's thought as an evolving whole, though one not exempt of synchronic and diachronic contradictions. In particular, the connection between Russell's second and third passions becomes clear: the epistemological foundations of knowledge often relate in interesting and complicated ways to imaginations of progress and decay in a world saturated by science and its products.

UTOPIA AND APOCALYPSE:
OUR APPROACH TO RUSSELL'S PUZZLE

Russell changed intellectual opinions almost as often as he changed wives. Both in *My Philosophical Development* (1959) and in his *Autobiography* (1951–1969), Russell presented many of these changes as "epiphanies" or "conversions". To name a few of those, Russell moved from the idealistic monism of his youth to a realism sustained in an ontological pluralism, from the objectivity of Moore's values to an ethical utilitarianism, and from a strong Platonism to the belief that mathematical equations are just mere tautologies. Alfred North Whitehead, Russell's collaborator and friend, joked that Russell's work was a Platonic dialogue in itself. Philosopher C. D. Broad was no less kind: "as we all know, Mr. Russell produces a different system of philosophy every few years" (for a review, see Pérez-Jara 2014). There were, it seems, "several" Bertrand Russells, at times even coexisting simultaneously and ready to provide their master with a more or less *ad hoc* position in the context of this or that particular discussion.

The point, however, should not be overdone. After leaving his youth's idealism (first Kantian and then Neo-Hegelian), Russell developed a series of philosophical theses that, in their main lines, remained more or less stable throughout his philosophical career. They revolved around empiricism, skepticism, realism, ontological pluralism, criticism of religions and superstitions, and the belief that physical and psychological sciences (with physiology as a necessary link between them) are the epistemological basis of our rational knowledge of the universe. On this last issue, however, lies the one schism within Russell's thought that motivates this book.

The early Russell viewed science as the mother of all intellectual and practical virtues; intellectually, science was a privileged form of knowledge destined to redeem humankind from a past (but still present) kingdom of darkness, repression, and evil represented by religion. Practically, technologies resulting from science's applications would bring unlimited progress and happiness to humankind. This narrative reached perhaps its zenith in his 1913 article "The Place of Science in a Liberal Education". In it, science and technology announced a new world of love, peace, and prosperity.

Russell never abandoned his rather simplistic view of religious historical and social phenomena. But he drastically revised his understanding of the relationships between science and progress. During the Great War, Russell became a peace activist. As many others, he pointed his finger at the unthinkable power that modern science and its technology bestowed upon 20th century tyrannies. His view of science as the almighty savior that would erase the darkness of ages gradually turned into ironic skepticism and a warning of the perils of unleashed science. This radical shift is most visible in Russell's article "Icarus or the Future of Science," published in 1924. There, he vigorously criticized the image of a future of human happiness guided by scientific discoveries. His own experiences with statesmen and governments, Russell argued, compelled him to fear that science would be used to promote the despotic power of dominant groups. As an answer to Haldane's use of the figure of Daedalus, the great mythical inventor of technological artifacts, Russell paralleled his view of human scientific and technological progress with the mythical story of Icarus. Using a pair of wings made out of wax by his father Daedalus, Icarus was destroyed by his own hubris and lack of sense, approaching the sun and choosing not to hear his father's warnings that it would melt his feeble wings. Similarly, this could be the destiny of scientifically developed human race. For the rest of his career, Russell insisted on the necessity of moral and philosophical reform to avoid a future of science-led apocalypse. His work is full of this dramatic opposition between bright and brilliant futures, with science and technology at the center of this unfolding and definitive drama.

An unexpected commonality thus waves Russell's intellectual career: the application of the binary opposition between utopia and apocalypse to the role of science and technology in human life. In Allan Ryan's words: "The world might become Paradise or hell according to human choice, and it was up to individuals to decide. It was noticeable that he hardly considered the possibility that things might go on in much the same way, a good deal sub-paradisiacal, but a good deal super-infernal" (Ryan 1988, 186).

The present book addresses the problem of why Russell consistently chose to ignore the possibility of a middle ground between utopia and apocalypse. This problem is related to others to which Russell scholars have raised. In a different part of his book, Ryan poses a different but related puzzle: Why did Russell, an icon of rationality, insisted in mobilizing religious language throughout his career? He did so when referring to mathematical practices as a "sacred fire," to political rivals as incarnations of absolute "evil," and to his own philosophical development as a series of "epiphanies". Most strikingly, he used the religious rhetoric of salvation and doom to condemn the irrational way of thinking that according to him religions had imposed for millennia.

Ryan's own answer is that this was a "rhetoric" that came "naturally to him" (Ryan 1988, 54). We believe, on the contrary, that it was much more than a rhetorical device (which it certainly was): Russell's radical binaries and semi-religious overtones served as a structure of meaning that organized some of his most influential philosophical ideas. This, moreover, helps explain the social success that some of these ideas enjoyed in a non-reductionistic way. Our goal is to explore why did these binary codes (utopia/apocalypse, good/evil, sacred/profane) come so naturally into Russell's writings and speeches, their relative independence of social and material factors, and their power of influence in the cultural and social world.

To that aim, we develop a multidimensional theoretical approach. Although ours is a cultural sociological analysis of Bertrand Russell as a dramatic intellectual, we equally draw from other disciplines, specifically history and history of science. And from philosophy. Because we want to emphasize that both cultural sociology and the history of science rest on philosophical assumptions. Philosophy grounds many of the ontological and epistemological discussions in both cultural sociology and cultural history of science—think of critiques of both holism and individualism, for instance. When the authors of scientific theories are not fully aware of the philosophical nature of some of their core assumptions—whether epistemological, methodological, or ontological—they risk overlooking inconsistences within those assumptions (Romero, Pérez-Jara, and Camprubí 2022). We try to make ours explicit. Philosophy also enables us, we hope, to place Russell's ideas within their own tradition and to discuss some of their virtues as well as their limits. We are particularly keen in pursuing the question of how the various parts of Russell's changing philosophical edifice relate to one another.

Philosophy informs our approach to the ancient epistemological problem of the relationships between the world and our knowledge of it. We acknowledge that scientific knowledge presupposes complex historical, technological, and sociocultural developments. Likewise, we are aware of the significant degree of contingency of many of these formations, along with their relationships to complex networks of political, economic, and ideological interests. As such, far from merely mirroring an absolute previous reality, sciences are always given at a human or "anthropic" scale (Bueno 1992). A scale that is supported on powerful symbolic attributions and a significant degree of epistemological distortion. The dream for ontological transparency in human knowledge is an epistemological fairy tale. Nevertheless, and without falling into naive realism, we also criticize the inverse myth of total ontological opacity. What we could call an anthropic matrix or anthropic illusion has fascinated thinkers from the radical Greek Sophists, Buddhist phenomenalists, and classical skeptics, all the way to the Nietzsche, the radical pragmatists, and most postmodern thinkers. A classical critique to these approaches is that, according to their own assumptions, they are unable to justify themselves.

There is no need for this simplistic binary between total ontological transparency and total ontological opacity. Throughout this book, we distance ourselves from realism, while introducing the concept of "reality's muzzle" to limit the excesses of constructivism and relativism. Such excesses lead to self-contradictory epistemologies—according to their own assumptions, these epistemologies are unable to justify themselves. We hold that several of the "anthropic realities" offered by scientific knowledge have important convergences and strong analogies with reality in itself (Romero, Pérez-Jara, and Camprubí 2022). If that is the case, we can assume ontological asymmetries against idealism and radical social constructivism. Political realities, for instance, imply biological, chemical and physical dimensions. Physical realities (such as nuclear explosions), on the contrary, do not have biological or social properties (Bunge 2010). Of course, sociocultural realities, for instance, are constantly influencing certain biological processes, and these ones, some chemical and physical realities. The current times make us all too aware of how political, economic and social decisions can either trigger or slow down climate change or the spread of the coronavirus. But such undeniable influences between ontological orders do not deny the asymmetrical relationships between them. Structural asymmetries separate our analysis from the flat-ontologies proposed by Actor-Network Theory, among others. Bruno Latour, for instance, called for studying ensembles of humans and non-human actants—say scientific instruments, ideas, unconscious psychological processes, ultraviolet light, social performances and famous speeches, geographical determinations, and diseases. These contingent relational assemblages would provide the world's ontological structure. While these flexible methodology enables flat ontologies to avoid both simplistic materialism and idealism, symmetrical relationism is a dangerous theoretical quicksand.

History of science, on its part, helps us to situate Russell within larger contexts of the late 19th and 20th centuries. There is a growing literature on how scientists, philosophers of science, science fiction authors, and the general public have relied on science and technology to imagine bright and grim futures (Rees and Morus 2019; Bud et al. 2018). Furthermore, as Sheila Jassanoff and others have argued, political anticipations of imagined futures shape scientific and political priorities (Jasanoff and Kim 2015). More generally, many historians of science of the past four decades have been very good at overcoming social reductionism and technological determinism and at tracing instead the interweaving between materialities and meanings in ways that emphasize their relative independence.

Exploring cultural symbols and meanings in all their "thickness," relative autonomy, and causal power of influence provides social and cultural theorizing and science studies with a middle ground between the respective reductionisms of materialism and idealism (Geertz 1973; Porter 2012). Cultural idealism holds the *absolute* independence of culture, which implies naively hypostatizing symbolic codes and actions. Some of Max Weber's approaches provide good examples. Cultural realism, in turn, postulates a no-less naive ultimately homologous relation between "mental representations" and "outside structures": Thrasymachus's definition of justice as the rule of the stronger is a good example of this. Reductionistic mechanism approaches symbolic and semiotic structures as secondary, epiphenomenal entities, fatalistically determined by material factors or by social structures and class struggle. And this from Thrasymachus all the way to many of Karl Marx's and Pierre Bourdieu's approaches.

Our approach, moving away from cultural idealism, naive realism, and reductionist materialism, holds that the "textual" or "ideal" dimension of culture constitutes a major moment in a complex imbroglio of a multidimensional interwoven series of determinations that cannot be reduced to each other.

This brings us to the three main specific theses which structure our book and to which different chapters of the book come back. First, the scientific and political events that Russell commented upon became socially significant or mere individual memories not by themselves and their intrinsic nature, but through complex and contingent processes of cultural codification and narration. Second, these codes and narratives, we argue with Jeffrey Alexander and others, often followed binary structures with millennia-long histories.

This gives a much deeper significance to Russell's otherwise unexplained rhetorical preferences. Finally, the success and social repercussion of public intellectuals such as Russell depends, rather than on the intrinsic quality or logical coherence of their ideas, on intellectuals' ability to connect their positionings to existing social codes, narratives, and emotional attachments (Baert 2012). As such, we strongly emphasize here the relative independence of the intellectual sphere: there is a great deal of contingency in both intellectuals' ideas and dramaturgical performances as well as in the sociocultural factors that allow their potential audiences to glorify or repudiate them.

In what follows, we elaborate further on each of these three theses and on how they inform our approach to Russell's changing understandings of science.

CONSTRUCTING ABSOLUTE EVIL

Russell himself, and many commentators after him, have argued that the intrinsic horrors of the First World War (and later the Second and the Cold War) were enough to curb optimist assumptions about the joint paths of scientific and moral progress. Russell and others did become increasingly skeptical about both the power of sciences to reconstruct reality and the role of techno-scientific progress in bringing peace, freedom, and justice to humankind. But considering this an immediate effect of the experience of evil would be a form of the naturalistic fallacy. As the likes of David Hume and G. E. Moore denounced, this fallacy consists in jumping from what ontologically *is* to the axiological *ought*. The naturalistic fallacy is common in mechanistic or deterministic theories of culture, and also one of the forms of realism we consider commonsensical but wrong. According to this view, the cultural categories of "good" and "evil" rise from the actual facts of social life in a more or less deterministic way. This is an illusion. Things and events *become* good or bad because of complex and contingent cultural processes of coding, signification, and narration. As such, good and evil are epistemological categories, not ontological ones (Alexander 2003). Good and evil as "ontological" categories could only be rescued in a phenomenological or correlationist sense (Pérez-Jara 2022). Depending on varying contexts and circumstances, the same or very similar events will be perceived as good and even salvific, or, alternatively, bad and even embodied evil. These processes are intertwined with multiple cultural spheres, from the obvious ones represented by religion, politics, and economics to the relatively autonomous discourses and narratives of different civil spheres around the world. Obviously, individual and group psychological factors tangled with cultural symbols also play an important role in the Gordian knot of evil. The problem of evil, therefore, demands a multidisciplinary approach (Effron and Johnson 2017).

That good and evil mean different things for different peoples is of course recognized by virtually all philosophers and social theorists. And yet, mechanistic explanations are still the preferred ones when discussing perceptions of 20th-century disgraces as incarnations of absolute evil. Russell scholars fall in this trap when retrospectively sympathizing with Russell's pacifism in World War I or condemning Russell's pacifism before World War II. They tend to be more divided on his late approach to the US as the "universal empire of evil". Some consider this to be an example of "common sense" (Broncano 2015, 25) and others a proof that Russell's political thinking was embarrassingly simplistic (Monk 2001). In all these occasions our question is prior. What were the cultural circumstances that turned these events into social traumas in the symbolic arena of which Russell was a part? (For the notion of "trauma" in the cultural sense that we will use it, see: Alexander 2001; Eyerman 2001, 2011; Eyerman, Alexander and Breese 2013.)

The two World Wars or the Vietnam War did not, in and by themselves, create collective heroic feelings or social traumas. This required lots of symbolic work. Reality can constrain symbolic attributions, but not in a direct way—we come back to the dialectic between "reality's muzzle" and "culture's symbolic plasticity" in the book's conclusion. There are two important corollaries to this argument which are worth making explicit. The first is that symbolic coding is not always a conscious or spelled-out process, as Jürgen Habermas seems to suggest. Many cultural processes through which some historical events *become* evil are invisible or unconscious even to the majority of social actors who contribute to their crystallization—and it is the task of social theorists to unearth these processes in their analysis. Russell was particularly good at making his thinking explicit, often in private letters. But both when invoking personal experience of the suffering of others or utilitarian calculations comparing greater and lesser evils, Russell's thought is full of implicit assumptions and biases that can be explained only by analyzing their wider cultural context.

The second corollary is that "evil" is in no way a secondary category with respect to "good". In traditional theological metaphysics of Greek inspiration, evil was often classified as the absence of the good. Essentialist or naturalist thinkers such as Plotinus and Saint Augustine are good examples of this tendency. But the approach persists in constructivist theories. Constructivist social scientists and philosophers regard the category of the "good" as a cultural product, not an absolute metaphysical reality. But they have often viewed "evil" as a mere deviation from socially constructed good values, broadly defined as the set of internalized norms and codes that make social equilibrium and sustainability possible. Even Talcott Parsons's structural functionalism of the mid-20th century, heavily inspired by Émile Durkheim's social theory, follows this tendency of downplaying the cultural weight of evil.

Regarding evil as a secondary or residual category misses the rich cultural and historical work of interpretation its construction requires (Alexander 2003). Russell oscillating attributions of science and technology as good and evil are best understood in a strong Manichean tradition in which both poles of the opposition are symbolically substantive. And the classics of social theory already refereed this Manichean tradition to ancient codes of thought. Durkheim, for instance, argued that modern moral and political codes are built upon millennial religious and mythical cultural structures. This thesis, to which the next section turns, inspires modern cultural sociology and our own theoretical framework of interpretation of Russell's legacy.

A SACRED DISENCHANTMENT

The early Russell mobilized the discourse of the Enlightenment and of Saint-Simonean and Comtean positivism: the advances of science announced a new era of reason with no place for mythical and religious thinking. Sociologist Max Weber contributed to solidify the identity between Modernity and what he called the "rationalization of the world". The process of rationalization consists in the growing replacement of past obscure traditional values and emotions with the transparent tools of scientific rationality. This rationality sheds its light (or casts its shadow, depending on the point of view), in all the cultural spheres, from government bureaucracies to the family. Although Weber tracked this rationalization introduced by modern capitalism back to its Calvinist theological roots, he thought that such roots ended up being incompatible with their former religious background, being eventually discarded. According to Weber, this sociohistorical process led to a "disenchantment of the world," a term he borrowed from Friedrich Schiller (Weber 1993). Modernity had buried religious-inspired categories distinguishing the profane from the sacred. But authors from sociologist Emile Durkheim to anthropologist Lévi-Strauss have argued that binary categories and other cultural structures link modern myths to archaic ones, so that millennial-old structures of meaning organized the way contemporary societies interpret the world (Durkheim 1995[1912]; Durkheim and Mauss 2010[1903]; Levi-Strauss 1974, 1975, and 1983). The very idea of historical progress which announced a disenchanted world followed the same mythical structure it claims to overcome (Josephson-Storm 2017).

This is also true for the thick variety of practices, instruments and results put under the umbrella of a single unified idea: modern science. Philosophers and historians have spelled out different contexts in which the idea of science has been bestowed with ancient mythical qualities, including in particular the prophetic and messianic character of the sacred as opposed to the social and ethical perils of the polluted and wicked profane (Walsh 2013). In this fight for modern science, the main global enemies were religion and metaphysics. The precedents of this opposition are already visible even before the ideas of religion and science acquired their contemporary form as institutionalized activities in the 19th century in 18th-century enlightened thinkers, who often presented their new natural philosophy as incompatible with both natural and revealed theology—for instance Baron d'Holbach's "system of nature," on which Russell relied to shape his own enlightened ideas.

Nevertheless, as historian Peter Harrison has argued, the modern terms of the conflict between science and religion and its status as a binary opposition were established in the 19th century (Harrison 2015). In Russell's own context, Great Britain, the "conflict thesis" appeared in a very specific moment of professionalization and institutionalization of science. According to historian Jaume Navarro, prominent members of the X-Club such as Thomas Henry Huxley, John Tyndall and Herbert Spencer would have felt the need of creating a global enemy for their new fragile community, rather new and divided by increasing specialization (Navarro 2017). Like national foundational myth makers, these scientists required a nemesis, a shadow against which to cast their lights. As elsewhere, and seemingly paradoxically, from the 19th century onwards the successful narrative of the modern technoscientific desacralization of the world was supported on mythical and religious categories.

In France, August Comte's famous "Law of Three Stages" presented modern science and technology as the main developers of the positive or scientific stage. This historical stage would overcome the previous metaphysical and theological ones. Comte nuanced this sharp division of world history, recognizing that, although in different proportions, the three stages of thinking could coexist in modern societies. But he (and, often to a larger state, his followers) held that science and technology would finally bring us a complete positive worldview, based on clear and transparent observations, experimentation, and logical comparisons (Bourdeau, Pickering, and Schmaus 2018).

In Germany, Marx famously held that modern industrial technologies, despite their role as instruments for the exploitation of workers, were also engines of the progress of history, helping to overcome past ages of primitive religious and magical thought (Marx 1963a [1867]; 1963b). In announcing a future redemption of an ancient sinful schism, Marx relied on Christian eschatology as much as on his own scientific socialism.

Once the cultural classification of science and technology as transparent activities called for spreading rationality over a world of shadows into the present and the future was fully available, it could take on pessimistic interpretations. Martin Heidegger, one of the most influential philosophers of the 20th century, identified modern "planetary technique" with the consummation of metaphysics. This "consummation" consists in the "ontification" of everything, forgetting "being" itself, and believing that calculative thinking exhausts the essence of everything "real". This process, Heidegger thought, started when the Greeks used the ideas of ποίησις and τέχνη to understand φύσις (Sheehan 2014). Although Heidegger's identification between modern techno-scientific thinking and the "consummation of metaphysics" is clearly contradictory with Comte's and Weber's ideas, these authors share the assumption that modern rationality has expelled the sacred and the divine from the realm of modern culture. If Weber, borrowing the term from Friedrich Schiller, talked about a "disenchantment of the world," Heidegger, following Hölderlin, talked about "the flight of the gods". These were just poetic ways of stating that scientifically and technologically-driven Modernity had buried the sacred, i.e., all ontological dimensions of reality that escape exhaustion by rational calculative thinking. Against the dangers of this kind of modern rationality, Heidegger held in the famous *Der Spiegel* interview of 1966 that "only a god can save us" (Sheehan 2009).

Despite their important differences with Heidegger, the members of the Frankfurt School approached the modern techno-scientific world in similar terms. Max Horkheimer's and Theodor W. Adorno's theories of "instrumental reason," Herbert Marcuse's "one-dimensional man," and Jürgen Habermas's thesis of "technology and science as ideology," in one way or another, agree in expelling the sacred and the profane from the domains of the modern techno-scientific world (Marcuse 1991[1964]; Habermas 1968). In contrast to Heidegger, and excepting Horkheimer, these authors did not hope for a return of the sacred and the divine. Adorno's and Horkheimer's *Dialektik der Aufklärung* illustrates our argument. Through the thesis that "myth is already Enlightenment, and Enlightenment reverts to mythology," *Dialektik* exposes the paradox that the Enlightenment's attacks to religion end up being utterly mythological (Adorno & Horkheimer 2002, xviii).

But all these authors did agree that modern techno-scientific thinking is an oppressive and simplistic approach to the human world that should be under critical theory's severe scrutiny. Habermas, for instance, held that the ideology of science and technology has displaced all previous ideologies, and, specifically, the religious and mythical ones: "the older mythic, religious, and metaphysical worldviews [that addressed] the central questions of men's collective existence [such as] justice and freedom, violence and oppression, happiness and gratification (. . .) love and hate, salvation and damnation" cannot longer be asked (1968, 96).

The narrative of the technoscientific expulsion of the sacred and the divine thus restored the ancient mythical binary between the sacred and the profane. Historical developments in the sciences do not speak for themselves: they always require an interpretation. And the historicist storytelling came to identify "modernity" with European science and progress (Daston 2006, 2016). Some astonishing technical advances in certain theoretical and practical disciplines might make this decision understandable. They do not, however, justify the salvific overtones attributed to an alleged new epoch of science with a capital S. This logical leap borrowed already existing oppositions, as it often happens when new ideas or institutions struggle to make for themselves a social and political niche (Alexander 2003). In a view that has crossed continents and epochs, science is the new gospel, and scientists the chosen prophets to mediate between its powers and humankind (for some examples: Elshakry 2007; Kendrick 2012; Farrell 2017).[1]

The sacred and the profane, the pure and the polluted, the salvific and the apocalyptic, messianic heroes and their diabolical enemies are all alive and well in technologically-driven societies (Douglas 1966). The 20th century begun with epistemologically optimistic movements such as logical positivism, descriptive phenomenology, and classical sociology. It ended with hermeneutics, postmodernism, and radical social and scientific constructivism, all of which revolve around the impossibility of accessing reality in its own terms. Politically, the dream of human progress brought by science, technology and democratic values was constantly challenged by dark nightmares of total warfare, tyranny, and environmental disasters.

The transition between these dimensions of temporality was poetically coded by the ancient Romans in the figure of the god Janus. And like this ancient deity, intellectuals of the 20th century have looked at opposite sides: barbarism and human progress, a golden age and an imminent apocalypse (Alexander 2013). The *ethos* of this dual and paradoxical understanding of the 20th century still sheds light on our present day. Public figures such as Bruno Latour, Noam Chomsky, Steven Pinker, Byung-Chul Han, Sam Harris or Greta Thunberg paint the world in bright or grim colors. This is partly a product of intellectuals' individual optimistic or pessimistic tendencies organizing their selective memory or confirmation biases. Optimists focus on astonishing achievements in science, technology and cultural progress in terms of life expectancy, literacy rates, rights for formerly oppressed social groups, and decline in world violence. Pessimists stress new forms of unprecedented totalitarian control, warfare, genocide and environmental catastrophes. But the problem runs much deeper. It is not a matter of a psychological tendency to cherry-pick some events over others. The real issue is that a given historical event—a revolution, a war, a scientific discovery, a technical invention—always gets interpreted through stable cultural structures of meaning that precede it.

This is not to say that symbolic structures of meaning are *a priori* or fatally imposed through the ages, as in some kind of cultural Kantianism without a metaphysical transcendental subject. As when discussing the relative independence of culture regarding reductionism and idealism, we also embrace a middle ground between historicism and structuralism. We recognize the values of the extremes but also their pitfalls. Claude Lévi-Strauss was right in that certain structures of meaning seem common to all cultures; binary codes between sacred-good and profane-evil, for instance, can be more or less simplistic and radical depending on the "social glue" that holds groups together. That said, these cultural structures of meaning do not boycott agency; rather, they make it possible. Social actors are not *mediums* through which the *spirits* of ancient cultural structures (or the logic of their respective fields, as in Bourdieu) speak up. They are also not creating Abrahamic gods. Against these extremes, Alexander and Jason Mast have emphasized the transcendental agential importance of social performances and their contingency—in opposition to the traditional idea of ritual, where the outcome is predetermined beforehand (Mast 2012; Alexander and Mast 2016).

Binary codes pervade and structure a significant part of social action and meaning. Nevertheless, through history new cultural structures of meaning also emerge (such as some of the ones around the most abstract elaborations from science and philosophy, unthinkable in simpler societies). Bertrand Russell reflected on realities that were new to his age, such as industrialism, quantum mechanics, and analytic philosophy. But, structuring several of Russell's reflections on these novelties, we still find ancient binaries between the pure and the polluted, the utopian and the apocalyptic. Crucially, we want to argue that the sharp binaries that structure public discourse in general, and Russell's public discourse in particular, are *powerful* in an undeniable way (Alexander 2011). "Symbolic power" is at times opposed to "real" or "factual" power. Even Max Weber, one of the fathers of political sociology, offered a scrawny definition of power as the factual ability to carry out one's wishes against the will of others. Weber's insistence on "legitimacy," true, nuanced his otherwise reductionistic definition of power. "Legitimate power" implies a powerful symbolic dimension. But Weber offered little insight to clarify it, usually focusing instead on the "factual" power implied by violence and coercion. Michel Foucault's and Bourdieu's views on power, despite their apparent complexity and nuances, and extraordinary influence in sociological theorizing, are not less reductionistic and simplistic: they only capture one of the multiple dimensions of power. This could be seen as an example of the consequences of starting from the wrong philosophical assumptions.

According to some accounts, philosopher Ortega y Gasset exclaimed that "governing is not pushing!" But even when it is, the brute power of violent pushes would be hardly effective without symbolic attributions. In the drama of social life, myths, legends, and narratives carry with them a hypnotic and magnetic power, producing strong emotional attachments in their receptors. This helps explain consent and voluntary compliance, but also the fanatic desire of killing or dying in the name of the wishes of the political or religious rulers—as well as the desire of opposing them through violent revolution and terrorist attacks, or by means of pacific civil performances. This also helps explain why contenders in wars for symbolic interpretation can still have power even if, after losing an election or a battle, they do not have access to governing institutions, economic means of production, or military force. A multidimensional conception of power ought to incorporate the role of performative power and emphasize that power is much more than a top-down relationship (Bueno 1991).

BERTRAND RUSSELL AS A DRAMATIC INTELLECTUAL

The last question we want to address in this introduction comes rather naturally at this point of the discussion: What is the role of concrete intellectuals amidst the powerful symbolic performances, codes and narratives that form the backbone of our cultural lives? When trying to influence public opinion or political decision-makers, Russell liked to present himself as a "private man". By this he meant that he had not the material power of party representatives or world leaders. But on several occasions of his life, he became well aware of his own symbolic power. "I find," Russell confided with his characteristic irony, "that the whiter my hair becomes the more ready people are to believe what I say" (2011[1960], 80). Despite being considered one of the most important influential intellectuals of the 20th century (Harrison 1989), Russell, as many other English-speaking thinkers and agitators, despised the notion of the intellectual. "I have never called myself an intellectual," he is said to have stated, "and nobody has dared to call me one in my presence. I think an intellectual may be defined as a person to have more intellect than he has, and I hope this definition does not fit me" (Collini 2002, 210). Against Russell's own opinion, in this section, and in the rest of the book, we pursue the making of Bertrand Russell as a powerful dramatic intellectual.

Once again, we embrace a middle ground—perhaps safer, but certainly more productive than sticking to an *a priori* alternative in a false dilemma.

Holism and individualism have both their grains of truth. Their respective pitfalls, however, should be avoided in favor of more nuanced understandings of how individuals become active participants within their wider contexts of symbolic production and attribution. Such participation, as we have stressed, often involves a significant degree of unpredictable contingency. Among privileged social actors that contribute to this process, we find the intellectuals. In pre-state societies, usually shamans were the ones in charge of the task of configuring social maps of chaos and order, impurity and purity, profane and sacred. More complex societies require more complex systems of coding. Priests and prophets first did the work, and then poets, theologians and the first historians. For millennia, these key social actors planted the seeds through which "intellectuals," in the late-19th century sense of the word, would rise (Alexander 2016). Therefore, although the figure of the public intellectual is a relatively new cultural phenomenon, it draws from millennial structures of meaning.

Moreover, while at its origins the Dreyfusan notion of "intellectual" was limited to left-wing writers, the notion has been extended to all social actors able to organize the relationships between ideas and events that wave the social fabric (Gramsci 2011; Camprubí 2020). Intellectuals, in their broadest sense, become public intellectuals when they jump to prominent social stages where they, as dramatic actors, exercise their power through their *performances*.[2] And sooner than later public intellectuals find themselves trapped in social dramas in which audiences, far from being passive receptors of stories, very often impose their own decisions and judgments, sometimes in an unpredictable way, as we will see through several key examples of the 20th century. The role of intellectuals, as dramatic social actors, is thus constrained by their audiences as well as by their means to reach those audiences.

Individual intellectuals cannot hope to situate themselves at the center of cultural symbolic attributions by their own means. They need access to stages on which to perform. Intellectuals necessitate to go through the gatekeepers of the means of symbolic production, including media and other institutions. The man of flesh and bone behind the cultural construction of "Marx" as a totem (one that embodies either good and salvation or evil and apocalypse) only reached large audiences through, among other means, the organization of the First and Second International, and later mass political parties (Alexander 2016).

Dramatic intellectuals' audiences are rarely homogeneous, but they tend to group around binaries which help glue their group identities in opposition to those of other groups. It won't come as a surprise to anyone with a scant interest in history, religion or politics that the social success of ideas is far from being explained only by their logical quality or coherence (Baert 2012). Simplistic oppositions and ideological packages sell well.

Sophisticated audiences attentive to philosophical complexities tend to be smaller than those attracted by simple and compelling narratives supported on Manichean binaries. Social ideas are much more than pure logical products; they inspire love, hate, fear, hope, and anxiety. The simpler the ideas, the stronger the emotional attachments they gather around them. Thus the pervasive success of well-defined binaries between the sacred-good and the profane-evil. In this fascinating and often tortuous weaving of the tapestry of social drama, the construction of meta-adversaries is usually a key element in the success of dramatic intellectuals. These meta-adversaries can of course have different masks: paganism, the political left, imperialism, the industrial civilization, fascism. But all of them have in common to gather heterogeneous groups with different interests and ideas into meta-enemies that give the impression, to the audiences that are consuming these narratives, of an unbreakable unified embodiment of profanity and evil. Throughout his long life, Russell constructed several meta-adversaries as the unholy bringers of apocalypse.

In the cultural process of providing master stories of social transformation, most intellectuals just become totemic mirrors reflecting pre-existing narratives of sacred-good and profane-evil. Charismatic political and religious leaders and famous journalists also fulfill some of these functions. They navigate social anxieties. On occasions, however, the most successful intellectuals also bring some new ideas, analyses and recipes—or at least they do so in the collective imaginary of a significant part of their audiences. By doing that, they move the conversation, add symbolic complexities, and, more likely, displace the binary oppositions structuring civil discourse (Alexander 2006). These performers create powerful intellectual and emotional attachments among their audiences. They can become popular heroic figures. In the collective imaginaries of their audiences, intellectuals raise above the mortals. They become meta-characters of the social life. They can, though, fall from grace. Dramatic intellectuals tend to play all or nothing. Their dramaturgy usually includes presenting themselves as saviors of a society facing absolute evil. They narrate social aspects as unbearable civil deficits of their national societies and inspire civil repair and justice through a set of salvific-sacred prescriptions. They call for a specific form of social action as the only means of avoiding immeasurable danger. Either you follow dramatic intellectuals' prescriptions, or you automatically become a passive or active accomplice of the forces of darkness. This helps explain intellectual's preferred choice of literary genre. Philip Smith (2005) has linked Northrup Frye's archetypical narratives to social action. Romance inspires reform, comedy and irony civil dissent, and apocalyptic and utopian narratives legitimate strong political actions, be it the way of defending regimes against their enemies or completely transforming them. Notwithstanding common combinations of genres, dramatic intellectuals have overwhelmingly privileged utopian/apocalyptic codes and narratives.

Despite their warnings of coming apocalypse, or even total annihilation, dramatic intellectuals also present themselves as forces of hope: they point the way towards a future Arcadia, Camelot or earthly Valhalla. They narrate the present as the hinge between utopia and apocalypse, total disaster and salvation. Intellectuals' uses of these binaries vary in their degree of radicality. And this depends partly on their personality and psychological situation. But there is also a specifically crucial cultural side to their performances. In Alexander's words:

> When intellectuals create narratives that juxtapose heroic protagonists with dangerous antagonists, the tension is portrayed not only as social struggle but as storied plot. Sacred and profane binaries thus become dramatic, energized by all or nothing battles that decide our shared human fate. (Alexander 2016, 344)

This general framework fits Russell perfectly. It also resituates some of the protests made by followers of Russell's more philosophical works. Monk, for instance, starts the second volume of his monumental Russell's biography declaring that Russell

> did *not* bring to politics the qualities that made him a great philosopher and logician. His best philosophical writing is subtle, nuanced, and unafraid of complexity . . . In most of the journalism and political writing that he produced in the second half of his life, however, these qualities are absent, replaced with empty rhetoric, blind dogmatism and a cavalier refusal to take the views of his opponents seriously. The gulf in quality between Russell's writings on logic and his writings on politics is cavernous. The question that must be raised, therefore, is why he abandoned a subject of which he was one of the greatest practitioners since Aristotle in favor of one to which he had very little of any value to contribute. (Monk 2001, 6)

Monk goes on to mention love, financial needs, and the shock of Ludwig Wittgenstein's philosophy as possible culprits of Russell's departure from philosophical rigor. While Monk's disappointment is understandable, describing the problem as one of expertise misses the point: Russell was willing to pay the price to become a public intellectual. The intellectual sphere is relatively independent from other cultural structures of meaning, such as logical and internal coherence. Entering this sphere often demands the sacrifice of logical coherence, nuance and philosophical complexity on the altar of public diffusion and collective emotional attachments.

Therefore, at times, Bertrand Russell the philosopher appeared to his contemporaries and later commentators as rather different from Bertrand Russell the public intellectual. But the divide cannot be located in a certain moment of Russell's biography or limited to certain parts of this thought. As the chapters below show, both Russells coexisted in different degrees from the onset and cut across Russell's system of thought. In his 1914 essay "Mysticism and Logic," for example, Russell built a radical binary to distinguish the forces of light from the "perverse" forces of dark in the history of philosophy—a distinction he had used before and would abuse in his famous *History of Western Philosophy*. Science versus religion, scientific philosophy vs mystical philosophy, logical atomism versus logical holism, skepticism versus dogmatism, tautologism versus Platonism, and other radical binaries structured Russell's metaphysics and epistemology for decades, as we will explore in the chapters of this book. As such, we do not agree with the extended opinion according to which Russell's binaries where more radical when discussing ethics and politics than ontology and epistemology.

Russell drew a sharp distinction between philosophy and politics and, as most non-theist thinkers, he explicitly limited utopian and apocalyptic dilemmas to the world of humans. "To conceive the universe," he wrote, "as essentially progressive or essentially deteriorating, for example, is to give to our hopes and fears a cosmic importance which may, of course, be justified, but which we have as yet no reason to suppose justified" (Russell 1913). Russell's distinction between "pure philosophy" and political and ethical thought certainly constrained—though by no means devalued—his use of simplistic binaries when discussing ontological or epistemological problems.

Some of Russell writing on ethics and politics raises well beyond simple Manichean dichotomies. The degree to which Russell sacrificed nuances and consistency in his public performances depended more directly on the larger context of his performance, intended audiences, and the media he used: from esoteric books to more exoteric TV interviews, newspaper articles and street speeches. What we want to stress now is that simplified positionings on certain social stages allowed Russell's performances to reach larger audiences. This was not necessarily a result of a conscious strategy—although at times it clearly was. On many occasions it was just something in between. Dramatic intellectuals play an agential role shaping a culture which at the same time is shaping them. Even when they strategize, intellectuals are very often hypnotized by the magnetic power of the most prominent codes and narratives that surround them. Even as meta-characters of the social life, intellectuals are not above the "rules" of culture.

Following his self-declared third passion ("unbearable pity for the suffering of mankind") led Russell to devote many of his best energies to an intellectual dramaturgy of the kind we have described above. He became a totem for several movements throughout his life, embodying the symbolic representations of the hopes and fears conveyed in his own narratives. The sociologists of intellectuals Patrick Baert and Alan Shipman (2012) distinguish three ideal-types of public intellectual—authoritative, professional, and embedded intellectuals. Russell became an authoritative intellectual in that he gained for himself vertical authority and seized the Papist prerogative of speaking *Urbi et Orbi*—to the city and to the world. At a time in which only a small percentage of the Western population received higher education, Russell's impressive number of intellectual interventions on many different topics, together with his distinctive public charismatic qualities, enabled him to engage in some of the main symbolic battles of his time.

Russell's interventions were obviously controversial. As such, their symbolic power needs to be gauged against that of the ideas he fought against. Rom Harré (1993) employs "evolutionary logic" to explain the diffusion of ideas in an ecology of intellectual products struggling for survival and dissemination. This "logic" is more Lamarckian than it is Darwinian, because ideologies constantly change and adapt to new circumstances (both material and symbolic) to survive and succeed. This furnishes intellectual positionings with a permanent element of negation and confrontation.

Baert (2011b) puts it clearly: "most intellectual movements arise at the expense of others, not only because a limited number of such movements can co-exist but also because intellectual currents tend to define themselves in opposition to what preceded them." What this means from our cultural sociological approach is that if intellectuals' staging fails, counter-performances are likely to emerge and undermine their legitimacy (Alexander 2011, 2–4). Russell's efforts to position himself and his ideas in the polemical context of his time were not homogeneously successful, but on certain occasions they were undeniably so.

Positioning theory is important for our book. When we talk about how Russell positioned himself in this way or in this other, we use the term mainly in Rom Harré's and, more recently, in Patrick Baert's sense (Harré 1993; Baert 2017, 2012, 2011a, 2011b). Positioning theory fits in the general performative framework of Austin's speech-act theory, whereby language is not only used to assert things, but also to do things. Positionings inside the intellectual sphere belong to these kinds of uses of language. Nevertheless, we employ positioning theory, adapting it to our general cultural-sociological framework, which stresses the relative independence of the intellectual sphere against any kind of reductionism to social structures and institutional struggles.

Among Russell's many positionings on the role of science and technology for humanity's future, the most striking one is his shift from utopian to apocalyptic. Such repositioning entailed risks and made Russell loose important protectors and patrons—most notably, his opposition to World War I, what he would later narrate as an industrial war, got him out of Cambridge. However, Russell was able to turn this to his favor and consolidate his fame as an intellectual. There are several factors relevant for spreading the resonance of intellectual interventions, such as getting access to the relevant media in a context of crisis which predisposes audiences to emotionally connect with promising ideas (Baert 2011b). And we say this in a non-structural, deterministic way: there are often social crisis without crisis of values and vice versa (Bueno 2010).

Russell made many enemies along his life, but also remained well connected to publishers, propagandists, and was ready to make alliances with public figures such as H. G. Wells or Albert Einstein, and with political leaders, ranging from the British socialists and the CIA to Ho Chi Minh's Viet Cong—needless to say, these required compromises and focusing on symbolic commonalities rather than on differences. Also, throughout his life, Russell was able to connect with the fears, anxieties, and hopes of large chunks of the Western populations, presenting himself as a salvific force against imminent evils.

Russell's intellectual authority regarding science and technology depended to a great extent in the role of science in the making of his public persona. Science was both the object of many of Russell's interventions and what made people listen. As such, the history of Russell the public intellectual is part of larger shifts in scientists' and philosophers' public engagement. In places like revolutionary France or industrializing Prussia, it was expected from savants to participate in public life not only as experts but also as engaged citizens. By the late 19th century, increasing specialization and public scrutiny had an important role reinforcing ideals which would become in the 20th century: technicality, disengagement, and a value-free approach to scientific problems (Shapin 2008; Porter 2009). Far from a retreat from public life, this armed scientists with a powerful tool to gain political authority.

On several occasions throughout his public career, Russell insisted that what made scientists able interlocutors to both national and world leaders was that science itself was politically neutral. This discourse on science and politics drew from a long tradition which was especially strong from World War I to the early 1960s, in the years of the Vietnam War (Schroeder-Gudehus 2016). In many other occasions, however, Russell encouraged scientists to become partisans and defend the view or the country he considered indispensable to save civilization. Of course, Russell self-identified more often as a philosopher than as a scientist. But one of the very specific kind practicing "scientific philosophy" and justified his own political engagements using "science" as a totem—in this strategy he had an unlikely partner: Henri Bergson (Somsen 2020).

Russell became the very icon of the philosopher—an icon repeated in the cover of most of his late books and many books about him. And he did much to rejuvenate, sometimes against the analytic tradition he had helped to build, the image of the philosopher overlooking humankind from a watchtower of wisdom and compassion. In a world full of inevitable distortions, "the supreme duty of the philosopher" was to show the way towards the best-available interpretations (Russell 1959a). Russell had the self-invested responsibility of filtering the world of his day to his contemporaries. Starting with his own self-representation, he was much more than a witness of the development of science and technology. He contributed to the cultural perception of 20th-century science and technology, weaving them into wider cultural networks of meaning.

STRUCTURE OF THE BOOK

This book combines a chronological and a thematic organization. While our goal is to track the overall trajectory of Russell's views regarding the utopian promises and apocalyptic threats of science and technology, this takes us to the different cultural spheres in which this process took place. This reveals new connections as well as discontinuities and arrhythmias. That Russell aimed to build a systematic approach to the world of his time does not mean that he was always successful. Discovering mismatches and incoherent developments enables us to delve more deeply in the limitations and lessons of his project. Chapters are relatively independent. Although they might be best read together, each of them provides a self-contained analysis of an important moment of Russell's evolving thoughts on science, technology, and the fate of human civilization.

Chapter 1 starts from the beginning: the making of Russell's wings of Icarus. It traces his early confidence in the power of science and technology through his own evolving perception of the work he and others were doing in mathematical logic and the philosophy of mathematics. Inspired by mathematical discoveries totally incompatible with his early Neo-Hegelian worldview, Russell embraced a realist and pluralist metaphysics supported on updated scientific knowledge and heavily influenced by Enlightenment and British empiricism. On his new approach, though, logic became the root of true scientific and philosophical knowledge. Russell kept this epistemological ideal until the end of his life, even after his rejection of logicism and Platonism.

Chapter 2 is not about World War I; it is about the sources of Russell's symbolic interpretation of this war. In particular, we ask how did the perception of the war contribute to Russell's increasing skepticism about the salvific powers of science and technology, which now he often described in a rather apocalyptic language. Russell's famous "conversion" from Boer imperialist to pacifist did not at the beginning affect his views on science and technology. Russell's shift in this regard was the product of later experiences and debates which then led to retrospective reconstructions of his own repositioning. Russell narrated the events of the Great War in strong traumatic terms. As if the Janus-faced Russell were a coin, the cultural interpretation of the Great War flipped it over: the face looking at the future no longer was expecting a coming Golden Age produced by the discoveries of science and technology. Rather, his gaze was now submerged into an apocalyptic view of the times to come.

The next chapter deepens into Russell's philosophy of science and scientific ontology. It does so by delving into Russell's epistemology of physics and psychology, on the one hand, and ontology of mind and matter, on the other, as developed mostly in the interwar period. For almost all of Russell's philosophical career, mind and matter provided reality's structure (i.e., the "the furniture of the world"). Conversely, psychology and physics (with physiology as the epistemological link between them) constituted for Russell the scientific pillars of our knowledge of the universe. But both in his realist and empiricist epoch and after embracing neutral monism, Russell was haunted by skepticism and idealism regarding the existence of the external world and the fallibility of sciences. Moreover, his psychological understanding of society and politics gradually curtailed any hopes he may have entertained on the uses of scientific knowledge for the betterment of human life.

Chapter 4 traces Russell's evolving thought on nuclear weapons from a time when they were only a distant imagination to the 1960s, when their power and numbers announced the imminent destruction of human civilization—or at least so thought Russell. Russell's nuclearization of political discourse provides rich examples of the power of sociotechnical imaginaries in the making of cultural traumas.

In the fifth and last chapter we dive into one of Russell's most controversial interventions, the International War Crimes Tribunal. The chapter explores the main sociocultural factors through which Russell contributed to the process of narration and signification wherein a good portion of the Western public came to perceive the Vietnam War as one of the most traumatic events of the 20th century.

The conclusion is a reflection on how some of the book's main findings may point towards lessons which might be helpful to interpret current understandings of the cultural analysis of ideology. The main question is about the strengths and limitations of the categories of utopia and apocalypses when imagining historical pasts and futures.

NOTES

1. The sacredness of allegedly disenchanted technique has received both scholarly and popular attention. Think of Alejandro Jodorowsky's comic books *The Metabarons* (1992–2003) and *The Technopriests* (1998–2006), which ironizes with "techno-bishops" and the "techno-Vatican". More recently, the best-selling PS4 video game *Horizon Zero Dawn* depicts technology as acquiring sacred or profane dimensions depending on different communities.

2. Starting out just as a theater-specific metaphor (Burke 1974[1941]; Schmidt 2004) the "performative turn" fully flourished in the 1990s to become a general methodological principle for understanding human behavior in a variety of social sciences. The performative approach can also be applied to understand the concept of "pure science" as the kind of language that is allowed in some social contexts in specific historical situations (Bud 2014).

Chapter One

The Dying Sacred Fire of Mathematics and Logic

In 1953 Russell published a collection of short stories containing imagined nightmares haunting relevant real or fictional characters. Among them was Dr. Squarepunt, an "eminent mathematician" whose admiration for the physicist Sir Arthur Eddington was tempered by "the mystical, cosmic powers which Sir Arthur ascribed to the number 137" (Russell 1953a). Eddington advanced in the late 1920s a theory by which the arithmetic powers of "137" became physical, demonstrating, he hoped, both the total numbers of protons in the universe and a solid ground for both cosmology and physics. This was for many, including the elderly Russell, an extremely Platonic interpretation of mathematics, by which mathematical entities such as numbers inhabit an abstract or ideal world while at the same time ordering and governing the empirical one.

In Dr. Squarepunt's vision, he is surrounded by numbers exhibiting physical characteristics in accordance with their abstract properties: odd numbers were male, even numbers female, and "the squares were tiles, the cubes were dice . . . and the perfect numbers had crowns". The mathematician, together with 137, engages in a dispute with the rest of the numbers. Numbers, led by no less than Pi, proclaim their Platonic eternity. In defense of this metaphysics, they physically attack the mathematician. After a moment of panic, Squarepunt recovers his nerve and exclaims "You are only Symbolic Conveniences!" The numbers then disappear "and, as he woke, the Professor heard himself saying, 'So much for Plato!'"

What Russell was ridiculing in 1953 were his own Pythagorean beliefs of some decades earlier. Since he always viewed mathematics as having a central role in science, mapping Russell's changing views on the meaning of mathematics is crucial for the purposes of this book. Moreover, mathematics was, together with logic, at the center of the most crucial transformation of Russell's ontology and epistemology: the move from holistic monism to atomistic pluralism. From his childhood years, Russell became fascinated by the necessity of geometrical proof, which he took as an example of the explanatory and transforming powers of scientific rationality. It was precisely to understand the grounds of this logical necessity that he decided to become a mathematician.

As his early Christian faith receded, he embraced first the Kantian view of geometry and arithmetic as intuitions given by the transcendental forms of our spatial and temporal perceptions. The rise of non-Euclidian geometries in the mid-19th century, however, had greatly undermined the transcendental interpretation of geometry. In his years as a Cambridge student of mathematics, Russell approached the so-called British idealists in their neo-Hegelian rejection of the objective independence of mathematical truths and in their understanding of logic as dialectical metaphysics. The philosophical project behind Russell's first publications built on allegedly insurmountable contradictions within mathematics in order to reach a monist synthesis.

After completing his mathematical education at Cambridge, however, Russell abandoned neo-Hegelianism. Along with many other thinkers of the time, Russell became convinced that the foundations of mathematics were to be sought in formal logic. Until the late 1920s, Russell thought that logic had to be understood as a synthetic a priori science studying all the kinds of structures there are. This made logic turned into the anti-monist science by excellence.

Russell's early logicism was a realist program. He understood the logicist imperative as a Pythagorean engagement with the objective reality represented by mathematical relations. In the period from about 1900 to the mid-1910s, Russell's views were much closer to Platonism than they were to the conventionalism his Dr. Squarepunt vindicated in 1953. Russell had understood mathematics as the gateway to a Platonic reality that provided shelter against worldly chaos. This is the view of an article he wrote in 1902 but was first published in 1907:

> In a world so full of evil and suffering, retirement into the cloister of contemplation, to the enjoyment of delights which, however noble, must always be for the few only, cannot but appear as a somewhat selfish refusal to share the burden imposed upon others by accidents in which justice plays no part. Have any of us the right, we ask, to withdraw from present evils, to leave our fellow-men unaided, while we live a life which, though arduous and austere, is yet plainly good in its own nature? When these questions arise, the true answer is, no doubt, that some must keep alive the sacred fire, some must preserve, in every generation, the haunting vision which shadows forth the goal of so much striving. (Russell 1907)

We will return to that 1902 text. What matters now is that this "sacred fire" was fueled by Russell's confidence on the power of logic as the science of relational structures, and on the ideal existence of mathematical entities.

By the early 1920s, however, Russell had already rejected Platonism and embraced a view of mathematics as tautological conventions. While some weaker version of Russell's logicism survived, it was no longer part of his earlier realist program. Russell often presented his own developments as "conversions" and "epiphanies". This is exactly the rhetorical framework he used to account for his withdrawal from a Platonist-realist interpretation in favor of an empiricist one reducing mathematics to tautological truisms. Russell's *Autobiography*, for instance, speaks of a "more or less religious belief in a Platonic eternal world" (Russell 2010[1975], 701). In his 1959 *My Philosophical Development*, Russell recalled that a significant part of his entire intellectual career consisted on the abandonment of his early Pythagorism towards the acceptance that mathematical truths are but tautologies. Moreover, he retrospectively accounted for his "retreat from Pythagoras" as a response to two blasts: World War I and Ludwig Wittgenstein.

The war's horrors would have made it impossible for Russell to keep seeking refuge in a world of abstractions. He emphasized his new position in contrast to his 1902 reliance on mathematics as a cloister against sorrow:

> I used to watch young men embarking in troop trains to be slaughtered on the Somme because generals were stupid. I felt an aching compassion for these young men, and found myself united to the actual world in a strange marriage of pain (...) All the high-flown thoughts that I had had about the abstract world of ideas seemed to me thin and rather trivial in view of the vast suffering that surrounded me. The non-human world remained as an occasional refuge, but not as a country in which to build one's permanent habitation. (Russell 1975[1959], 157)

In the next chapter we analyze the effect that Russell's symbolic interpretation of World War I had upon his confidence on science as an engine of moral progress or a shelter from worldly horrors. For now, it suffices to say that one should avoid taking for granted Russell's own recollections of the effects of the war's shock. Late Russell became eager to present his politics as passionate enough to shake the entire edifice of his epistemology, including what he thought at the time were its foundations: logic and mathematics. Because of Russell's own insistence in the effects of World War I on his approach to abstractions, other authors have (understandably) accepted this narrative (including for instance Copleston 1994). But many other scholars have questioned this account in view of Russell's more complex approach to mathematics both before and after World War I (Monk 1996).

As for the second blast, the influence of Wittgenstein's view of mathematics as tautologies, scholars have also noted that it was only effective because of Russell's own difficulties in grounding Platonism and logicism on the one hand, and because of Russell's partial misunderstanding of Wittgenstein's stances on mathematical entities on the other. It is tempting to follow Russell's own account of Wittgenstein's enormous influence in his views of mathematics. According to it, Wittgenstein, who had travelled to Cambridge to study under Russell in 1911 under Frege's recommendation, would soon present such strong criticisms to his professor's theory of types that Russell was forced to accept the painful fact that mathematics are just tautologous and true by convention. But it is not the case that for Wittgenstein mathematics were just tautologous and truth by convention. It is true that Wittgenstein's *Tractatus* states that "[t]he logic of the world, which is shown in tautologies by the propositions of logic, is shown in equations by mathematics" (6.22). Moreover, Wittgenstein explicitly held that "mathematics is a method of logic" (6.234). But there are important differences between Wittgenstein's and Russell's views on the nature of mathematics that Russell tended to downplay. In the *Tractatus*, Wittgenstein characterized mathematics as a purely formal calculus of operations. Mathematical propositions are analogous to logical propositions in that they *show* their correctness rather than *saying* anything with content which could be either true or false (Mays 1967; Rodych 2018). But this does not mean that mathematical propositions should be considered tautological and just true by convention; rather, they are instead equations which *show* the logic of the world (*Tractatus* 6.22). But Russell, like Ayer and other analytic philosophers, rejected Wittgenstein's saying/showing distinction. The obvious consequence of this is that Russell did not accept Wittgenstein's characterization of mathematics as "showing the logic of the world" in equations (Nakano 2021). Of course, the similarities between Wittgenstein's and Russell's views on mathematics are very strong: Russell, like Wittgenstein, came to deny that mathematical propositions have any kind of truth-evaluable content or what other analytic philosophers, such as Ayer, called "factual meaning" (Frascolla 1997, 2017). But, even so, the difference between considering mathematics as true by convention rather than as showing the logical structure of the world, should not be overlooked.

It is thus apparent that Russell's retrospective narrative oversimplifies his actual development (Gandon 2012; Korhonen 2013). Thus, Russell's retreat from Pythagoras was rather gradual and largely due to internal reasons preceding both the war and Wittgenstein's attacks. We would like to stress that, despite Russell's own binary recollections, important passages in early Russell's work are closer to conventionalism than they are to Platonism: Russell's early Platonism was rather selective. Reciprocally, late Russell defended, for instance in his 1927 *The Analysis of Matter,* that the ultimate structure of the world seemed to be mathematical (if in a rather ambiguous way). And yet, his rhetorical shift for presenting mathematics as tautologies was, we argue, an effect of the Manichean structures that pervade Russell's thoughts. That is, in the face of the complexity and richness of mathematics, only a false dilemma between Platonism/empiricism can explain Russell's embracement of tautologism.

For this book's argument, it is particularly interesting to enquire about the changing rhetoric of Russell's approach to the philosophy of mathematics, which drove him to overemphasize first his Platonism and then his empiricism both in his daily work and in his later recollections of it. As we have argued in this book's introduction, the effect of social and political events on intellectuals are often not as direct as their own recollections indicate nor as historians of ideas would sometimes like to think. Events require cultural interpretations to enter a system of ideas, which in turn must be re-organized to host that interpretation, even if logical coherence is not always kept in the process. For us, the significance of Russell's recollections over his own changes of view on the status of mathematics reveal the central role logic and mathematics played in Russell's early scientism. Finding an internal (mathematical and philosophical) source of skepticism, in turn, makes it easier to understand why he could then interpret the tragic events of World War I in ways that fundamentally shaped his approach to science and technology.

In this chapter we tackle Russell's main changing views on mathematics, logic, and language vis-à-vis science and philosophy. Russell's program of reducing mathematics to symbolic logic has received an enormous amount of attention by philosophers and historians of philosophy, logic and mathematics. As one of the founding fathers of analytical philosophy, the ontological and epistemological import of his understanding of logic has also been widely discussed by historians and practitioners of that tradition of thought. Drawing on that literature, what we aim at offering here is not an original appraisal of Russell's logicism but an account of Russell's shifting views on science, its foundations, and its repercussion. While not entirely novel, this is important in building our book's argument and in introducing the reader to early Russell's take on science and philosophy. As such, the questions we ask have often to do with the making of his public thought and persona.

Russell's presentation of logic as foundational of mathematics emerges as part of a larger strategy for elevating the public role of science. As the first section explores, this view was deeply embedded in late 19th-century scientific and philosophical developments. In keeping with our cultural-sociological analyses, we pay attention to the public interpretations that philosophers and pure mathematicians put forward of their own work. Russell approached mathematics with philosophical questions that, for an early period, he sought to solve with the tools provided by British Hegelian philosophers. But Hegelian monism and holism soon became the mystic past against which Russell rebelled. For the rest of his career, he looked for firm foundations of science in individual entities and their external relations. "Pure" mathematics acquired for him a dual technical and axiological inception, which separated Russell's own work and epoch from prior periods of impure intellectual darkness and polluted superstition.

The second section presents a broad overview of Russell's logicist program, with special attention to its meanings, nuances, and transformations. Attending more to his public expositions (both to academic and popular audiences) than to his technical works, we trace Russell's apocalyptic and semi-religious language as mobilized to create new binaries between science and non-science. As in other cases, this confronted Russell with some logical inconsistencies as the necessary price to pay in order to achieve a greater symbolic effect. Russell gradually abandoned his Platonic realism towards an empiricist view of mathematics as tautological. Moreover, despite decades of strenuous efforts, important parts of Russell's logicist program of reducing mathematics to logic failed. As logic and mathematical philosophy had played a role in his understanding of the place of science in human knowledge and society, this relative failure fed Russell's skepticism. This provides the background to the apocalyptic overtones Russell would soon be applying to science vis-à-vis society at large. Logic was no longer the key to absolute reality. However, we argue, Russell did never abandon important aspects of his logicist program nor his confidence in that, though limited, science was the best available tool to access reality.

The chapter's third and last section stresses the role of logic beyond logicism. It briefly sketches Russell's philosophy of language, particularly in contrast to Wittgenstein's. Insisting on the ontological import of Russell's logical analysis, we emphasize the role of logical atomism within Russell's pluralist metaphysics. That Russell's pluralism was sometimes at odds with his foundationalist impulses is apparent in several landmarks of his career, including, of course, neutral monism, which will be the subject of Chapter 4. The main point for now is to signal the various meanings of logic and the lasting legacies of the logicist program in Russell's philosophy and approaches to science.

LOGIC AND MATHEMATICS AS *PURE* AND FOUNDATIONAL SCIENCES

When Hegel published the two volumes of his *Science of Logic* between 1812 and 1816, he intended to offer a complete doctrine of the most fundamental structure of what exists or can exist. According to Hegel, Aristotelian syllogisms gave way to the insurmountable contradictions exposed in Kant's antinomies of reason. Kant understood logic as the rules of judgment. As opposed to the object-dependent special logics, "pure general logic" comprised for Kant the most abstract of these rules, dealing with the pure forms of thought (Korhonen 2013, 161–165). In contrast to Kant, Hegel's absolute idealism linked logic not only to human thought but to the very structure of reality. Influenced by Fichte's and Schelling's developmental metaphysics, Hegel did not interpret the antinomies of Kant's transcendental logic as limits to human reason, but as steps towards a holistic and unitary theory of reality encompassing both subjects and objects, the spirit and nature. Hegel's *Logic* approached reality's main structures through this dialectical metaphysics.

Hegel, however, was no absolute monist. Through his critiques of the classic ontological principle "natura non facit saltus" he defended the existence of structural ontological discontinuities in reality. And yet, most of his idealist heirs did embrace a more radical form of monism. For Russell's early understanding of logic, the most relevant of these were the British neo-Hegelians, whom Russell approached as a young student of mathematics at Cambridge University. In particular, Francis Herbert Bradley (Oxford University) and John M. Ellis McTaggart (Cambridge University), although very different from one another, situated themselves outside of the empiricist and utilitarian trends that characterized British philosophy from John Locke and David Hume to John Stuart Mill.

At Cambridge Russell became friends with his fellow student George E. Moore and both of them came to be close disciples of their professor McTaggart. It was McTaggart who introduced Russell to the works of Bradley and other British idealists like T. H. Green. Russell, Moore, and McTaggart were soon known as "The Mad Tea-Party of Trinity", McTaggart representing *Alice's* Dormouse (Wiener 1953). The three were also active in the so-called "Cambridge Apostles". This Cambridge organization had been founded in 1820 and, accepting only 12 members simultaneously, had an enormous influence for many generations of intellectuals. Closely working with the neo-Hegelians took Russell to idealism and what we could call the "hubris of the psyche" (Pérez-Jara 2014), by which the mental ends up drowning all reality. This early commitment had lasting sequels in Russel's intellectual career (Clark 1975).

McTaggart's *Studies in the Hegelian Dialectic* (1896) argued that only the absolute was real.[1] That absolute is composed of immaterial individual selves. Philosophy ought to rationally justify a mystical embracement of unity. The method was logical synthesis, not analysis. McTaggart later abandoned the Hegelian dialectical method, but the idealist premises remained in both his epistemology and ontology. Nevertheless, it is important to note that, unlike the majority of British idealists, McTaggart was an ontological pluralist: against Bradley, he believed in the reality of relations (Griffin 1991). For McTaggart, absolute monism is contradictory, because if there were only one absolute thing without any kind of plurality (and therefore no properties), that thing would be indistinguishable from nothingness. Matter and time are illusions, but eternal plural relations of spiritual nature are not. It is very reasonable to think that, aside of Moore's influence, McTaggart's metaphysics of the reality and plurality of relations had an influence in Russell's later conception of logical atomism. By contrast, Bradley's 1897 *Appearance and Reality* presented a very Parmenidean picture of reality, although with less mystical overtones. The parts cannot be understood without the whole; their independent existence is an illusion. Relations do not make sense if understood as links established between preexisting entities. Only internal constitutive relationships are "real"; the rest are but subjective illusions of the limited human mind.

Russell's approach to neo-Hegelian philosophy was from the onset related to his interest in mathematics (Griffin 1991, 2003). He had developed an early concern with foundational problems, motivated by his dissatisfaction with undemonstrated geometrical proofs. Already as a child, Russell sought refuge in Euclidean geometry from an infancy of detachment and loneliness. According to Russell's own account, mathematics had apotropaic powers which saved him from committing suicide.[2] Young Russell became interested in the possibilities of science to transcend the realm of worldly uncertainty. Geometrical proof was for him, as for many philosophers before him, the example of the power of logical necessity and truth. But as soon as he became aware of his century's discussions on non-Euclidean geometries, the basis of the solid edifice of Euclidean geometry seemed less solid. He embraced first his family's Christianity and later deism, but soon abandoned them for their lack of intellectual coherence. It was then that Russell decided to study mathematics at Cambridge precisely searching for solid grounds in which to base scientific and philosophical truths.

At Cambridge, however, Russell found instead applied mathematics and little skeptical questioning of mathematical principles. Foundations were not something most British mathematicians were too worried about. Following in part the Scottish example, Cambridge mathematical education was directed towards practical problems, concerning mostly physics and, to a lesser extent, engineering. According to Andrew Warwick, the student *ethos* of applied mathematicians needed no more foundation than musculation and mechanics. This *ethos* began to fade only with Russell's generation, when a growing interest in importing German so-called pure mathematics accompanied the rise of young professors like Alfred Whitehead. Only then did problems become examples of pure mathematical analysis (Warwick 2003, 221).

The situation had been different in Germany. From the first half of the 19th century onwards, non-Euclidian geometries (and their interpretation) had redirected attention to foundational issues. In an academic context of high prestige of pure knowledge and of strong interactions between mathematics and philosophy, Carl Friedrich Gauss, Farkas Bolyai, and Bernhard Riemann played the role of both developers and commentators of geometry and arithmetic (Ferreirós 2007a). Among these "pure" mathematicians, Riemann took seriously the truth-value of the geometries he developed, and this led him to speak of both his own and Euclid's axioms as hypothetical. Instead of the necessary truths through which God spoke to contemplative souls or through which *a priori* forms organized the world, the door was now opened to seeing mathematical entities as playful creations of the human mind. Coherence became as important as truth. As historian and philosopher of mathematics José Ferreirós argues, an important component of this turn was informed by Kantianism while departing from it: looking for mathematical objects in *a priori* structures, but without an ideal transcendental logic, led German mathematicians to see logic, and particularly set-theory, as foundational (Ferreirós 2007b, 17).

Riemann's reading of the mathematical developments did not gain critical mass acceptance until later in the century. But from the 1870s onwards the embracing of the implications of non-Euclidean geometries became more widespread and shook the confidence in mathematical axioms. This drew mathematicians and philosophers to interpret "pure mathematics" rather differently than before. For some, the goal became to find and justify axioms that avoided contradictions, and not only in geometry but also in arithmetic. What followed were some turbulent decades of foundational debates, which the growing general prestige of German science contributed to extend (Ferreirós 2008).

As he endured his applied mathematical training, Russell's philosophical take on mathematics and logic underwent dramatic changes. He first embraced the Kantian view that Euclidean geometries provided the *a priori* forms of human perception. This view, however, had already been severely questioned by the development of non-Euclidean geometries, which left little reason to think that Euclidean space was so universal as Kant had thought a century earlier. In 1893, when he was about to finish his final exams (Tripos), he abandoned the Kantian interpretation of mathematics for a neo-Hegelian one inspired by McTaggart and Bradley. He also followed the neo-Hegelian notion of logic as the dialectics by which absolute spirit developed itself.

Mathematics were an attempt of the spirit to gauge control of worldly empirical appearances. Following McTaggart's dialectical and holistic understanding of logic, Russell's first serious incursions into the philosophy of mathematics and mathematical logic aimed at showing how the inherent contradictions of mathematics (regarding continuity and the infinite) could only be solved by physics. Physics' own contradictions would in turn be solved by psychology, which in turn would resolve into metaphysics. At the end of the process, the sciences, for all their seemingly spectacular developments in the 19th century, would reveal themselves to be mere façades veiling a unitary reality accessible only through dialectical philosophy.

Pursuing mathematics' internal contradictions, Russell thought, was the first step towards reaching the one and absolute reality, a sort of non-personal God like the one imagined by Spinoza. In this picture, philosophy emerges as superior to the sciences. While mathematicians ignored the contradictions pervading their own field, philosophers embraced them. In 1896, Russell wrote that philosophical antinomies were covered by mathematical fallacies, pervading the calculus and "even the more elaborate machinery of Cantor's collections". "Cantor's transfinite numbers", he added, "are impossible and self-contradictory" (Russell, "On Some Difficulties of Continuous Quantity", quoted in Monk 1996, 111). In 1897, Russell published his first epistemological book: *An Essay of the Foundations of Geometry.* This work realized his neo-Hegelian program. Discussing at length non-Euclidean and projective geometries, the book concludes that the antinomies of continuity, which had haunted philosophers since Zeno, could only be solved by moving on to physics.

Later in the same year, however, Russell began to gain confidence in the powers of pure mathematics. Only one year later he was already writing privately that "Mathematics could be quite true, and not merely a stage in dialectic" (Monk 1996, 122). Soon after he became an enthusiast of the role of logic in grounding mathematical science. His most fervent declarations in favor of the Platonic existence of mathematical entities come from this time. When the already famed physicist and mathematician Henri Poincaré took the time to review Russell's *Essay* in no-less than thirty pages, Russell had already abandoned the Hegelian dialectical metaphysics that had inspired it. Poincaré's defense of conventionalism, however, was no less incompatible with Russell's newly adopted Platonism. The exchange that followed, together with Russell's controversy with his (then still) friend Moore over this same book, consolidated Russell's academic fame.

The years 1898 and 1899 were the defining time for his conversion to pluralism and realism. There were several reasons for this radical change of mind. First, Russell often recalled ironically that reading Hegel directly showed him that neo-Hegelian speculations on both logic as dialectical metaphysics and the nature of mathematics were pure nonsense (Russell 1959).

Second, Russell came to think more closely on the theory of relations. Replacing McTaggart while he was abroad, Russell lectured on Leibniz at Cambridge, a course which would result into his book *A Critical Exposition of the Philosophy of Leibniz* (1900). Perhaps unfairly, Russell viewed in Leibniz an example of the problematic metaphysical implications of the Aristotelian traditional logic considering all propositions as being formed by subjects and predicates. But, because mathematical relations (like whole and parts, or smaller than) were not of this kind, Russell thought that Leibniz was forced to claim that they were mere ideal constructions of the mind (Goethe 2007). Russell extended his accusation to Bradley and McTaggart: their limited understanding of logic made them unable to understand relations, and thus forced them to deny relations as mere appearances. Recall that in the neo-Hegelian view there are only "internal relations", i.e., relations that are essential or constitutive to the relata. This monistic doctrine, Russell now saw, was just incompatible with the "external relations" that he was studying in mathematics and that Moore was developing for philosophy of language.

If external relations were real, that means that reality should be considered as a real plurality of independent things, rather than as a monolithic and continuous whole, as British idealism postulated. In Russell's new philosophical worldview, the independent entities that constitute reality should be considered in isolation from both their relations to other things (pluralism) and their relation to the mind (realism). Instead of logical holism, Russell turned to a pluralistic ontology which he would later call logical atomism (see below), in contrast to the logical holism of the British idealists.

Russell abandoned his conception of logic as the dialectics of the spirit and became interested in pure logic as the science of relational structures, something extremely useful for the analysis of propositions. While he was following the British creators of symbolic logic, a more distant but influential source were Bernard Bolzano's works on logic of the early 1800s. Bolzano rejected Kant's idea of pure general logic as the formal rules of human thought. Logic was always concerned with propositions about the world but dealt with kinds of propositions rather than with particular ones (Korhonen 2013, 165–174). Following Bolzano and Moore, post-idealistic Russell understood logic as the most universal science in that it studies what remains constant in certain classes of proposition, including those of pure mathematics (Korhonen 2013, 174–177).

Contemplating his former idealistic and monistic beliefs as polluted ways of thinking, Russell went to the extremes of metaphysical pluralism and realism. In such extreme, Russell understood that points of space and instants of time are mind-independent entities that belong to an eternal world of Platonic essences. Two quotes make explicit Russell's own later recollection of his turn to Platonism:

> Hegel and his disciples had been in the habit of "proving" the impossibility of space and time and matter, and generally everything that an ordinary man would believe in. Having become convinced that the Hegelian arguments against this and that were invalid, I reacted to the opposite extreme and began to believe in the reality of whatever could not be disproved—e.g., points and instants and particles and Platonic universals. [. . .] I came to think of mathematics, not primarily as a tool for understanding and manipulating the sensible world, but as an abstract edifice subsisting in a Platonic heaven and only reaching the world of sense in an impure and degraded form. (Russell 1959, 10, 155).

As we will see in the next section, this 1959 account retrospectively exaggerated Russell's own Platonist position to produce the impression of a sharper contrast with his previous idealism and his later empiricism. But what is clear is that Russell's own work on the foundation of arithmetic contributed much to his abandonment of his former neo-Hegelian interpretation of mathematics. In particular, also in 1898 he studied the foundational works of Karl Weierstrass, Richard Dedekind, and Georg Cantor. In the early 1870s, both Dedekind and Cantor published different approaches bridging the divide between natural and real numbers that had hunted mathematicians since the Greek's discovery of irrational numbers—at the heart of the problem was reducing the continuity of geometry to the discrete nature of arithmetics. While their methods differed greatly, their approaches had in common dealing with the actual infinity of the set of the rational numbers (for a complete discussion, see Ferreirós 2007b). This enabled them to redefine the infinite and also to compare different infinite sets, concluding things so remote from common sense as that the whole is not necessarily larger than the parts or that there exist hierarchies of infinite numbers, some being larger than others.

Russell was fascinated by this. As he delved into this mathematical and logical work on continuity and infinity, he took it to put an end to millennia-long philosophical disputes. In 1901 Russell published a popular article "Recent Work on the Principles of Mathematics". The title with which the paper was republished in 1917 (as a chapter of *Mysticism and Logic*) is telling: "Mathematics and the Metaphysicians". Indeed, the article's takeaway message was that 19th-century mathematicians had solved (or dissolved) traditional metaphysical disputes. "For the philosophers", Russell stated provocatively, "there is now nothing left but graceful acknowledgments" (Russell 1901a).

Russell, though, never suggested to do away with philosophy. Even after abandoning British idealism, philosophy was always for Russell a meaningful rational discipline necessary for our (always tentative and incomplete) understanding of the world and our knowledge of it. But only in so far as it followed closely the rules of logic and scientific novelties. The 1901 article argued that philosophers had followed neither. They had, since Greek times, overlooked logic when accepting Zeno's attacks on the infinity and continuity. These attacks rested on the unproved assumption than the whole has more terms than the part. "As the conclusion is absurd, the axiom must be rejected, and then all goes well. But there is no good word to be said for the philosophers of the past two thousand years and more, who have all allowed the axiom and denied the conclusion" (Russell 1901a). The axiom's rejection was precisely Cantor's merit.

As for the philosophers' disregard of scientific novelties, Russell's examples were his own Kantian and Hegelian conundrums of only a few years before. "This difficulty", Russell explained when discussing infinity, "led to Kant's antinomies, and hence, more or less indirectly, to much of Hegel's dialectic method. Almost all current philosophy is upset by the fact (of which very few philosophers are as yet aware) that all the ancient and respectable contradictions in the notion of the infinite have been once for all disposed of" (Russell 1901a). Moreover, mathematicians had proven Kantian philosophy wrong, based as it was in considering arithmetic and geometry as *a priori* intuitions. Russell's article thus concluded with a plea for philosophers to follow the example of mathematicians and base their works on philosophical logic. The language was prophetic, promising great triumphs for the near future (Russell 1901a).

In the Western tradition, mathematics had long been associated to the divine. A sense of divine reverence surrounded mathematical entities. Plato's divine demiurge was somehow subordinated to mathematics. Even for Christian philosophers, mathematics was seldom presented as capricious products of God's mind. From St. Augustine to St. Thomas, theologians had defended that mathematical entities and truths were co-eternal, always present in God's infinite understanding. This divine character might have been also present in the origins of formal logic in mid-nineteenth century Victorian England. Historian Daniel J. Cohen argued that "the 'father' of pure mathematics," as Bertrand Russell would later refer to George Boole, had not been purely interested in mathematics, nor was his mathematics free of the "'impurities' of extra disciplinary concerns, in particular, religious ones" (Cohen 2007, 77). Unlike in the French tradition after the early modern period, in Britain necessary truths in pure mathematics had been linked to theology (Richards 2011). This was extended to formal logic. According to Cohen, both George Boole and Augustus De Morgan developed symbolic logic and the logic of relations in part as a way of grounding an ecumenical universal faith that would offer a way out of sectarian strife in the Victorian age.

The religious aspects of formal logic should not be exaggerated. There are many other sources for the focus on logical form, including the traditions of Kant and Bolzano. And indeed, late nineteenth-century professionalization and a strategic retreat from public theological debate stripped pure mathematics of its religious envelop. Nineteenth-century Platonism did not need to refer to the divine anymore. And yet, we want to argue, even for a non-religious philosopher of mathematics like Bertrand Russell the eternal nature of mathematical entities retained their status of godly beauty and pureness. Moreover, in keeping with this book's perspective, it is easy to track the dual scheme sacred/profane as a framework structuring Russell's foundational project. Russell's appropriation of the theological rhetoric is perhaps most visible in his article "The Study of Mathematics", written in 1902 but rejected and left unpublished till 1907:

> In every age the finest intellects have vainly endeavoured to answer the apparently unanswerable questions that had been asked by Zeno the Eleatic. At last Georg Cantor has found the answer, and has conquered for the intellect a new and vast province which had been given over to Chaos and old Night. (Russell 1907)

There is no reason to see irony in this exposition of pure mathematics through the ancient binary between the pure light and the polluted night. Russell held that "the nature of the postulates from which arithmetic, analysis, and geometry are to be deduced was wrapped in all the traditional obscurities of metaphysical discussion." Instead, "mathematics, rightly viewed, possess not only truth, but supreme beauty". He explicitly endorsed the statement by the *Athenian* of Plato's *Laws* that mathematical necessity "is divine and not human". Russell elaborated further:

> Philosophers have commonly held that the laws of logic, which underlie mathematics, are laws of thought, laws regulating the operations of our minds. By this opinion the true dignity of reason is very greatly lowered: it ceases to be an investigation into the very heart and immutable essence of all things actual and possible, becoming, instead, an inquiry into something more or less human and subject to our limitations. The contemplation of what is non-human, the discovery that our minds are capable of dealing with material not created by them, above all, the realisation that beauty belongs to the outer world as to the inner, are the chief means of overcoming the terrible sense of impotence, of weakness, of exile amid hostile powers, which is too apt to result from acknowledging the all-but omnipotence of alien forces. To reconcile us, by the exhibition of its

awful beauty, to the reign of Fate—which is merely the literary personification of these forces—is the task of tragedy. But mathematics takes us still further from what is human, into the region of absolute necessity, to which not only the actual world, but every possible world, must conform; and even here it builds a habitation, *or rather finds a habitation eternally standing*, where our ideals are fully satisfied and our best hopes are not thwarted. It is only when we thoroughly understand the entire independence of ourselves, which belongs to this world that reason finds, that we can adequately realise the profound importance of its beauty. (Russell 1917, 18; the emphasis is ours)

Against psychologism, pure mathematics takes us beyond the human into a reign of absolute necessity. There lies its moral force. In face skepticism, mathematics "edifice of truths stands unshakable and inexpugnable to all the weapons of doubting cynicism." The article was intended as a plea to reform the way mathematics was taught at all levels of education. Likely reacting to his Cambridge education in applied mathematics, Russell proposed to save mathematics from its usefulness. The obsession with applications, thought Russell, forced students to accept principles without questioning and then to quickly proceed to solve particular problems.

Let us be clear: Russell was not against technology, which he considered to result from theoretical scientific advances, i.e., applied science. Mathematics served as an engine of technical and social progress: "the use of steam and electricity—to take striking instances—is rendered possible only by mathematics". It was a matter of emphasis. Fundamentals and deductions show the "intellectual beauty of the whole . . . with all the overwhelming force of a revelation." Focusing solely on applications obscured that

> Every great study is not only an end in itself, but also a means of creating and sustaining a lofty habit of mind; and this purpose should be kept always in view throughout the teaching and learning of mathematics. (Russell 1918).

Russell's logicist program, to which the next section turns, thus mobilized a traditional view of mathematics as the bridge between human frailty and divine solidity. It rested on a cultural tradition of interpreting pure mathematics that had been growing with the century. In this tradition, "pure" had a double meaning, technical and moral.

RISE AND FALL OF RUSSELL'S PLATONIC LOGICISM

Russell devoted the first years of the 20th century to demonstrate his newly acquired confidence in pure mathematics by attempting its reduction to philosophical logic. The stakes were high. In his 1901 article "Recent Work in the Philosophy of Mathematics", Russell emphatically argued that "the nineteenth century, which prided itself upon the invention of steam and evolution, might have derived a more legitimate title to fame from the discovery of pure mathematics." Moreover, he concluded:

> There is every reason to hope that the near future will be as great an epoch in pure philosophy as the immediate past has been in the principles of mathematics. Great triumphs inspire great hopes; and pure thought may achieve, within our generation, such results as will place our time, in this respect, on a level with the greatest age of Greece. (Russell 1901)

The language is of optimistic confidence and hope in a bright future. In his prologue to the article's 1917 reprint in *Mysticism and Logic*, he felt obliged to blame his 1901 editor for the article's "romantic tone". By 1917 much of Russell's Platonic faith was fading. But his separation from the epic language of ancient myths was far from severe. After all, the whole volume *Mysticism and Logic*—to which we return in this chapter's conclusion—aimed to build a dichotomy between two ways of thinking, the rational and the mystical. Rationalist Russell endeavored to sanctify science and demonize religion.

Russell's philosophical logic thus went well beyond grounding mathematics. Mathematics would provide both a ground and a model over which to build the edifice of empirical sciences. The empirical sciences, in turn, were for the post-Hegelian Russell the best available tools to understand reality (despite their inability to provide definitive answers due to their empirical character). In the always tentative ways of empirical science, mathematics was a powerful backbone. The wings of Icarus were fully spread, reaching for the sun, as Russell prepared the first draft of his *Principles of Mathematics* around 1900. Three years later, the publication of this book would serve as a powerful announcement of the logicist program. In it, Russell held that mathematics and logic are identical:

> The fact that all Mathematics is Symbolic Logic is one of the greatest discoveries of our age; and when this fact has been established, the remainder of the principles of mathematics consists in the analysis of Symbolic Logic itself. (Russell 1903, 5)

The equation of symbolic logic and pure mathematics was not self-evident. Those advancing symbolic logic in the mid-19th century did not identify it with pure mathematics. Some, for instance, defended that logic was the necessary formal rules of thought and mathematics the necessary matter of that thought (Merrill 1990, 170–195). However, as Dedekind and Cantor approached pure mathematics with the tools of set theory, and set theory was regarded as a branch of logic, the foundational approach to axioms came to be seen by many as a problem of advanced and sophisticated logic.

In particular, from the 1870s onwards, German and Italian pure mathematicians interested in foundational problems set to develop tools from formal logic in an attempt to deduce the arithmetic axioms–some of these mathematicians extended the project to include the principles of geometry. This program is known as logicism. However, logicism came in different shapes. And, importantly for this chapter, it was compatible with a variety of ontologies. In the late 19th century, most logicists shared some strong form of Platonism. In Italy, Giuseppe Peano developed a logical notation and operational rules to both arithmetic and geometry. While "the usefulness of symbols comes to light and its measured by its applications", mathematical logic referred to truths in themselves rather than conventions (Peano 1900; quoted and interpreted in Rodríguez-Consuegra 1991, 92–105). Logic was a useful tool to *find* mathematical axioms.

In light of the former, Gottlob Frege's statement that Boole had offered a *calculus raciocinator* without *lingua characteristica* and Peano a *lingua characteristica* without *calculus racioncinator* was clearly unfair. And yet, it speaks for the importance that the reference to Leibniz's *mathesis universalis* had acquired among many of the authors involved in the foundational program. Frege explicitly wanted to do both things: offer a clear set of axioms for arithmetic (his approach to geometry was heavily inspired by Kantian intuitionism) as well as the rules to work with these axioms. For him, this meant abandoning both ordinary language and the psychologist understanding of logic. Against the idea that logic described human thought, Frege's metaphysics rested on the assumption that logical entities and relations were eternal and independent from empirical and historical circumstances (for a discussion of the many subtilities of this position, see Kluge 1980). Frege's rigorous analysis of logical concepts, along with the tools provided by their formalization, became essential to Russell's and Alfred Whitehead's *Principia Mathematica* (3 vols., 1910–1913), but also to Russell's epistemology of descriptions.

The ontological meaning of Russell's logicism changed throughout time. By 1899 he had clearly embraced the program of finding *The Fundamental Ideas and Axioms of Mathematics,* as he titled a first draft of what would later be *The Principles of Mathematics.* Between that first draft and the book finally published in 1903 went many revisions of both the texts and Russell's approach to the foundational effort (the successive drafts and approaches are available at Russell 1993). At the heart of this text's three big successive re-elaborations lied Russell's understanding of Cantor. In the first draft he rejected Cantor's approach to the continuum. Before long, however, he had fully accepted it. A turning point was meeting Giuseppe Peano in Paris in the summer of 1900.

In a 1901 unpublished paper, Russell praised Peano's axioms for arithmetic as the finest result of a decade-long effort to understand numbers as a specific type of more general series or progressions (Russell 1901b). This enabled Russell to reinterpret the 19th-century long-path to pure mathematics. Here it is useful to turn again to Russell's own words in the above-mentioned "Recent Work in the Philosophy of Mathematics":

> Zeno was concerned, as a matter of fact, with three problems, each presented by motion, but each more abstract than motion, and capable of a purely arithmetical treatment. These are the problems of the infinitesimal, the infinite, and continuity. To state clearly the difficulties involved, was to accomplish perhaps the hardest part of the philosopher's task. This was done by Zeno. From him to our own day, the finest intellects of each generation in turn attacked the problems, but achieved, broadly speaking, nothing. In our own time, however, three men—Weierstrass, Dedekind, and Cantor—have not merely advanced the three problems, but have completely solved them. The solutions, for those acquainted with mathematics, are so clear as to leave no longer the slightest doubt or difficulty. This achievement is probably the greatest of which our age has to boast; and I know of no age (except perhaps the golden age of Greece) which has a more convincing proof to offer of the transcendent genius of its great men. Of the three problems, that of the infinitesimal was solved by Weierstrass; the solution of the other two was begun by Dedekind, and definitively accomplished by Cantor. (Russell 1901a, 68)

Russell then went on to explain at some length how infinitesimals had been avoided, the infinite redefined, and continuity savaged. Cantor appeared as the hero who had proven that, for infinite sets, the whole is not greater than the parts. Cantor had discovered that there were different kinds of infinity. Set theory had also enabled a new approach to arithmetic by providing new definitions of numbers. Looking at numbers as cardinal rather than ordinal enabled their intensional definition as collections; this was a nominalist definition: number 3 is just the name we give to the set of things that come in trios—more on this below. While this was in explicit opposition to Dedekind's ordinal (that is, relational or structural) approach, Russell went back and forth many times before embracing his own nominalist position (Heis 2020). And here the final step had been given by Peano and his collaborators who had produced the definitions of all natural numbers in purely formal terms. Russell rewrote the draft of *The Principles of Mathematics* with the program of reducing all of Peano's fundamental notions to that of class (Korhonen 2013).

By early 1901, however, Russell was convinced that his approach was frail. In the same 1901 paper Russell already introduced for the first time the reason behind his new doubts. It had to do with Cantor's very solution to the problem of infinity through a hierarchy of infinities. In this early formulation, the problem was with Cantor's proof that there is no greatest number. Russell attributed this to a "subtle fallacy" and promised to explain it in future work (Russell 1901a, 74). Throughout 1901 he elaborated instead a more complete understanding of what would soon be known as the Russell's Paradox: the class of all classes cannot belong to itself. The theory of classes was not complete as he had hoped for. In 1902 he encountered the works of Frege, whose project he immediately identified with his own—despite an important difference regarding geometry, which Frege thought was unreducible. The term "logistique" was introduced by Couturat and others in the early 1900s. Russell appropriated the term to designate Frege's program, helping promote Frege's work and also making boosting the concept's fame. As it is known, however, when Russell communicated to Frege the difficulties posed by his newly found paradox, the German abandoned logicism.

Russell spent the entire 1902 working on his contributions to *Principles of Mathematics*, oscillating between optimism and despair. As Russell's biographer Ray Monk points out, it seems paradoxical that it was precisely in this period of hesitation that he wrote the triumphalist "The Study of Mathematics" analyzed in the previous section (Monk 1996, 159). By this time, Russell was starting to doubt his own declarations of Platonic faith. Russell's logicist program was realistic in a Platonic sense only with respect to certain structures, while in many others his logicism followed constructivism. That in "The Study of Mathematics" (as well as in retrospective recollections) he chose to emphasize only the former is one of the first clear instances in which Russell's public persona was more ready to suppress doubts and subtilities than his private self. As in other instances of this strategy analyzed in this book, it is then no wonder than his partisan public declarations chose to follow the Manichean rhetoric of good and evil. In *My Philosophical Development* (1959), he picked again his mystical language, but this time with evident irony, to explain his crumbling faith in the face of the paradox: "I felt about the contradictions much as an earnest Catholic must feel about wicked Popes" (Russell 1959, 212).

Russell's solution to his paradox was his theory of types. Drawing on set theory, Russell argued that there existed a hierarchy of phrases that justified distinguishing phrases devoted to individual objects and phrases about classes. The class of all classes is of a different logical order to the classes contained in it. In the final and published version of *The Principles of Mathematics,* Russell acknowledged that much work still needed to be done so that this theory could effectively constitute the solid principles for the edifice of mathematics that logicists hoped for (Russell 1903).

This is clearest in some later developments by other authors. As Mancosu has shown (Mancosu 1999), Russell's foundational work entered David Hilbert's school in Göttingen through Hilbert's student Heinrich Behmann (for Hilbert's earlier logicism and changing positions in mathematical philosophy, see Ferreirós 2009). This is important because Behmann's interpretation tried to combine concreteness of experience, *a priori* truth, and the fictional character of numbers as part of a formal system. According to Mancosu, these are the seeds of Hilbert's own turn from foundational logicism to a peculiar formalist approach in which the concrete individuals are the mathematical signs themselves. Referring only to the set of signs as opposed to all other concrete individuals seemed to have the advantage of accounting for operationability.

Even within Russell's early foundational work, there are significant traces of both empiricist intuitionism and, most importantly, a formalism that precedes that of Hilbert. Actually, in Russell's 1901 paper "Recent Work in the Philosophy of Mathematics" there is little mention of the realist Platonism of his later "The Study of Mathematics", written in 1902. The theory at work here has become known as *if-thenism*. In Russell's own words:

> Pure mathematics consists entirely of assertions to the effect that, if such and such a proposition is true of anything, then such and such another proposition is true of that thing. It is essential not to discuss whether the first proposition is really true, and not to mention what the anything is, of which it is supposed to be true. Both these points would belong to applied mathematics. We start, in pure mathematics, from certain rules of inference, by which we can infer that if one proposition is true, then so is some other proposition. These rules of inference constitute the major part of the principles of formal logic. We then take any hypothesis that seems amusing, and deduce its consequences. If our hypothesis is about anything, and not about some one or more particular things, then our deductions constitute mathematics. Thus, mathematics may be defined as the subject in which we never know what we are talking about, nor whether what we are saying is true. People who have been puzzled by the beginnings of mathematics will, I hope, find comfort in this definition, and will probably agree that it is accurate. (Russell 1901a)

In this oft-cited text, axioms need only to be sufficiently amusing and coherent. Truth about anything external to the formal system is superfluous and distracting. Russell went on to add, contrary to his earlier Euclidean faith, that geometry did not say anything about space: "thus the geometer leaves to the man of science to decide, as best he may, what axioms are most nearly true in the actual world. The geometer takes any set of axioms that seem interesting, and deduces their consequences" (Russell 1901). This approach to geometry was very far from Platonic realism. But Platonism re-emerged only two years later when referring to arithmetic:

Arithmetic must be discovered in just the same sense in which Columbus discovered the West Indies, and we no more create numbers than he created the Indians. (Russell 1903, 451)

Struggling to understand the true nature of numbers, sets, classes, and types, Russell abandoned this Platonism regarding numbers some few years later. This can be seen clearly in *Principia Mathematica* (1910–1913). There, Russell, like Frege, defined natural numbers in terms of sets and classes, i.e., a natural number n as the collection of all sets with n elements. From this point of view, the number ten, for instance, is the set of all sets with ten members, while the number seven is the set of all seven-membered sets, and so on and so forth. Despite its popularity, it is not difficult to see how Russell's definition of number implies a clear begging of the question—it tries to define a number presupposing what a number is: the number "six", for instance, cannot be successfully defined through the "set with six members". Because, after all, what is the meaning of *six* here? Furthermore, since sets are a kind of classes, and classes, for Russell, are logical constructions, it means that the incompatibility of Russell's philosophy of mathematics with radical Platonism is already present in Russell's definition of number. Russell could continue hypostatizing some logical relational structures. But, according to his own definition of class, numbers cannot exist beyond human cognitive operations.

We could make the political joke of Russell's "abolition of all classes" in Platonic terms. Russellian classes are (epistemologically) polluted to enter into the Platonic Kingdom of Heaven. But Russell insisted time and over in that, although classes are just logical constructions, they are totally necessary to understand and classify the processes we find in the world. It is just that, when possible, we would replace these logical constructions with inferred realities. But we will return to this thesis in Chapter 3, when we analyze Russell's epistemology and ontology of mind and matter. Before being abandoned completely, Russell's Platonism progressively narrowed within a few years.

Regarding Russell's logicism, the philosophical difference between geometry and arithmetic regarding realism is an interesting aspect to consider. When discussing geometry, Russell often accepted the conventionalist views put forward by Poincaré and against which Russell had fiercely argued only a few years earlier. Moreover, while for Poincaré the axioms were not completely gratuitous but somehow related to our bodily experience, for Russell, geometry, and even more projective geometry, was purely formal and unrelated to figurative or bodily experience. And yet, Russell's flirtations with intuitionism are well known. According to Sébastian Gandon, Russell's philosophy of mathematics did not exactly correspond to his actual mathematical analysis (Gandon 1912). While finishing *The Principles of Mathematics*, Russell agreed with Whitehead to work together in a foundational work, the famous *Principia Mathematica* that they would only finish in 1913. According to Gandon, when both works deal with actual mathematical problems preceding philosophical logic, they forget about pure logic and adapt axioms and principles to the existing concepts. This would be especially true for geometry, particularly given that Russell did not share the program of arithmetization of geometry launched by Dedekind (Gandon 2012, 7).

Despite continued triumphalist logicist claims, Russell's logicism was therefore never quite absolute. It is thus hardly surprising that, in *Principia Mathematica*, Russell referred to axioms as based on inductive evidence, as useful to derive not contradictory propositions (Ferreirós 2016, 155). Equally interesting, logicism played a rather minor role in the foundational crisis of the interwar period. The competing views were intuitionism and formalism (Hesseling 2003, 89). By this time, Russell was not very active in the foundational debate. But in the introduction to the 1937 edition of his *Principles of Mathematics* he despised formalists. A formalist, Russell wrote, is like "a watchmaker who is so absorbed in making his watches look pretty that he has forgotten their purpose of telling the time, and has therefore omitted to insert any works" (Russell 1937, vi). There he considered intuitionism "a more serious matter".

However, Russell's publicly declared position in the 1930s was, in several points, similar to that of the empiricism of the Vienna's Circle (excepting Carnap's own logicism). Based to a great extent on an interpretation of Wittgenstein's *Tractatus Logico-Philosophicus* (1921), the idea was that mathematics and logic were no more than linguistic tautologies. Observational data produce new knowledge. Mathematics and logic, on the contrary, have no reference outside of themselves.

The program was still that of logicism. But of course very different from the Platonic contemplation of the beauty of pure, eternal, and necessary truths he promised in his first public writings about mathematics and the power of science. And yet we should not admit, as it is too commonly assumed, that Platonism had no further role in Russell's thought. As we advanced above, it reentered Russell's wider ontology and philosophy of matter as late as 1927. In his *The Analysis of Matter*, Russell defended that the ultimate structure of the actual objects studied by physics was mathematical rather than material. This position was common to many physicists in the period, who retreated from mechanics relegating physics to a mathematical construct. But it introduced an important ambiguity for Russell, because mathematics can be seen as either the structure of the world or of our finite and incomplete knowledge of it. Furthermore, and as we will see in Chapter 3, Russell considered for many decades *mind* and *matter* as "logical constructions"; that is, as complex epistemological constructs rather than immediate, ontologically transparent realities.

Absolute reality (that is, reality as it really is) was no longer represented by Platonic objects; rather, it had become almost unknowable for Russell.

In any case, Russell's 1927 claim about the ultimate mathematical structure of physical objects is hardly consistent with the view he held at the time of mathematics as man-made tautologies. While he had moved away from Pythagoras in his explicit mathematical philosophy, the very Pythagorean idea of an underlying mathematical structure below worldly appearances still played a role in other areas of Russell's thought. As any other scientist and philosopher, Russell was vulnerable to incoherencies when attempting to interpret different realms of reality.

In 1919, Russell published *Introduction to Mathematical Philosophy*, "intended for those who have no previous acquaintance with the topics of which it treats, and no more knowledge of mathematics than can be acquired at a primary school" (Russell 1919, book's blurb). To such popular audience, Russell emphasized once again pure mathematics as the greatest human achievement since Ancient Greece. The promise that logicism would eventually produce answers to the conundrums still present in his theory of types was still alive. The praise of the work of Weierstrass, Dedekind, Cantor, and Peano was also unmoved. They had redefined old-standing problems in a way that dissolved alleged contradictions which had puzzled philosophers for millennia. With this, they had set the example of the power of analysis coupled with formal logic. Even as late as 1937, when Russell had long abandoned his earlier Platonism, he wrote in the first page of the second edition of the *Principles of Mathematics* that: "the fundamental thesis of the following pages, that mathematics and logic are identical, is one which I have never since seen any reason to modify" (Russell 1937).

Thus, while Russell lost interest in pure mathematics and partly abandoned his logicist project and many of the hopes he had invested in its development, some of the logicist's legacies remained very active in his thought throughout his entire life. Most importantly for us, Russell always retained his commitment to scientific rationality. He also maintained the view that the scientific approach should remain the best model for philosophical thinking. The next section turns to Russell's broader notion of analysis and its changing roles as the basis of his philosophical thinking beyond mathematics.

ANALYTICAL PHILOSOPHY AND LANGUAGE'S METAPHYSICAL IMPORT

Russell's departure from neo-Hegelianism and his abandonment of dialectical logic entailed a rejection of holism and monism in favor of atomism and pluralism. We already mentioned that for Bradley all relationships were internal and constitutive. The idea that two independent things come into some sort of relationship external to their respective ready-made beings was the result of our limited understanding of reality. In 1898, the same year that Russell was disappointed by Hegel and taken by Dedekind, Moore presented a theory of propositions as objective (not mental) complex combinations of distinct entities. Relations were real in mathematics, logic and linguistic analysis of propositions. This enabled Russell to elaborate his own doctrine of external relations against logical holism (Russell 1959; Pérez-Jara 2014). Doing logic and philosophy of language was doing ontology.

These were the origins of what soon came to be known as analytical philosophy. There were important precedents. Russell repeatedly referred along the years to Hume's analytical empiricism and Leibniz's ideal of the "*mathesis universalis*". Of course, the immediate model of the prowess of logical analysis was the work being done in pure mathematics (Linsky 1999). Again, Russell's interpretation of that work was not merely technical, but deeply ingrained in epistemological and ontological choices regarding the possibilities of human knowledge. Russell's early understanding of analysis relied on his theory of parts and wholes and on the possibility of breaking complex propositions down to their logical components. In this metaphysics, ultimate logical facts (considered by the epistemological analysis as "atoms") are the ones that cannot be divided any further, each of which can be independently analyzed of other facts. Logical atomism's methodological side can perfectly be understood as a powerful endorsement of analysis beyond Hume. For a given domain of inquiry (be it biological, physical or social), a logical atomist attempts to identify the most basic concepts and vocabulary that epistemologically support the other concepts and vocabulary of that given domain as well as the most general and basic principles from which the remainder of the truths of the domain can be derived or reconstructed.

As he developed the various drafts of the *Principles of Mathematics,* this theory became intertwined with the theory of types. It enabled Russell to distinguish the types of terms and objects which referred directly to units of knowledge from those which where inferential. This resulted from Russell's discussions with Frege about the nature of propositions and, in particular, about how to explain the unity of complex propositions and the reality of false propositions. Russell's initial reaction against idealism entailed a complete realism of propositions. Propositions are a transparent structure composing the very things indicated in them. In the course of his exchanges with Frege and others on the problem of false propositions, he realized this was untenable (Korhonen 2013, 195). Something else was needed to distinguish propositions from the facts they refer to. In his 1905 "On Denoting", he took the important step of distinguishing phrases with direct meaning—proper names—from phrases which only acquired meaning in a given logical context: the definite descriptions (Russell 1905). This provided an early account of Russell's theory of descriptions, which, for many, is Russell's most significant contribution to the 20th-century philosophy of language—despite, or because of, the criticisms received through the years by philosophers such as P. F. Strawson, Keith Donnellan, or Saul Kripke.

Russell's theory of description was mainly focused on the logical structure of linguistic expressions that involve denoting phrases, and it was linked to his emerging theory of knowledge. Specifically, Russell's "On Denoting" already contains a first attempt to what would become the epistemological theory of *sense-data*, key to Russell's philosophical understanding of language. As we will explore in depth in Chapter 3, for Russell sense-data are the physical properties or objects that we are directly aware of through our psychological perceptions. Logically analyzing the contents given in our sense-data, we can arrive to the "logical atoms" of philosophical analysis. In his 1911 "Le Réalisme analytique", Russell coined the term "logical atomism" to refer to this new philosophy. From 1911 on, the term appears in texts that irradiate confidence in science. The possibilities of advancing scientific and philosophical knowledge seemed as bright as ever.

Epistemology was intertwined with the philosophy of language in a specific way: through our sense-data, we have a direct cognitive relation to the objects of our perception, which are the primary source of our knowledge.[3] Russell called this knowledge by *acquaintance*, in contrast to knowledge by *description*, which is always indirect and therefore (as Russell will later say), "inferred". Direct knowledge (or by acquaintance) is the root of the intelligibility of every language. At the same time, there is no language without descriptions. "Logical atoms", as the final goal of philosophical analysis, are reached through the interaction of both kinds of direct and indirect knowledge. In these times, Russell linked the philosophy of language to his general understanding of "logic". As we will see in Chapter 3, though, Russell later strongly psychologized philosophy of language, especially after abandoning Platonism and embracing neutral monism. In both stages, however, Russell's philosophy of language had strong empiricist roots. In 1912, Russell published *The Problems of Philosophy,* which was more systematic and much more widely read that his 1911 book. It took Russell's academic image beyond that of a logical-mathematical philosopher. This image would soon be indissolubly linked to Wittgenstein's critiques.

Wittgenstein's early philosophical insights were key in the development of Russell's philosophy of language and the theory of knowledge (Stevens 2018). Wittgenstein attacked the multiple-relation theory of judgement that

Russell had been developing between 1906 and 1913. According to this theory, judgment is a two-place relation between the judging subject and the proposition. A judgment is true when the proposition it is supported on is true. But this theory was contradictory with other stances that Russell held during that time, from the intentionality nature of every mental act to the correspondence theory of truth itself as Russell had defined until that moment (Lebens 2017). Wittgenstein's critiques made Russell abandon his 1913 *Theory of Knowledge manuscript* and rethink several points of his epistemology (Connelly 2021). That led to the publication in1914 of the book *Our Knowledge of the External World as a Field for Scientific Method in Philosophy*. Important continuities exist between this book and previous ones, from its empiricist premises to the role of logic as the purest form of scientificity. Russell aptly dubbed one of the book's main chapters "Logic as the Essence of Philosophy"; this was precisely one of the book's main thesis, and a central one for Russell's thought on the role of science and philosophy:

> Every philosophical problem, when it is subjected to the necessary analysis and purification, is found either to be not really philosophical at all, or else to be, in the sense in which we are using the word, logical. But as the word "logic" is never used in the same sense by two different philosophers, some explanation of what I mean by the word is indispensable at the outset. (Russell 2009[1914], 51)

He went on to divide logic into two main parts. The first one is the analytical investigation of propositions, specifically the study of the different forms and properties of atomic, molecular, and general propositions (Stevens 2005). The second is the study of the most general true propositions, which are those of pure mathematics. Both meanings of logic are supported on the general notion of logic as the rigorous and systematic discipline that studies all kinds of relations there are. In the remainder of the chapter, we demonstrated the centrality of the first meaning of logic for Russell's "logical atomism" even after he lost interest in the second.

Although Wittgenstein's *Tractatus Logico-Philosophicus* was published in 1921, in 1918 Russell acknowledged the influence of conversations with Wittgenstein in the final form of his *Philosophy of Logical Atomism* (Russell 1956; Stevens 2018). This new philosophy was the result of the publication in 1918 of a series of lectures Russell gave in the years 1916 and 1917. According to this general approach, reality is made of particulars and so is language. Propositions are the result of the combination of those particulars. Doing philosophy is to a large extent working (logically) on the philosophy of language.

Russell's 1918 *Philosophy of Logical Atomism* contains important differences with Wittgenstein's version of logical atomism (Galuagher 2013; Elkind and Landini 2018). Russell's emphasis on language and logical analysis does not mean that his logical atomism does not have a strong metaphysical side: Russell emphasized radical ontological plurality and contingency as a true feature of reality. In Russell's metaphysical worldview, reality consists in a plurality of discontinuous (i.e., independent and discrete) particulars. A single particular that exhibits a simple quality form a fact: an "atomic fact". Particulars, though, are constantly forming more complex realities, which are also *facts*. From this point of view, multiple particulars that stand in a simple relation also form an atomic fact. For Russell, we express a fact when we say that a certain thing has a certain property (including for instance a specific relation to another thing). Things and events, therefore, are not "facts" for Russell. Atomic facts, accordingly, belong to epistemology and its "logical analysis", rather than to metaphysics.

Although Russell's logical atomism had an undeniable metaphysical side, Wittgenstein's metaphysical atomism went even further. Specifically implying that the (semantically) simple symbols that appear in a proposition really refer to *simples* in reality. It is true that, despite its apparent precision, Wittgenstein's *Tractatus* is loaded with important ambiguities; one of them is about the metaphysical nature of logical atoms. Nevertheless, Wittgenstein's famous metaphysical "Argument for Substance" (TLP 2.0211–2) clearly seems to imply the metaphysical view of the existence of simple objects. But for Russell, and although in 1911 "Le Réalisme analytique" he held that he believed in the existence of simple things in the universe, and in 1915 he had published an article called "The Ultimate Constituents of Matter" (to which we will come back in Chapter 3), the metaphysical goal of arriving at ultimate simples ended up being impossible. Russell (1975[1959]) arrived at the conclusion that nothing can ever be known to be simple. Even if they exist, we do not have direct access to simple things as such; "atoms" are always in relative terms to the logical analysis. Whenever scientific investigation has reached an atomic element, it was only to realize its complexity and multiple parts. This meant that the simple elements we reach through logical atomism are not to be confounded with simple and absolute ontological elements: the empiricist Russell always defended the tentative and incomplete character of scientific knowledge. Therefore, and in a similar way as in the case of the "the ultimate constituents of matter", Russell's notions of *ultimate* or *atoms* only make sense here for the logical analysis, rather than for an optimistic metaphysical picture about how reality is. Therefore, logical atoms, rather than metaphysical absolute units, should be seen instead as epistemological units open to be broken down into simpler parts in future scientific empirical investigations. In Russell's metaphysical picture of reality, only the general structure of reality can be really known.

In Wittgenstein's logical atomism, reality has a timeless logical structure which is *shown* in the logic of language. In this general picture of reality, atomic facts consist of objects. For Russell's logical atomism, on the contrary, an atomic fact consists of the combination of at least one simple sense datum and at least one universal. In Wittgenstein's logical atomism, facts are also central. The *Tractatus* famously starts stating that the world is the totality of facts and that every fact is contingent. But in Wittgenstein's notion of fact, properties, understood as universals, do not have the importance we find in Russell. Furthermore, Wittgenstein's above-mentioned "Argument for Substance" implies a metaphysics hardly compatible with Russell's event ontology and tendency toward skepticism.

Russell held that many metaphysical mistakes stem from lacking a clear hierarchy of types. For instance, he attacked Wittgenstein's claim in the *Tractatus* that philosophical language is nonsensical because it does not refer directly to empirical events as scientific languages do. This, Russell pointed, would lead Wittgenstein to the contradiction of classifying his own non-scientific thesis as nonsensical. The trouble could have been avoided, Russell held, by his theory of types; that is, by acknowledging that philosophical languages are of a different type from scientific ones. Philosophical sentences could also be true or false, both in epistemology and ontology. This separated Russell from the logical empiricists. Language and ontology are necessarily related; but reducing the latter to the former is excessive. On these bases, Russell's well-known criticisms of the linguistic investigations of the second Wittgenstein were even harsher. Nevertheless, Wittgenstein complained in a private letter to Russell that the British philosopher did not understand the main philosophical idea of the *Tractatus*: the distinction between what can be *said* and what can be *shown* (Pulido 2009). There are things that, for their very nature, cannot be expressed in propositions. But they can be shown: for instance the mystical experience that things *are*. But also how propositions that are nonsensical can *show* things. It is important to remember that Wittgenstein's *Tractatus* clearly distinguishes between the concept of "nonsense" (*Unsinn*) and "senseless" (*Sinnlos*). Senseless propositions, for instance, are ones that lack truth-conditions (as Wittgenstein had defined them in empircal terms), such as tautologies and contradictions. But even these propositions "show that they say nothing" (TLP 4.461). We could say that, according to the *Tractatus*, Wittgenstein's nonsensical philosophical propositions try so hard to *say* what can only be *shown*. But in doing so, help the reader understand the nature of the world and of our knowledge of it. Later, the reader can throw away the *Tractatus*, in a similar way (Wittgenstein famously stated) as someone throws away a ladder after climbing up it.

For Russell all this was just contradictory. Russell did not accept Wittgenstein's binary saying/showing, claiming that it left with an undeniable "intellectual discomfort" and was not useful for him (Pulido 2009). But, since Wittgenstein held that in his *Tractatus* that the distinction between saying and showing is the chief means to explain how language is used, Russell's rejection of such distinction only meant that he was unable to accept Wittgenstein's core philosophy. It is important to note that Wittgenstein, in one way or another, kept this distinction until the end of his philosophical career, long after he had rejected his previous logical atomism and naive theory of truth (Pulido 2009; Stevens 2018).

Russell's differences with Wittgenstein's views of logical atomism went so far that, after their friendship vanished, Russell even ridiculed Wittgenstein's peculiar views of atomic facts as independent of one another, along with the thesis that all deductions must be formal. Thus, in "The Limits of Empiricism" (1936) Russell stated that "no one in fact holds these views, and a philosophy which professes them cannot be wholly sincere."

We have delved extensively on Russell's relationship to Wittgenstein's philosophy of language to stress that, even after having abandoned his interest in logicism and pure mathematics, Russell continued to work on logic as applied to philosophy of language. More centrally for our book's main interest: Russell understood logic as the best way of analysis of scientific propositions in general. A good example of this continuity is *An Inquiry into Meaning and Truth* (1940), which Russell wrote for the courses he taught at the University of Chicago in 1938 and 1939. Starting with some of the classical topics of philosophy of language, including language acquisition and the meaning of words, Russell built an argument about the reach and limits of human knowledge. Russell was no longer satisfied with his own theory of sense-data, and yet the role of atomism for logical analysis was central to his argument. His main tool was once again the distinction between object-language and logical or second order language. Object-language named experiences which are directly available. It was Russell's way of preserving a weak form of the realism through which he had opposed the neo-Hegelian idealism of his youth (Broncano 2015). Propositions and negations, on the contrary, already imply logical constructions and a reference to the linguistic possibilities. Propositions are the result of logical abstractions. When we use "no" to point that something is false, our reference is a phrase which is logically possible but has no correlate in reality. Analyzing how logical connectors enable complex linguistic propositions is the philosopher's tool to determine truth and falsehood beyond sensed experience.

Russell's approach to analytic philosophy was thus very different from that of the logical positivists, who had built a "scientific worldview" partially based on their reading of both Russell and Wittgenstein. In the 1920s and 1930s, Russell grew increasingly distant from what he thought to be Carnap's exaggerated emphasis on the empirical origin of all propositions. Another relevant point of contention concerned the power of linguistic analysis as dissolvent of (almost) all philosophical problems. For Carnap, philosophy should only focus on the logical analysis of scientific propositions: ontology and metaphysics should be discarded.

As such, philosophical propositions are neither true nor false. Russell could not accept this. Right after his abandonment of idealism, Russell (together with Moore) embraced a "primitivist theory of truth". This is analytical philosophy's first theory of truth, and considers "truth" an irreducible concept that is presupposed in every attempt of the definition of truth (Asay 2013). In his 1905 "On Denoting" it is already clear that Russell had shifted to the correspondence theory of truth, which he sustained until his death (Russell 1959). In both stages, though, he held that philosophical propositions can be true—for instance the main ontological principles of logical atomism.

The logical positivists, and particularly Carnap, presented their empiricism as ontologically-adverse: only epistemology can be truly philosophical. Against this reductionistic view of philosophy, Russell insisted instead in the ontological choices and backgrounds supporting his analytical methods. He presented his differences with some of the central tenets of the Vienna Circle with increasing clarity through the years. In 1948, for instance, Russell made clear in his *Human Knowledge: Its Scope and Limits* that philosophy should not be reduced to technical and detached linguistic analysis:

> Logic, it must be admitted, is technical in the same way as mathematics is, but logic, I maintain, is not part of philosophy. Philosophy proper deals with matters of interest to the general educated public, and loses much of its value if only a few professionals can understand what is said. (Russell 2009[1948], 13)

One interesting contribution to the critique of the Vienna Circle's approach to language and philosophy was Russell's 1949 paper *Logical Positivism*. There he collected classical arguments against naïve empiricism: induction, as Hume had already defended, only gives probability, and true knowledge requires extra-empirical assumptions. Experience thus could not be the only guide for truth. For instance, we do not experience past events which, however, inform our understanding of present physical or biological configurations. The same happens with predictions that we believe to be meaningful even though we cannot verify. This problem had of course come up in the discussions within the Vienna Circle about the dark side of the moon. But Russell used an example which will acquire its full significance in later chapters: the belief that atomic warfare could annihilate all life on Earth. "Who would then remain to verify this opinion?" (Russell 1949). Most importantly, linguistic reductionism was shortsighted. Philosophy was not exhausted by clarification or by ignoring all problems not directly checkable through experience; rather, it needed to be developed with reference to the sciences, including physics and, in stark contrast to Comte and most logical positivists, psychology.

Chapter 3 explores in more detail the epistemological and ontological development of Russell's thought, including in particular his turn to neutral monism. Many authors have pointed out to some incompatibilities between this monism and logical atomism (Bikson 1967, 206). After abandoning the theory of sense-data, the notion of object-language as presented in *Meaning and Truth* is not completely clear. Nevertheless, in Russell's philosophy analysis retained its status as the key philosophical tool. For Russell, this analysis was "logical" in its broadest sense (i.e., beyond the concept of symbolic logic). Moreover, mathematical logic remained for Russell one of the key scientific disciplines on which to support rigorous philosophy, truth continued to be defined by the correspondence between some forms of language and a plural and mainly discrete reality, and important dosages of skepticism and empiricism were a key part of epistemology. But the most pervasive continuity amidst Russell's rhetorical changes was, we think, that metaphysical pluralism kept providing the ontological framework of his worldview. As such, in a way Russell never truly abandoned the main premises of the "logical atomism" that he started to build after 1898. As we have been arguing throughout this chapter, Russell's approach to science and its role in society rested to a great extent on this complex combination of confidence and mistrust.

Arguments by Gödel, Hilbert, and others came to undermine the logicists' reductionist ambitions. Russell would never be able to recover logicism from these attacks.[4] Nevertheless, in a way Russell continued to endorse a different form of logicism, that is, a defense of logic against its perceived enemies. If we can say that Russell held some kind of logicism even after abandoning logicism is because the term "logic" is far from being univocal. Russell explicitly recognized this by separating modern scientific logic from the traditional one—the main difference being precisely the treatment of relations introduced in modern logic by de Morgan and others. In his essay "The Art of Drawing Inferences", written during World War II, but published in book form much later in 1968, he offered the following admonishment:

> If you wish to become a logician, there is one piece of advice which I cannot urge too strongly, and that is: Do Not learn the traditional formal logic. In Aristotle's day it was a creditable effort, but so was the Ptolemaic astronomy. To teach either in the present day is a ridiculous piece of antiquarianism. (Russell 1990[1968])

But even in the realm of modern scientific logic there are different types of logic—and different interpretations of them. Symbolic logic's realm of action, for instance, is constituted by a very reduced set of marks (which are non-arithmetic symbols), along with a few "logical" axioms. How to interpret these axioms has profound implications as to the reach and meaning of symbolic logic and still is an open problem in philosophy. If logical axioms are understood only as laws of thought, then the hiatus between reality itself and our knowledge of it increases. On the other hand, if the "laws of logic" are interpreted as absolute laws of reality itself, like in Parmenides or Hegel, it is easy to fall into some form of "panlogism" threatened by the ghost of subjective idealism.

Russell, aware of this conundrum, opted for some kind of blurry middle ground. Science, based on logical axioms, methods, and forms of analysis, is not descriptive of an absolute reality. But it is the best way available to us in our attempt to access reality's main structure and contents. A way, Russell insisted throughout his life, incomparably better than "polluted" ways of thinking, such as religion, superstition, or mystical philosophy.

Russell's logical atomism was pegged to his logicist program, but only partially. Analysis was at the heart of both. What this specifically entailed changed throughout the years. But the commitment to logical atomism as a way of philosophically grounding scientific propositions remained.

For our book's narrative, what we want to emphasize is Russell's pervasive commitment to logic in connection to science. Let's come back to the essay "Mysticism and Logic", which gives the name to Russell's book *Mysticism and Logic and Other Essays*. Originally published in 1910, this essay divides the history of philosophy through the radical binary of logical and mystical ways of thought:

> Metaphysics, or the attempt to conceive the world as a whole by means of thought, has been developed, from the first, by the union and conflict of two very different human impulses, the one urging men towards mysticism, the other urging them towards science. (Russell 1910)

Logic remained at the core of science. But logic, as crucial as it was for Russell, could be tainted by human ignorance, stupidity or malevolence. Such polluted logics were obviously to be avoided. Thus, although Russell recognizes the existence of a "logical mysticism" (such as Parmenides's or Bradley's), he clearly states that "mystical logic" is a prominent example of polluted logic. In Russell's own words: "the logic used in defence of mysticism seems to be faulty as logic, and open to technical criticisms". And even more radically: "the logic of mysticism shows, as is natural, the defects which are inherent in anything malicious". With changes of emphasis and nuances,

Russell maintained this thesis until the end of his life. According to it, the "logical holism" that he defended until 1989 was an oxymoron. Only a "logical atomism", or a "scientific logic", is truly *logical*.

For Russell, "mysticism", "holism", and so on, embodied the most dangerous mistakes in ontology and epistemology (such as denial of plurality, temporality, and the importance of empirical data). After Russell abandoned his logicist program, he continued to defend this strong binary—clearly visible, for instance, in his immensely popular *Religion and Science* (1935) and *A History of Western Philosophy* (1945).

CONCLUSION

When thinking about the foundational efforts of late 19th-century mathematics, historian Jeremy Gray proposes to take "modernism" seriously as a historical period (Gray 2006). Without wanting to reify a *Zeitgeist* cutting across different spheres of life, he nevertheless situates the various ideologies informing the practice of foundational mathematics in a larger context in the arts and sciences governed by a search of new disrupting principles set up against the old traditional ones and as immanent to the discipline in question as possible. That is, reference to the external world (of experience, of applications . . .) was not forbidden, but was often considered secondary relatively to the attempt to ground mathematics upon itself. The social background of this inner-looking had likely to do with the professionalization of mathematics—which, however, was still not compartmentalized by overspecialization (Ferreirós 2021).

The question of the broader cultural factors of the late 19th century turn to pure mathematics evades any easy answer. Discussing a later foundational moment which occurred twenty or so years after this first one in the interwar period, historian Dennis Hesseling asks directly whether World War I can be said to provide a cultural context relevant to the then prevalent talk of "crisis" (Hesseling 2003, 301–344). His answer differs from the classic one that Paul Forman applied to the crisis in physics in the same period on empirical grounds: there was simply no hostile social environment mathematicians were answering too. Hesseling's own response that the linkages to the broader culture were merely metaphorical and applied to events that otherwise might be explained in purely internal grounds is, however, not completely satisfactory either. Other replies to Forman might prove more fruitful. Norton M. Wise, on top of the empirical countering of Forman's hostile environment thesis, put forward a more general objection regarding historical causation (Wise 2016). For him, rather than seeking for "influences" of the external world upon the practitioners of a given science, it is more productive to look at scientists as active participants of the broader society with their own agendas and (socially informed) motivations and who are ready to appropriate the ideological resources they see most suited for their purposes.

In this general context, Bertrand Russell, and the transnational group of mathematicians he engaged with, is better seen as someone trying to shape his own times than merely passively responding to them. In the case of Russell, his approach to the foundational debate aimed to ground a new science-based ontology and epistemology. After rejecting neo-Hegelian dialectics as a polluted way of thinking, Russell turned to defending the superiority of science and logical analysis as a sacred form of thought. He combined this ardent defense, however, with his skeptical and empirical conviction of the tentative and changing nature of scientific theories and discoveries. This chapter has explored the place of mathematics and logic in Russell's dual approach to science and technology. The rise and fall of Russell's logicist and Platonic programs undoubtedly factored in whether he chose to stress optimism or pessimism regarding science. The "sacred fire" gradually extinguished itself.

Clearly, Russell's magnificent attempt to solve the ontological and epistemological problems posed by mathematics through logic did not succeed as he expected. But the project rendered lasting results and, more importantly for our book, it helped shaping Russell's intellectual life and his public persona. Russell's logicist agenda grounded his optimistic confidence in the power of science to understand and control the world. The problems it encountered, however, proved insurmountable. After abandoning British idealism, he combined his logicism with a form of selective Platonism, consisting on the reification of logical relations. This Platonism was selective in that, even after accepting some sort of conventionalist if-thenism for many regions of mathematics, there was some sense in which other mathematical entities or structures maintained for Russell a sense of eternity until reading Wittgenstein's *Tractatus* in 1919 (see, for instance, his 1917 private correspondence quoted in Monk 1996, 504). As this chapter has shown, however, Russell's Platonism was already by the 1910s much more limited than it had been in his turn of the century writings.

The collapse of Russell's Platonic logicism delivered a hard blow to his confidence in the sacred values of science. We have seen that logical analysis remained for Russell the most powerful philosophical tool. But he now understood logic itself, along with mathematics, as a set of man-made conventions and tautologies. This view fit into a simplistic binary: if knowledge mainly comes from empirical sources, mathematics and logic (or "mathematical logic") had to be reduced to harmless tautologies that do not inform us about anything in the world.

The gradual fading of his Platonic logicism showed Russell that science did no longer necessarily embody sacred values against the mystic's ignorant philosophy. During his most Platonic era, Russell used mathematics as some kind of safety room in which to escape from the pain, sorrow, and stupidity of the real world. World War I—or rather his interpretation of it—would show Russell that, on the contrary, science and technology could become the profane engines of destruction and suffering. And what is even more important: once the dream of Platonism collapsed, there was no escape from such profane evil. Russell, therefore, felt obligated to "return to the cave", becoming a well-known social and political activist.

Russell's abandonment of Pythagorean and Platonic epistemological and ontological optimism in favor of the rather more (epistemologically) pessimistic theory that the whole set of mathematical and logical propositions are nothing else than man-made empty tautologies thus played an important role in his later presentation of science as a more-than-probable harbinger of apocalypse. And yet, in the first two decades of the 20th century, Russell became one of science's most vocal advocates, and an inspiration to a new way of presenting philosophy as a logical analysis free from outdated metaphysical presuppositions.

Moreover, Russell's retrospective declaration that his intellectual career can be seen as the gradual abandonment of Platonism towards the view of mathematics as tautologies—in which we demonstrate what we have already assumed in our axioms—rests partly on a false dilemma. As in other cases, Russell seems to use a simplistic binary (in the case of mathematical objects: realism-conventionalism) which oversimplifies the actual positions he adopted across time. He transited other options. The intuitionist position of his Kantian youth re-emerged from time to time with the empiricist lenses of Poincaré (for instance when considering figures as pedagogical devices useful to picture abstract mathematical relations). As we have seen, even early Russell was ready to acknowledge that geometry was not completely reducible to logic and that the utility of axioms is demonstrated by the coherence of their results.[5]

For this book's interest—Russell's dual approach to science through utopian and apocalyptic imaginaries—mathematics and logic are at the core of the process of Russell's thinking. Science was the mother of the most important human practical and intellectual virtues; the sacred harbinger of human unlimited happiness and progress. In this picture, mathematics, understood in the logicist sense of *Principia Mathematica*, was the queen of the scientific kingdom. This picture had its days numbered; and when the sacred fire of mathematics became progressively weaker until finally dying, Russell ran out of any psychological or existential safety room from the darkness of human despair, evil and decadence. And yet, the soteriological role of "science" survived the ashes of mathematics' and logic's sacred fire, remaining as the most powerful weapon against the kingdom of darkness represented by human ignorance, stupidity and malevolence.

As the next chapter shows, in Russell's imagination, science became increasingly tainted from the Great War on. Like the God of the Old Testament, science developed a terrifying schizophrenic nature. Science was for Russell both the main source of humanity's good and evil, utopia and apocalypse, salvation and condemnation.

NOTES

1. McTaggart would later abandon the Hegelian dialectical method, but the radical idealist premises remained in both his epistemology and ontology.

2. In Russell's own words: "In adolescence, I hated life and was continually on the verge of suicide, from which, however, I was restrained by the desire to know more mathematics" (Russell 2013[1930]). "There was a footpath leading across fields to New Southgate, and I used to go there alone to watch the sunset and contemplate suicide. I did not, however, commit suicide, because I wished to know more of mathematics" (Russell 2010[1975], 32).

3. A relevant context for Russell's theory of language and epistemology is the *modernism* of the Bloomsbury group, epitomized by the literature of Virginia Woolf and other good friends of Russell and adepts to his and Moore's philosophy. For them, the challenge was to articulate an objective image of the world through concatenations of subjective sensations (Broncano 2015, 76–77).

4. Gödel, the author of the Theorem of Incompleteness that had so undermined logicism in 1931, attempted to bring Russell to his own form of Platonism in an essay he wrote in 1943 and that Russell chose to ignore (Monk 2001, 269).

5. We are not blaming Russell for essaying different approaches to the philosophical problem of mathematical reference. It is to this day an open problem (see some of the debates in Romero, Pérez-Jara, and Camprubí 2022). Platonism is still strong among mathematicians (but often in a methodological sense rather than in a strong ontological one: see Ferreirós 2016, 170–176). The alternative of *if-thenism* (also embraced by conventionalist and fictionalist philosophers) recovers a sort of formalism by which formal coherence with the premises is the only limitation as to what counts as doing mathematics and as mathematical entities. While Kantian forms of transcendental intuitionism are rather out of fashion, a more empirical intuitionism is alive and well in the empiricist view that mathematical entities derive from our worldly experience. In particular, the authors who emphasize the turn to practice in mathematics attend to bodily operations and material techniques which embed mathematical objects in spatial-temporal realms. This does not need to take the reductionist turn of claiming that the only reference for mathematical objects are diagrams and signs themselves. As Moritz Epple has argued, the practical and technical (and thus histori-

cal) configurations through which mathematical objects emerge are not incompatible with the abstract nature of those objects (Epple 2011). As opposed to *if-thenism*, an attention to historical practice attempts to answer the question of why some formal systems have been pursued and not others (Ferreirós 2016, 158–159).

Chapter Two

World War I and the Dethronement of Science

"When the War came", Russell recalled years later, "I felt as if I heard the voice of God" (Russell 1975, 227). At forty-two years old, he finally knew something with certainty: he had to do something to stop the war. The war, he went on, changed everything for Russell, including his conception of human nature: "I ceased to be academic and took to writing a new kind of books" (Russell 1975, 247). He gave this intellectual and personal transformation the form of a religious conversion. Russell notoriously opposed religious fundamentalists who based their political decisions on their alleged familiarity with God's voice. That he chose this metaphor becomes thus more revealing of the epiphanic nature of his conversion to anti-war pacifism. There was no room for doubt.

Importantly for this book's enquire, Russell also reconstructed World War I as a decisive point in his views on science and technology. The young neo-Hegelian Russell was long-gone, and the empiricist already well established and enjoying growing academic fame devoted to the promotion of science. The horrors of the war, according to his own recollection, would have curbed Russell's enthusiasm for science and technology as the bearers of progress and happiness.

In this chapter, we reinterpret the significance of World War I in cementing Russell's fame as public intellectual and social activist in transforming Russell's views on science and technology. Our main point is that the effects of the war's impact on Russell's approach to science and technology took longer to emerge than Russell would later acknowledge. Rather than an intrinsic association between the techno-scientific sphere and evil during the war, we argue that this association was the product of a traumatic interpretation of the conflict linked to industrial technology and national identities. This cultural interpretation required a complex work of narration and signification by a variety of authors and groups. In this process, Russell took longer than other public figures to accept the link between science and evil. This delay is understandable given his deeply rooted trust in science and technology as the most powerful tools for solving both intellectual and social problems.

What led Russell to accept the association between science and mass destruction and tyranny at the cost of his former confidence in science as bringer of progress and happiness? Russell had not always been a pacifist and was never an absolute one. In 1900 he had fiercely defended in front of friends and colleagues the necessity of British imperialism in the name of peace as well as of "the spread of civilized government" (Ryan 1988, 33–35). By 1903, however, he and many of his contemporaries sided with the Boer's guerrilla warfare against British imperialists. The reasons had to do with the much-publicized horrors of the war and international opinion on the role of Great Britain.[1] This early pacifist stance did not divert Russell from British liberalism. This would change in World War I. Since the very beginning of the Great War, Russell supported British neutrality in the conflict; and, from 1916 onwards, he joined socialist anti-war activism through a number of talks, international voyages and pamphlets. Eventually, this cost him imprisonment and a temporary removal from his position at Cambridge. He came back as a public figure of growing international impact.

Russell's fame in academia was well grounded after the publication of *The Principles of Mathematics* (1903) and *Principia Mathematica* (written along with Alfred North Whitehead and published between 1910 and 1913). But his extra-academic essays, such as the 1903 atheist-agnostic declaration *A Free Man's Worship*, became popular only once he had become a public intellectual. We argue that Russell's public activism and anti-war public discourse gradually led him to point to science and technology as forces of evil, an association increasingly common among some of his main pacifist allies. The very Manichean categories he often used to defend science against superstition, he now put to the service of attacking science and technology as irrational forces against moral and social progress. While other public thinkers shared this trajectory, Russell is perhaps unique in embracing the dualism in which science appears both as savior and wicked. Audiences and contexts could mark the difference between black and white, sometimes ignoring all the scales of gray.

The dual valuation of science would accompany Russell as a public figure throughout the rest of his career. Russell's theoretical attachment to "science" as the golden standard of knowledge and reasoning survived throughout the Great War. On the 18th of November 1914, just some months after the war had started, Russell delivered a Herbert Spencer lecture at Oxford titled "On Scientific Method in Philosophy", which was published by the Clarendon

Press as a pamphlet the same year, and reprinted in the second edition of *Mysticism and Logic* published in 1917, just months before World War I finally ended. In this lecture, Russell famously stated:

> When we try to ascertain the motives which have led men to the investigation of philosophical questions, we find that, broadly speaking, they can be divided into two groups, often antagonistic, and leading to very divergent systems. These two groups of motives are, on the one hand, those derived from religion and ethics, and, on the other hand, those derived from science [. . .] The adoption of scientific method in philosophy, if I am not mistaken, compels us to abandon the hope of solving many of the more ambitious and humanly interesting problems of traditional philosophy. Some of these it relegates, though with little expectation of a successful solution, to special sciences, others it shows to be such as our capacities are essentially incapable of solving. But there remain a large number of the recognised problems of philosophy in regard to which the method advocated gives all those advantages of division into distinct questions, of tentative, partial, and progressive advance, and of appeal to principles with which, independently of temperament, all competent students must agree. (Russell 1917a)

This binary opposition between "scientific philosophy" (linked to rigor, clarity and truth) and "non-scientific philosophy" (linked to obscurity, arbitrariness and superstition) was a constant throughout Russell's career. One finds it in *What I Believe* (1925), *Why I Am Not a Christian* (1927), *Religion and Science* (1935), *Human Knowledge* (1948), and even in his philosophical testament, *My Philosophical Development* (1959). This pervasiveness makes Russell's embracement of the association of science to mass destruction and tyrannical oppression all the more intriguing. This optimism coexisted with certain degrees of skepticism from the onset. But after World War I, the combination of science, technology, and tyrannical politics became one of Russell's main targets. In the last years of his life, Russell became an activist against nuclear weapons and a ferocious attacker of the US war in Vietnam. As Chapter 5 of this book explores, it was then that Russell's narrative of techno-scientifically produced universal evil reached its full apocalyptic dimension.

The contradiction between utopian an apocalyptic interpretation of science is rampant. It might be tempting to scape it by pointing that Russell distinguished between science and its uses and applications. But this does not solve the problem. Because, even if that were the case, the distinction between science and technology is not central in his public statements for and against science—excepting his early pleas for pure mathematics beyond the usefulness of applied mathematics. Rather than through pure logic, Russell's dual approach to science needs to be explored in its specific sociological contexts. Russell emerges not only as a privileged witness of the history of 20th-century science and technology, but also as a key actor in the moral codification of science in this convoluted period.

In the first section we overview Russell's anti-war activities from 1916 until after the war. These activities had two immediate effects: new books and ideas and a growing fame as a political agitator, fueled by his imprisonment and dismissal from Cambridge. Our main point here is that Russell's stance against British involvement in the war was not self-evident. Rather, it was the result of a traumatic interpretation of the war advanced mainly by socialist groups opposing the Victorian order. As ideologies often come in packs, Russell's activism took him to political positions that he had hitherto criticized and which will also inform his new approach to science and technology.

The second section shows that Russell did not immediately extend his negative interpretation of war to science and technology. This argument was already available during the war, with anti-war thinkers blaming both science and its applications for mass-destruction. Russell, until then convinced that science (and its applications) announced a new bright future for humanity, took a bit longer to reposition. Starting in 1920 he grew more vocal in his attacks to industrialist society. But his full-blown denouncement of the perils of science appeared in 1924 in a much-publicized discussion in which the mythical figures of Daedalus and Icarus provided a framework to imagine the future of a technified society.

RUSSELL AGAINST "THE WAR TO END ALL WARS"

Russell's certainty about the urgency of opposing the war contrasted sharply with the ambience around him. Before war was declared by the British Empire, Russell organized a petition, signed by over 60 Cambridge dons, expressing "their conviction of the supreme importance of preserving England's neutrality", since "no vital interest of this country is endangered such as would justify our participation in a war."[2] He was at the time certain that the majority of the British people opposed the war. He began to lose confidence as he witnessed popular joyful celebrations of Britain's declaration of war. At the very beginning of the war Russell had not completely lost hope that "some day we shall emerge into a saner world" (Griffin 1992, 525).[3] Russell was ready to justify wars of civilization, but it seemed to him that amongst civilized nations there is no possible justification. Only primitive psychological instincts like fear and pride could account for the continuing existence of these kinds of wars, and only education could promote the future annihilation of those feelings (Monk 1996, 366–402).

The war was much longer than he or anyone had anticipated. Russell's deep emotional and intellectual transformation due to his interpretation of the Great War gradually led him to depression and also to entertain mystical ideas once again, this time following his new friend, the young writer David Herbert Lawrence. As he grew less interested in academic philosophy and more in exploring the human passions that led to war, Russell agreed with Cambridge University for a leave of absence in the academic year 1915/1916.[4] He planned to devote his time to political work, part of it writing together with Lawrence a series of lectures called "Philosophy of Social Reconstruction". The two men argued over the text and Lawrence turned against Russell's democratic and pacificist ideals (Monk 1996, 403–431). Russell fell into a "black despair" and even considered suicide.[5] Russell could hardly endure the pain and bordered nihilism: "I hate the world and almost all the people in it."[6] This pathological hate led him to ask rhetorically: "how much good it would do if one could exterminate the human race?"[7]

There are good accounts of the personal and social contexts that made Russell's positioning seem so self-evident to him (Denton 2001). We should be careful, however, not to rely on the "horrors" of the war alone to account for this strong positioning. As trauma sociologists and psychologists have insisted, violence and suffering alone do not determine how armed conflicts are perceived. The political interests and projects of the groups able to put up successful narratives are often at least as relevant as the actual numbers of bombs, deaths, and rapes (Baumesiter 1999; Eyerman, Alexander and Breese 2016). As such, Russell's conversion did not occur in an ideological void. Rather than the result of an empirical observation of evil, it was linked to the discourses of the late Victorian positivists and socialists who opposed British imperialism and, by the end of the war, advocated for a world government as the only way of avoiding future wars (Claeys 2010). These discourses, in turn, opposed the more extended official nationalist and imperialist narrative, shared by colleagues and friends with whom Russell entered in intellectual conflict. This polarization, for instance, brought to an end the friendship between Russell and Whitehead, his co-author of the *Principia Mathematica*.

Again, no matter how sympathetic philosophers and historians of ideas might be to Russell's views, they should avoid taking them for granted. Not the least because there were intellectuals, in Britain and abroad, who saw "the war to end all wars" as the necessary lesser evil against German imperialism—the phrase was coined by no less than leftist H. G. Wells in an article showing his enthusiasm after Britain's declaration of war.[8] The idea was that a definite victory against the forces of evil would bring long lasting peace. Russell himself would make a similar argument during World War II, as we discuss in Chapter 4. In different parts of the world, the cultural impact of World War I produced competing ideological polarizations around the interpretation of the conflict. In a neutral country like Spain, progressive intellectuals such as writer Blasco Ibáñez pleaded the government and public opinion to enter the war by the allies' side (Navarra Ordoño 2014). Pacifism was thus not self-evident. As elsewhere, positions defined themselves against domestic and international rivals. In the United Kingdom, a significant slice of the public opinion supported the government's role in the war, hoping that Great Britain's victory would grant their country a politically and economically advantageous position. Against this stance, radical socialist movements organized a pacifist opposition. They saw in their fight against war an opportunity to end the weakening Victorian order. Despite government repression and media demonization, the British pacifist movement achieved a prominent presence within the British civil sphere (Hochschild 2011, 277).

In this specific cultural context, Russell positioned himself as a convinced pacifist. From 1916 on, he also became a prolific author of books which were partly academic and partly political. This was when, according to Russell, the war became fiercer and pacifism harder (Russell 1975, 233). Russell's pacifist ideas and lecturers appeared in the books *Principles of Social Reconstruction* (1916a); *The Policy of the Entente, 1904–1914: a reply to Professor Gilbert Murray* (1916c), *Justice in War-time* (1917b), *Political Ideals* (1917c), and *Proposed Roads to Freedom: Socialism, Anarchism, and Syndicalism* (1918).

During the summer of 1915, Russell finished alone the book he had planned to write with Lawrence, *Principles of Social Reconstruction*. In his *Autobiography* (1967–1969), Russell recalled (somewhat obscuring the book's real context), that he had not planned to write the book and it came to him rather spontaneously (Russell 1975, 229). He presented its chapters as lectures at the Caxton Hall during the fall and winter. The lecture's success among leftist and radical intellectuals proved to him that he could make a living outside academia and feel politically useful as the head of a regenerationist movement (Monk 1996, 455). The book appeared in 1916 and it is widely recognized as one of Russell's most solid political theorizations. Russell himself was taken by surprise by its success—and pleased by the economic rewards this success brought him (Russell 1975, 229–230). The *Principles* was Russell's first best-seller.

Loyal to his psychological approach to social problems, *Principles of Social Reconstruction* presented a political philosophy in which impulses have more weight than conscious purposes in shaping men's lives. This is likely why the book was called *Why Men Fight* in the United States, even without Russell's consent (Russell 1975, 229). Abstracting himself for the political details of World War I and from its debates, the book's wider focus was how to regenerate society after the war, offering "his vision of a society whose members would be too content with peace to be anxious to resort to war" (Ryan 1988, 32). Russell classified human impulses into "possessive" and "creative". According to his binary distinction, possessive impulses were the main things responsible for war and suffering, through the struggles between political nations and groups of power. The "Principles of Social Reconstruction", therefore, meant the criticisms and limitation of these "possessive impulses" in order to create a new and better society.

In December 1915 appeared Russell's 100-page pamphlet *The Policy of the Entente*, which was a public reply to Professor Gilbert Murray's endorsement of the war. Murray, a leading scholar of Ancient Greece's language and culture, was since 1908 Regius Professor of Greek at the University of Oxford. He had also been good friends with Russell. Disgusted by Russell's anti-war activities and with the support of the Foreign office, he wrote a pamphlet responding to Russell and others under the title *The Foreign Policy of Sir Edward Grey 1906–1915* (Monk 1996, 438). It was published by Oxford Clarendon Press in 1915 and the government secretly distributed thousands of copies among opinion makers (Monk 1996, 438). Russell's response triggered a public debate which consolidated Russell's public image. It also marked his public break with the Liberal Party's official line.

Departing from the abstraction of the *Principles of Social Reconstruction, The Policy of Entente* descends back to the political intricacies of World War I. Unlike Murray, Russell could not accept the argument that the only way for the UK to defend Belgium was declaring war on Germany. In his view, criticizing the political mistakes that led to the war was an act of patriotism. His love of England was undisputed, but the war represented a threat to European civilization (Russell 1916c, vi). Russell proposed in *The Policy of the Entente* alternative geopolitical scenarios in which the British Empire renounced further imperial expansions, surrendered its right of capture at sea, concluded arbitration treaties and used its political and cultural influence as a creditor nation to further liberal ideas, to prevent oppression and to promote democracy (Russell 1916c, 75).

As historian Alisa Miller argues, *The Policy of the Entente* "articulated the motivations behind Russell's engagement in the Union of Democratic Control, although he was underwhelmed by its effectiveness" (Miller 2015). While not explicitly pacifist, the Union sought to decrease military presence in the government, particularly in deciding on foreign affair issues, including waging wars. Russell's short-lived alliance with the Union thus speaks to his willingness to make his ideas socially and politically effective in the war's specific milieu. After the unexpected success of his first two books on the war, Russell continued targeting large audiences. The arguments were rather similar in his next books. Relying on a growing body of accounts of imperial struggle for resources, he distinguished between the real "egotistical" and "irrational" motives why powerful decision makers went to war and their ideological justifications. But the matter was one of utilitarian ethics: for the majority of people, the costs far exceeded the benefits. World War I, Russell concluded, is "trivial, for all its vastness. No great principle is at stake, no great human purpose is involved on either side" (Russell 1917b).

Russell's anti-war activism went well beyond these written contributions. The real personal, professional and political effects of his activities were the result of his collaboration with the No-Conscription Fellowship (NCF), linked to the Independent Labour Party. In January 2016 the British government approved the forced conscription of all single young men. The NCF became a leading movement for all opposing the war and willing to declare themselves conscience objectors against fighting the war or contributing to the war efforts. Russell joined the effort in the spring of 1916 and offered his intellectual prestige to its cause, eventually becoming chairman (in substitution of the imprisoned one). Russell acted as a ghost writer to some of the NCF's most important pamphlets, traveled abroad to build transnational networks, and mediated between different factions of the party (Vellacott 1980; Slot 2008; Miller 2015). He also became a notorious public speaker. By and large public opinion perceived objectors to conscription as traitors (Russell 1975, 241). But there was also an audience for pacifism. The Leeds Convention of June 1917 gathered over a thousand pacifists, most of them belonging to the Independent Labour Party and the Socialist Party. The convention had achieved a loud echo, and the international press reported that Bertrand Russell, the famous professor at the University of Cambridge, had preached the pacifist ethos together with prominent members of the Labour Party such as Ramsey McDonald and Philip Snowden. "To my surprise," Russell told his then-lover, the poet and activist Lady Ottoline Morrel, "when I got up to speak, I was given the greatest ovation that was possible to give anybody" (Russell 1995[1917], 34).

The alliances of his new activism took Russell to political positions which had been until then very foreign to him. Previously a (conservative) liberal, he had opposed socialism already in his first book, the rather unnoticed *German Social Democracy* (1896). Already at the beginning of the war he told Ottoline that "socialists are the hope of the world; they have gained in importance during this war. I would swallow socialism for the sake of peace" (quoted in Monk 1996, 382). During the war he became much closer to socialist and collectivists ideas as part of his opposition to World War I. Ideologies often come in packages or set menus—a theme to which this book returns. Liberalism had become the ideology of patriotic warriors.[9] By contrast, socialists (Marxist and non-Marxist alike), argued during the Great

War that capitalism led to imperialist and nationalist warfare. Socialism seemed a viable option to gauge against war (Ryan 1988). This enabled some socialists, including Russell's future wife Dora, to retain their faith in human progress despite the horrors they denounced.[10] Capitalism was to blame. Russell's critique of capitalism did not mean that he embraced the socialist faith in full (Ryan 1988). By 1917, Russell was proposing "guild socialism" as a way out of this conundrum (see, for instance, his *Political Ideals*). And yet, Russell interpreted the outbreak of the Russian as the announcement of a new and freer society; an optimism he lost after the Bolshevik turned over (Monk 1996, 497–502).

As Russell increased his anti-war visibility, the number of his enemies grew. In April 1916, Russell published the pamphlet "Two Years Hard Labour for not Disobeying the Dictates of Conscience" on behalf of Ernest Everett. Everett, a schoolteacher, was among the conscious objectors to be punished for avoiding the forced conscription under the Military Act. "Everett", Russell wrote in his defense, "is now suffering this savage punishment solely for refusal to go against his conscience. He is fighting the old fight for liberty and against religious persecution. Will you join the persecutors . . . ?" Russell's pamphlet led the Foreign Office to prosecute him under the Defence of the Realm Act (DORA) of 1914. Russell harshly criticized the Act because it gave the British government the power not only to requisite buildings or lands for the war, but also to censor criticisms against the government's policies. Both Russell's allies and enemies interpreted Russell's prosecution as a ruse designed to keep Russell from traveling to lecture in the United States (Miller 2015). Russell, on the other hand, took it as an opportunity to extent his fame and influence in the anti-war propaganda effort through his very political speech at court (Monk 1996, 463).

The scandal led to Russell's dismissal from the University of Cambridge's Trinity College. Outrage followed when the vast majority of the Fellows of the College opposed the decision (Hardy 1970, 57–58). Godfrey Harold Hardy, a well-reputed professor of mathematics at Cambridge and Oxford, wrote in 1941 a widely-circulated pamphlet titled "Bertrand Russell and Trinity". According to him, Russell's dismissal had deeply affected the College's reputation, even after the feud between Russell and the university was eventually solved (Hardy 1970, 59, 61).

Russell's anti-war activism included foreign relations. When the US was still neutral, Russell wrote to President Wilson urging him "to save the world" by staying out of the war (Russell 1975, 237). Censorship made it hard for the letter to travel. Nevertheless, the sister of a short-lived fiancée of Russell, Helen Dudley, took the document secretly to the United States, delivering the letter to the committee of American pacifists through which it was widely published (Russell 1975, 240). The letter appeared in various American newspapers on 23 December 1916. Despite this apparent success, it obviously did not help in reducing the scope of the war. Russell recognized this failure to change the course of events (Russell 1975, 248).

Disappointed by President Wilson's involvement in the war, Russell publicly lectured against the United States' role on Britain's side in the war. In an editorial he wrote in January 2018 for *The Tribunal* suggesting to accept German's peace offer as Russia was planning on doing, he included too many explicit insults against both the British and the American governments. This led to a second prosecution which resulted in Russell's imprisonment as a traitor (Vellacott 1980).[11]

Russell remembered his six months' imprisonment with certain nostalgia. It augmented his prestige and self-conscioussness as a public agitator while at the same time offering him time to write about things "less painful than the universal destruction" (Russell 1975, 242). Unlike many of his companions at the NCF, Russell certainly did not have a bad life in prison. Arthur Balfour, conservative politician who had served as Prime Minister of the United Kingdom (1902–1905), was the main person responsible for Russell's first-class treatment while at prison. He had returned as First Lord of the Admiralty in Asquith's Coalition Government (1915–1916). In December 1916, he became Foreign Secretary in David Lloyd George's coalition (Adams 2013). And, although Russell had opposed all his policies during the war, thanks to Balfour's intervention, Russell enjoyed a more than acceptable life in his imprisonment. He was allowed to read and write all he wanted, provided, of course, it was not pacifist propaganda. At the Brixton Prison, Russell wrote his *Introduction to Mathematical Philosophy* and started working on *An Analysis of Mind*.

Thanks to the social echo of his imprisonment, Russell's fame as public intellectual kept growing. Russell would never since then take out his public agitator hat. After the war, he was reinstated at the University of Cambridge in 1919. Although he later resigned in 1920, Russell became Tarner Lecturer in 1926 and Fellow again in 1944. But he had developed a taste for activism, journalism, and free-lance philosophy. In 1920, by invitation of the Trade Unionist, Russell travelled to the Soviet Union. The trip, during which he met both Trotsky and Lenin, killed all of Russell's expectations for both Russia and the Communist revolution (as he would make clear short after in his *Theory and Practice of Bolshevism*). It also increased his ambivalence towards socialism as both a hopeful alternative to industrial capitalism and a threat to individual freedom.

In 1922, Russell delivered and published a lecture titled "Free Thought and Official Propaganda" at the South Place Institute. In this lecture, Russell described the episodes of censorship he had to suffer for being a "free thinker" in different moments of his life, including his dismissal from Trinity College due to his opposition to the war. In 1924, Russell attended a celebration at the House of Commons with famous pacifist campaigners such as A. Lupton, who had been a Member of Parliament and was also imprisoned because of his pacifist activities during the war. This event granted Russell enormous press attention, increasing his fame as social activist and intellectual even further.

Before moving to the relationships between Russell's activism and his views on science and technology, it is important to stress that Russell's pacifist activism was completely colored with Manichean and messianic language. As discussed in this book's Introduction, *evil* is always the result of rich cultural processes of interpretation, narration, and signification. Already sociologist Émile Durkheim argued that the sociocultural processes of narrating and "embodying" evil are structured upon binary codes (Durkheim 2008[1912]). The radicality of these binaries depends largely on the social glue holding together those groups which label a particular phenomenon, event or rival as wicked. This binary logic often implies the sacrifice of theoretical or practical coherence in exchange of strong social positionings.

Russell's own philosophy comes to prove the point. Before reading of Santayana's *Winds of Doctrine* (1913), Russell's approach to the categories of good and evil was decidedly naturalist and essentialist. The ethical cognitivism of his 1910 *The Elements of Ethics* closely followed G. E. Moore's 1903 *Principia Ethica*. Ethical statements have truth-value. They are objective and universal. But Russell soon abandoned this ethical cognitivism for a more subjective and relativistic stance on ethical categories (Russell 1975, 504). What is significant for our analysis is that, despite this theoretical development, he continued presenting "good" and "evil" as absolute categories in his facet as public human rights activist of growing world fame. Moreover, as the next section shows, he would eventually come to apply this mythical binary logic to the political roles of science and technology.

THE APOCALYPTIC FLIP

Before World War I, Bertrand Russell fought squarely among the ranks of the historicists who shared the view of science as the main engine of human progress (see Chapter 1). In early 20th-century Britain, the conflict thesis between science and religion had given way to timid alliances in various fronts. Not for Russell (Bowler 2001, 340–349). Science and scientific philosophy represented a complete departure with previous religious and mythological thinking and the disappearance of religious thought in a philosophically-scientifically produced future seemed likely to him. It does not seem unfair to consider Russell's interpretation of science as "scientific fundamentalism". This concept appeared in 1928 in the American journal *Welfare Magazine* by analogy to religious fundamentalism (Bueno 2014). Through a simplistic binary code, religious fundamentalism holds that a specific religion has the monopoly of all intellectual, aesthetic and practical virtues and values. Scientific fundamentalism bestows this role onto "science".

Russell positioned himself as a progressive thinker since very early stages of his career. Drawing from the Enlightenment and positivism, Russell identified science with "Reason" and placed it as the main engine of progress. In this scheme, science played a similar role as the divine light did for medieval worldviews. It saved everything it touched. It was science which justified both technology and philosophy, which could be bestowed with the virtues of science by becoming scientific enough. By contrast, things outside science's radiating scope remained in the dark shadows of ignorance and evil. Religion and superstition were among them, but also traditional metaphysical philosophy. The holy duty of the true philosopher was to protect and encourage the virtues brought by science. A great example is his article "The Place of Science in a Liberal Education", which was a reprint of "Science as an Element in Culture" (*The New Statesman*, May 24 and 31, 1913):

> The increased command over the forces of nature which is derived from science is undoubtedly an amply sufficient reason for encouraging scientific research, but this reason has been so often urged and is so easily appreciated that other reasons, to my mind quite as important, are apt to be overlooked [. . .] Disinterested curiosity, which is the source of almost all intellectual effort, finds with astonished delight that science can unveil secrets which might well have seemed for ever undiscoverable. The desire for a larger life and wider interests, for an escape from private circumstances, and even from the whole recurring human cycle of birth and death, is fulfilled by the impersonal cosmic outlook of science as by nothing else. To all these must be added, as contributing to the happiness of the man of science, the admiration of splendid achievement, and the consciousness of inestimable utility to the human race. A life devoted to science is therefore a happy life, and its happiness is derived from the very best sources that are open to dwellers on this troubled and passionate planet. (Russell 1913, 33, 44)

Science emerges here as the means to dominate nature, but also as the all-beautiful and all-powerful fountain from where all kind of aesthetic, ethical and intellectual virtues flow. For all of his opposition to religion, Russell was ascribing the highest sacred value to science. Predictably, values classified in opposition to science became for Russell impure or polluted (in a word, profane). Thus, for instance, his criticism of those educated only in the arts, who in his view would tend to think that the past was superior to the present and that desires are stronger than logic and reasoning:

> In the study of literature or art our attention is perpetually riveted upon the past: the men of Greece or of the Renaissance did better than any men do now; the triumphs of former ages, so far from facilitating fresh triumphs in our own age, actually increase the difficulty of fresh triumphs by rendering originality harder of attainment; not only is artistic achievement not cumulative, but it seems even to depend upon a certain freshness and naïveté of impulse and vision which civilisation tends to destroy. Hence comes, to those who have been nourished on the literary and artistic productions of former ages, a certain peevishness and undue fastidiousness towards the present, from which there seems no escape except into the deliberate vandalism which ignores tradition and in the search after originality achieves only the eccentric. (Russell 1913, 40)

In contrast to Hesiod's decadent view of history, in Russell the nostalgia for the past has a very dark and dangerous side: it hides the fact that science, as the fire stolen by Prometheus from the gods, has brought the key for the ever-growing progress of humankind. Past ages, with all their undeniable achievements, were undoubtedly less scientifically developed. And science is the golden standard for progress. Therefore, contrasting to the light of his own times, Russell perceived his epoch's ancestors as bound to rely on superstitious, mythology, and theological metaphysics. Russell very drastically tamed this progressive view after World War I.

How did war force Russell to revise his faith in science? It did not in an immediate way. Just as the war's intrinsic brutality does not suffice to explain the anti-war narrative that identified it with absolute evil, making the techno-scientific sphere responsible for its violence required political and rhetorical work. After all, since at least the Renaissance, wars and exploitation had heavily relied on new technologies of transportation, communication, and mass destruction. None of this stopped Russell from embracing the so-called "Age of Reason" as a new era full of promises. It is also not enough to affirm that the scale and scope of suffering brought by World War I was unprecedented in absolute terms. Because many other British intellectuals kept intact their faith in science and technology as the harbingers of progress after the Great War (Bowler 2001, 32). Russell admitted in 1928 that the war had not put an end to optimism in England and America (Russell 1928, 1).

Later in his life, Russell repeated that his pessimism towards science and technology emerged during the war (Russell 1975). But even in *Proposed Roads to Freedom*, which was completed as late as April 1918 just before his anti-war activism took him to jail, the techno-scientific sphere does not appear as a menace to the world. Certainly, science and technology did not get in the way of a promising future in which guild socialism could help achieve "a new and younger world, full of fresh hope, with the light of morning in its eyes"[12] (Russell 1919).

Russell did eventually curb his optimism regarding science as the source of all epistemic and moral virtues. But he did so once the war was over, and particularly after his visit to the Soviet Union and during his trip to China. The key to Russell's changing interpretation of science was the association of industrialism and modern science. The ambivalence towards the place of science in society is already a "matter of life and death" in his 1922 article "Obstacles to free Thought":

> My plea throughout this essay has been for the spread of the scientific temper, which is an altogether different thing from the knowledge of scientific results. The scientific temper is capable of regenerating mankind and providing an issue for all our troubles. The results of science, in the form of mechanism, poison gas and the Yellow Press, bid fair to lead to the total downfall of our civilization. It is a curious antithesis, which a Martian might contemplate with amused detachment. But for us it is a matter of life and death. Upon its issue depends the question whether our grandchildren are to live in a happier world, or to exterminate each other by scientific methods, leaving perhaps to negroes and Papuans the future destinies of mankind. (Quoted in Monk 2001, 16)

This is precisely the duality that structures our book. From here onwards, Russell would, alternatively and depending on context, attach to science the promises of utopia and the prophecies of apocalypse. An even more elaborate argument blaming industrialism for mass destruction appeared in 1923 in *The Prospects of Industrial Civilization,* a book he partly wrote with his then wife Dora. They had started writing it during their trip to China in 1920. Russell contrasted his experience in China with his trip to Russia that same year.[13] With perhaps an anthropologically naïve look, the couple was fascinated by the morality and way of life of a country seemingly frozen in time—in a later text, Russell imagined a spatial equivalent to Well's time machine: China was 150 years back (Russell 1928). The industrial age of energy and factories produced automobiles and telephones, but also guns, bombs and poison gas. Linking it to nationalism, Russell and Dora presented industrialism as an explicit threat to human freedom. In the wrong hands, science could be fatally destructive for the human race. Industrialism created large populations which had to be subject to controls only made possible by new scientific and technological discoveries. To tame this new power, they continued, a world government was the only solution.

The argument was not new in the Wilsonian era of the League of Nations. In fact, linking war and untamed modern capitalist industry was part of the ideological pack of the British pacifist activists Russell had collaborated with during the war. And yet, Marx and other socialists tended to blame applications of science rather than science itself. That changed with the war. Borrowing from the sociological notion that political movements are bundles of narratives, historian Robert Bud has explored British narratives around "applied science" from the turn-of-the-century to the interwar period (Bud 2018). The concept, far from self-evident, moved across a variety of social movements. In political propaganda, industrial advertisement and educational reform, applied science announced an era of knowledge-led progress. With the outburst of World War I, liberal imperialists and conservatives alike made victory dependent on the efficiency of applied sciences. This association proved to be a two-edged sword. German strength was attributed to their leading position in applied sciences. And German poisonous gas came to embody the dangers of untamed science (Girard 2008). World War I became "the chemists war" (MacLeod 1993). Thus, Bud shows, already during the war applied science came under attack. While some scientists advocated for a retreat to the realm of pure knowledge untouched by military uses, religious movements in Britain resuscitated the science-faith debate with a vengeance. They now blamed science for the very applications it had hitherto been given credit for. Socialists opposing the war took on the discourse and added it to their denounces of industrial capitalism and their mistrust over machines replacing workers.

Given Russell's strong faith in science and technology, it is not surprising that it took him longer to adopt the whole anti-war ideological package. Amidst a polarized debate around applied science, Russell's strong anti-war positioning made it impossible for him to dissociate the mass scope of destruction he was denouncing from the modern scientific and technological discoveries which made it possible. Others put the blame on "machinic civilization", leaving science rather untouched and pure. But Russell had insisted throughout his career in the benefits carried by sciences through their application—to refer to them, he usually preferred to use "scientific technique" over technology (Schatzberg 2018, 124). Now, he feared that nefarious applications were practically unavoidable. In Russell's repositioning, peace and altruistic freedom became the sacred ideals, and science and technology the (at least potentially) polluting means through which profane powers aim to destroy them.

Once again, we encounter Russell's dual valuation of science. Throughout his career, Russell's ambivalence towards science and technology switched the axiological value he attributed to them often depending on contexts, arguments, and audiences. In late 1923, Russell participated in a series of lectures organized by the Fabian Society under the agonizing question "Is Civilization Decaying?" (Monk 2001, 28). Russell, who had time and again asked the same question in private and public, contributed with a lecture soon after published as a series of articles under the title "Science and Civilization". Birth control, scientific psychology, new apparatuses, all could be put to the service of mankind if men were rational. But they are selfish and brutal. Only the brute force of a nation like the United States could create a world Government and ensure a peaceful and democratic future (Russell 1923). This paper became the basis of what would be Russell's most vitriolic attack on the role of science in society: *Icarus: Or the Future of Science.*

Positionings need antagonists. Russell chose to make public his new interpretation of the place of science and technology in human progress in the context of a famous controversy. In 1923, John Burdon Sanderson Haldane published *Daedalus: Or, Science and the Future,* reproducing a lecture he had offered earlier on that same year at the Heretics Society, an intellectual club at the University of Cambridge. Haldane had been teaching biochemistry at the Trinity College since 1922 and was already a well-known scientist. His ideas on the bright future of biological control of human offspring had already circulated before *Daedalus* and had had a controversial reception: already in 1921 Aldous Huxley wrote a novel which announced some of the critiques to which he would devote *Brave New World* in 1932 (Bowler 2017, 194). The repercussion of *Daedalus* spread quickly, increasing Haldane's fame as an intellectual.

Russell capitalized on this prominence to promote his own views through Daedalus's counterfigure in a book published in 1924: *Icarus: Or, the Future of Science*. After having been taught to fly by his father Daedalus, the great mythical inventor of technological artifacts, Icarus was destroyed by his own hubris and lack of sense, approaching the sun without realizing that it would melt his feeble wings. Similarly, human hubris would ruin the bright prospects for a scientific and technological future imagined by Haldane. As the two texts generated a heated polemic at their authors' common intellectual home, the Trinity College, Russell's public position on the dangers of science attained a great visibility

Russell's article clearly articulated this new position. "Mr. Haldane's Daedalus", Russell stated, "has set forth an attractive picture of the future as it may become through the use of scientific discoveries to promote human happiness. (. . .) I am compelled to fear that science will be used to promote the power of dominant groups, rather than to make men happy" (Russell 1924). Russell invoked his experience with statesmen, governments, and as witness of the Great War to declare wrong and naive his own former views on science. Instead of bringing a future Golden Age, science would be mobilized by despotic governments as a powerful tool to control and repress their citizens, as well as to build weapons of mass destruction.

When read carefully, Haldane's *Daedalus* is more nuanced than Russell acknowledged. It contains certain warnings here and there about the possible dangers of scientific advances if not enlightened by similar progresses in ethics.[14] Nevertheless, Russell chose to focus on its overall optimistic tone about the role of science in building a golden future. The controversy gave Russell the opportunity of putting forward his new but long-lasting thesis: "science has increased man's control over nature, and might therefore be supposed likely to increase his happiness and well-being. This would be the case if men were rational, but in fact they are bundles of passions and instincts" (Russell 1924).

According to Russell's *Icarus*, physical sciences are responsible for the most significant changes in our control of nature. But the dark side of this process was felt in the way industrialization and technological development completely transformed human cultural and social development, generating a hostile environment where nations fight each other for the control of finite resources and markets. Russell was aware that competition and violence were also present in the pre-industrial era. But he highlighted that modern industrialized nations needed more resources and raw materials than former societies based on more basic ways of economic production and development. The growing and fierce struggle for resources between states and empires has war as its predictable and sinister outcome. Coal, iron and oil, Russell continued, had become the basis of modern power and, therefore, of wealth and economic progress. Nations without those resources are doomed to perish in the face of more scientifically and technologically advanced powers. An industrialized nation rich in resources, and Russell had very specific examples in mind, controls markets and imposes direct or indirect tributes on weaker nations. And economists too often underrate the role of war in economic progress.

Science and technology are at the heart of this process. Russell's key idea was that technology generates stronger dependencies on resources and simultaneously increases the destructive capacities of the countries that are fighting to extract and use them. Russell adhered to the lineal model according to which new technologies were the result of new scientific advances (on the linear model, Kline 1995). In particular, progresses in physics and chemistry accounted for the appearance of new weapons of mass destruction. And he also understood that particular techniques favored certain forms of governments over others, such that the technological advances made possible by scientific progress jeopardized political liberalism. Thus, communication and transportation allowed for the rise of more despotic forms of centralized governments hitherto unthinkable. In Russell's words:

> Without railways, telegraphs and telephones, control from a centre is very difficult. In ancient empires, and in China down to modern times, provinces were governed by practically independent satraps or proconsuls, who were appointed by the central government, but decided almost all questions on their own initiative. (Russell 1924)

Russell blamed not only the physical and chemical sciences as responsible of new ways of evils and tyranny: biology, psychology and medicine were not exempt from his bitter criticisms. Sure, developments in biological sciences made possible birth-control, which for Russell had significant social benefits regarding women's liberation. However, at the same time, birth-control also opened up new possibilities for eugenics, a technique with respect to which Russell also strongly repositioned himself. Before the war, the science-enthusiast Russell was very optimistic about eugenics' possibilities. But the post-war "traumatized" Russell argued that eugenics, instead of being put at the service of the common good, would be used by despotic governments with sinister goals. In Russell's sarcastic words:

> So, if eugenics reached the point where it could increase desired types, it would not be the types desired by present-day eugenists that would be increased, but rather the type desired by the average official. [. . .] I suspect that they would breed a subservient population, convenient to rulers but incapable of initiative. However, it may be that I am too skeptical of the wisdom of officials. (Russell 2005[1924])

Despite these precautions, only one year later, in *What I Believe*, Russell hailed scientific betterment of the human race, an idea he also cast in a positive light in his 1929 *Marriage and Morals*. Russell also oscillated between the poles of utopia and apocalypse regarding psychology, and in particular its applications to the control and manipulation of human populations. While in this period Russell envisioned a bright future built through science-led education, *Icarus* warned of the perils of scientific psychology. Advertisers in America were already employing eminent psychologists to instruct them in the techniques for producing irrational belief. These scientists, Russell stated, could also be able to persuade people that their wicked governments are wise and good. And, what is worse, rulers could also develop and deploy powerful drugs to control the hormones regulating human behavior.

Russell, once again, opened the door for some form of hope: "whether, in the end, science will prove to have been a blessing or a curse to mankind, is to my mind, still a doubtful question." The key to that door, we will see in the next chapter, lied in education. But he concluded his *Icarus* stressing that: "science has not given men more self-control, more kindliness, or more power of discounting their passions in deciding upon a course of action"

(Russell 1924). Quite the opposite, science has given communities incredible power to indulge their evil passions, and that is "why science threatens to cause the destruction of our civilization". As in *The Prospects of Industrial Civilization,* the only solid hope for a brighter future lies "In the possibility of world-wide domination by one group, say the United States, leading to the gradual formation of an orderly economic and political world-government. But perhaps, in view of the sterility of the Roman Empire, the collapse of our civilization would in the end be preferable to this alternative" (Russell 1924). Russell's ambivalence vis-à-vis the US as world power and empire would undergo further transformations in the future, taking him first to plea for a nuclear attack on the Soviet Union and then to systematically demonize US foreign policy during the Vietnam War—a development explored in further chapters (Woodhouse 1980). Science was no longer the palace of Siddhartha Gautama before becoming Buddha, a place where evil and suffering do not exist.

CONCLUSION

This chapter has followed the flow of Russell's ideas about science and progress before and after World War I. It has done so paying particular attention to the cultural riverbeds that canalized this flow and to their historical dynamism. Locating the precise nature of Russell's transformations is not easy. In his late book *My philosophical Development*, Russell repeated again the huge influence that World War I had in his intellectual career, making impossible for him "to go on living in a world of abstraction" (Russell 1975[1959], 157). But it would be much more accurate to say that during and after the war, Russell just increased the number of "abstractions" through which he interpreted the world. Russell's change of mind also had a powerful emotional side:

> In this change of mood [caused by World War I], something was lost, though something also was gained. What was lost was the hope of finding perfection and finality and certainty. What was gained was a new submission to some truths which were to me repugnant. My abandonment of former beliefs was, however, never complete. (Russell 1975[1959], 157)

We have sought to discern how and why Russell interpreted the events of the Great War in strong traumatic terms. Recall the book's three main theses as laid out in our Introduction—the importance of interpretation for providing historical events with meaning, the mythical structures of those interpretations, and the necessity of public intellectuals to connect to existing interpretations. Along those lines, and in pursuing the book's focus on Russell's changing views of science and technology, our main interest in this chapter has been in the impact that Russell's traumatic interpretation of World War I had on his public views of the role of science and technology in bringing either salvation or apocalypse to humankind. As if the Janus-faced Russell were a coin, the cultural interpretation of the war flipped it over: the face looking at the future no longer was expecting a coming Golden Age produced by the discoveries of science and technology. Rather, his gaze was now submerged into an apocalyptic view of the times to come. To be fair, Russell's thought was not nearly as consistent as this, and in the same year as he published his *Icarus* he continued in other venues preaching on several of science's bright promises—this led to the end of his friendship with Thomas Elliot, who had become even more radical than Russell in his mistrust of science. But there was no coming back from the dual characterization of science as savior or annihilator.

Before the Great War, Russell's optimistic narrative on science and progress was structured upon a set of easily identifiable simplistic binaries: a non-scientific past (which, from our perspective, could be classified inside the domain of the "profane/polluted") was placed in contrast with a scientifically driven present and future (which would fall into the "sacred/pure" category). With only very few exceptions, Russell had previously mainly focused on ontology and epistemology in his publications and lectures. Since the 1916 appearance of *Principles of Social Reconstruction*, he began to publish extensively on political philosophy and ethics. These essays, opposing violence and resource struggle, defended world peace and freedom. But Russell's darkest views of the role of science and technology in human future did not come to light directly during the war or right after it. Rather, it took several years of maturation, achieving its most complete and famous expression in his 1924 "Icarus".

At least in part, Russell's dramatic rhetoric on the increasingly dystopian dimension of science and technology belonged, we have argued, to the dramaturgical aspects of his pacifist positionings and their packaging in a particularly polarized intellectual arena. One could interpret Russell's imprisonment during the Great War as a kind of theatrical performance.[15] It greatly increased Russell's popularity among certain audiences who could emotionally identify themselves with the dramatic intellectual who, like a modern martyr, was unfairly punished for bringing a sacred message of peace and prosperity against the profane powers that were spreading the unbearable evil of the war. Of course, from both the British government and other public and private institutions, counter-narratives and counter-performances emerged to limit these interpretations, presenting Russell as a betrayer of his sacred nation and the brave soldiers who were sacrificing their holy lives to defend it.

But that these narratives did not succeed to obscure public sympathy towards Russell demonstrates that not only victorious groups get to narrate historical events. Opposition to the government questioned the legitimacy of the British Empire and its use of scientific and technological tools to preserve it, and it succeeded in spreading a traumatic understanding of the war and its associations to applied science. As a dramatic intellectual, Russell recognized that he had adopted the role of a prophet, proclaiming hopes about brighter futures in a way that was able to convince important parts of the public (Russell 1975, 366).

We will in further chapters see that Russell's prophetic ardor did in fact not fade in later periods of his life. But we would like now to return to the role of World War I in triggering it. The naturalistic fallacy appears when a too strong connection is drawn between facts (is) and values (ought be)—for instance, assuming that it was the intrinsic brutality of the Great War itself what flipped the coin of Russell's Janus-faced understanding of the past and the future, of Golden Age and darkness, of sweet dreams and nightmares. In contrast, we have emphasized the contingencies of interpretation and the work required for narratives to ignite. From the point of view of cultural sociology, these considerations could also be applied to other "traumatic" well-known historical and social events, from the Babylonian Captivity, the Discovery of America, to 9/11 attacks; in all of them, socioculturally mediated processes were always needed to unfold these events as devastating. Usually, these thick cultural layers of interpretation remain invisible or unconscious to the social actors who are shaped by them.

In the case of the Great War, this cultural attribution was made in real time, as the war unfolded. Nevertheless, as we saw, Russell's view on the apocalyptic nature of the techno-scientific sphere was a *post hoc* cultural reconstruction, after the Great War had concluded. In other occasions, a cultural trauma can be produced before an event occurs, or, what is more surprising, by an imagined event that has never occurred at all but *could* occur (Alexander 2001, 2003), as we will see when discussing nuclear weapons and nuclear apocalypse.

The cultural processes through which events are represented in traumatic ways tend to be deeply rooted in traditional mythical and religious codes and narratives. Thus, when Russell bestowed technology and science of new meanings after the Great War, he represented them as the terrifying profanation of the sacred values of human progress and freedom; as a set of evil powers that, in the hands of rulers, represented as tyrants, would pollute everything they touched. For Russell, the future had acquired darker tones.

Past, present and future are not absolute dimensions of being. Rather, they are, among other things, the product of complex cultural classifications. As a well-known social actor, Russell played a significant role in the cultural classifications through which a considerable part of the world populations came to think that the future was no longer what it used to be.

NOTES

1. According to David Blitz, and against Russell's own autobiographical recollections, Russell's anti-imperialist and pacifist shift occurred in the middle of the Second Boer War; more specifically, "in the course of Russell's debate with the French logician Louis Couturat during the year 1900. Not only was Russell unable to refute Couturat's pacifist arguments; but by his silence and lack of reply he acknowledged that Couturat had refuted Russell's own best efforts at defending imperialism and the rule of the most powerful" (Blitz 1999, 117).

2. This petition for neutrality appeared in *The Guardian* and *Daily News* on August 3rd 1914, accidentally the same day that Foreign Secretary Sir Edward Grey carried the House of Commons in support of a declaration of war, duly made the following day, August 4th. The same day that the war was declared, Russell had planned, along with the editor of the British Liberal newspaper, *The Nation*, to publish a letter which was finally withdrew. Nevertheless, after protests, it was printed on August 15th. In it, we can read: "Against the vast majority of my countrymen, in the name of humanity and civilization, I protest against our share in the destruction of Germany. A month ago, Europe was a peaceful comity of nations; if an Englishman killed a German, he was hanged. Now (. . .) he is a patriot [. . .] And all this madness, all this rage, all this flaming death of our civilization and its hopes, has been brought about because a set of official gentlemen, living luxurious lives, have chosen that it should occur, rather than any of them should suffer some infinitesimal rebuff to his country's pride." As is perhaps understandable, after this letter British mainstream newspapers were closed to Russell during the war.

3. From a letter to Margaret Llewelyn Davies, August 1914.

4. Russell felt increasingly uncomfortable at Cambridge, which did not welcome radical pacifists and he felt as oppressive; see his letter to Ottoline Morrell, May 15th, 1915 (Russell 1975, 262).

5. Russell spoke about his despair and depression during the war in many occasions; for instance Russell 1975, 237.

6. In his December 28th, 1916 letter to Colette, Russell spoke of the hate he felt to all of whom he considered responsible for the war and for the human race at large; "I am ashamed to belong to such a species" (Russell 1975, 289).

7. Letter from October 8th, 1917, to Lady Ottoline Morrell.

8. The motto "the war to end all wars" was adopted by H. G. Wells, who published a number of articles in British newspapers that were later collected in a book entitled *The War that Will End War*. In Russell's interpretation, Wells blamed the "Central Powers" for the coming of the war, with a specific target in German militarism (Rempel 2003, 10; Wagar 2004, 147).

9. In his writing "Some Psychological Difficulties of Pacifism in War Time," appeared in the book *We Did Not Fight: 1914–18 Experiences of War Resisters* (edited by Julian Bell in 1935) Russell recognized, referring to the Liberal Party, how painful was seeing how, "one by one, the people with whom one had been in the habit agreeing politically went over to the side of the war" (Bell 1935, 327). In his rejection of the Liberal Party and its stances during the war, Russell even unsubscribed from the Cambridge Liberal Association in 1915, writing them a letter explaining his decision (Russell 1975, 256).

10. Dora Black was a young pacifist activist and feminist intellectual who admired Russell's public anti-war campaign. The air initiated their romantic relationship in 1919 and got married on 25 September, 1921.

11. In the newspapers *The Daily News* and *Leader* from 2 September, appeared articles on Russell that read: "the Government have preferred to treat an Englishman of distinction as though he were an alien of suspicious antecedents, presuming apparently on the unpopularity of his views to protect their conduct from inconvenient criticism" (Miller 2015).

12. In *My Philosophical Development*, Russell downplayed the importance of *Roads to Freedom* as a book wrote quickly when he was already convinced that he had done all he could for pacifism and more interested in reissuing what he considered to be proper "philosophical subjects" (Russell 1975[1959], 95).

13. Dora had also travelled to Russia in 1920, although not with Russell, and she had become fascinated with the Soviet Revolution. Their disagreement on this did not conceal their agreement on China.

14. Although it is also interesting to note that some scholars have empathized that Haldane had a peculiar view of the role of ethics in human progress, as his admiration for Stalin would prove (Dronamraju 1995).

15. As we clarified in this book's Introduction, when we talk about dramaturgy and scenography, we do not mean at all that social actors are, somehow, "fake"; in some cases, of course, they can pretend and "calculate" their performances for personal or group benefit. But in others, on the contrary, they can intellectually and emotionally fully identify with the social roles and rituals they perform in front of a specific audience. In the majority of cases, though, social actors oscillate between strategy and unconscious identification with the roles they perform (Alexander 2004, 2011).

Chapter Three

The Tortuous Mazes of Mind and Matter

In his *Autobiography*, Russell situated the origins of his long-life fascination with the ideas of mind and matter was triggered by his grandmother's ironic dislike of metaphysics:

> When she discovered that I was interested in metaphysics, she told me that the whole subject could be summed up in the saying: "What is mind? no matter; what is matter? never mind." At the fifteenth or sixteenth repetition of this remark, it ceased to amuse me, but my grandmother's animus against metaphysics continued to the end of her life. (Russell 2010[1975], 33)

The puzzle of dualism structured much of Russell's evolving understanding of the possibilities and limits of science, both from the point of view of his epistemological theories of knowledge and of his ontological studies of mind and matter. Russell came back and again to this set of problems. His thoughts on mind and matter resemble a maze, full of conundrums and dead ends that forced Russell to try new paths and rectify his course. His Ariadne's thread was philosophical but made of scientific fabric. Russell was witness of the extraordinary development of physical and psychological theories such as the theory of relativity, quantum mechanics, behaviorism, and psychoanalysis. Russell always sought to mobilize scientific developments to inform and structure his own epistemological and ontological approaches to mind and matter.

Russell's efforts to analyze the ideas of mind and matter from a scientific philosophy and not get lost in the attempt, structure his entire epistemological and ontological thought. This is not to say that Russell always thought that everything that there is must be either mental (psychological) or material (physical). At different moments of his intellectual career Russell considered the existence of mathematical essences or structures and of a neutral reality prior to mind and matter. But, throughout his life, the main guiding ideas for ordering the ontological and epistemological space were the ideas of mind and matter. It is around these two ideas that Russell's changing and conflicting ideas on idealism and realism took place.

Russell attempted to overcome dualism in various ways throughout his long career (Leithauser 1997). In his Kantian and neo-Hegelian youth, the world of empirical matter is but an appearance. There is only the Whole or the Absolute, which has a spiritual nature. After abandoning idealism around 1898, Russell assumed the fundamental postulates of an empiricist philosophy of a realistic nature (Eames 1969; Ciguere 1970). Empiricism remained with him for the rest of his life, but with important nuances of interpretation. The main issue in Russell's empiricism revolved around the duality between sense-data, such as objects or objective physical characteristics, and perceptions, as subjective mental acts. This was different from traditional spiritualistic dualism. For Russell, the spirit makes little sense without the body: even if he held that incorporeal living beings are ontologically possible, he insisted that in humans and other advanced animals the brain seemed to be the basis for psychic life (Russell 2005[1921]). But the duality between perception and the thing perceived did reintroduce a strong division between mind (the subjective) and matter (the objective) that haunted Russell's philosophy.

Russell attempted to overcome this duality through the theory of "neutral monism," inspired by his reading of, among others, Ernst Mach and William James—whose approach Russell had previously argued against. *The Analysis of Mind* (1921) identified physical matter and the mind as aspects of a prior extramental reality. But neutral monism created problems of its own. Russell's empiricist psychologism led him to emphasize, time and again, the psychological aspect over the physical one. This reintroduced the specters of skepticism and idealism. Taking the mind and its perceptions as the point of departure, Russell struggled to justify the existence of the external world and of our knowledge about it beyond mere probability. Later in his life Russell hesitantly fell back to a sort of duality between the physical and the mental, which he manifested, but hardly developed, in *My Philosophical Development* (1959).

For the purposes of this book, Russell's philosophical tribulations around the external world and our knowledge about it are central to his changing views on the power of science in relation to society. This is so in two fundamental ways. First, after the sacred fire of Platonic essences had died out, Russell viewed mathematics as mere tautologies unable to inform us about the intrinsic nature of the external world. Natural sciences, on the other hand, became the only hope for grounding a philosophical worldview. Russell came to see philosophy as distinct from the sciences (in its generality and criticism) but at the same time dependent on them, particularly to mathematical logic, physics, psychology, and physiology as a bridging discipline between the two (Russell 1975[1959], 12). Philosophy's main goal is unveiling the "fundamental furnishing of the world" (Clack 1964, 159). As such, it relies on natural sciences and at the same time critically demarcates their limits. Philosophical knowledge is much more precarious than traditional metaphysicians like Hegel thought. Philosophy's very value lies in its uncertainty, which shatters dogmatic thinking and questions received common sense.[1] It is this critical stance which enables Russell to admit a much greater degree of certainty to the sciences than to philosophy while simultaneously ascertaining that the reality sciences describe is not absolute. There is thus a circular feedback loop between Russell's epistemology and ontology and his gauging of the truth-value of scientific knowledge.

Second, Russell's evolving understanding of the human mind was central to his fading hopes on human rationality. In his 1913 *The Place of Science in a Liberal Education* there is a strong sense of the liberating possibilities of enlightened rationality against ignorance and superstition. As World War I unfolded, Russell attributed an ever-larger role to primitive instincts in human affairs. As he delved into psychoanalysis and behaviorism he envisioned new possibilities for scientific education, this time in the sense of a science-informed set of educational techniques able to produce selfless rational civilized citizens. His own personal failures in this regard, as well as his continuing studies in human psychology, gradually replaced this utopian program with a darker view of the possibility of tyrannical manipulation of human primitive instincts and reason. In the hands of such irrational human beings, the prospect for science and technology were bleak. While Russell sometimes separated what he considered pure philosophy from his interest in politics, he made the link clear and explicit in 1924, and in a way which goes to the core theses of our book regarding his conception of the relationship between science and society:

> Science has increased man's control over nature, and might therefore be supposed likely to increase his happiness and well-being. This would be the case if men were rational, but in fact they are bundles of passions and instincts. (Russell 1924)

The first section of this chapter dives into the central puzzle haunting Russell's epistemological and ontological thought: the relationship between perceptions and percepts. Exploring Russell's early writings on sense-data and sensibilia, we then turn to his exposition of neutral monism as a crossroads between epistemology and psychology, on the one hand, and ontology and physics, on the other. Russell's confidence and skepticism towards the natural sciences is here at one with the idealist tendencies haunting his empiricism. Idealism casts its long shadow through what we have called the hubris of psychology (Russell's tendency to subjective idealism) as well as through a more Platonic sense of the concept of idea (the objective idealism regarding mathematical structures as the ultimate object of physics).

Section two studies Russell's philosophy of physics, in particular his reception of the novel quantum and relativity theories. Our goal here is to demonstrate Russell's enthusiastic but careful approach to these sciences. A sense of provisionality cuts across Russell's approach to physical theories. Furthermore, Russell makes it clear that our access to the physical reality is limited and mediated and we should not expect the physical sciences to provide a trustworthy picture of absolute reality.

The third and last section delves into Russell's philosophy of psychology and physiology. Physiology mainly provides the causal theory of perception, which poses the philosophical problem of the circularity of using physics to explain the perceptive apparatus which gives us access to the physical reality. This problem haunts Russell's 1927 *The Analysis of Matter*. Psychology, in turn, demonstrates for Russell that the soul, consciousness, and even the ego are to a large extent mythical constructs. Following and updating Hume's bundle theory, Russell thinks of the human mind as a mutable aggregate of mental events, often in precarious relationships with one and other and rarely in complete control of the human subject. This poses more challenges than opportunities when it comes to using science for the betterment of society and to make people embrace scientific reason in their social and political choices.

NEUTRAL MONISM AND THE HUBRIS OF PSYCHOLOGY

In Chapter 1 we mentioned the origins of Russell's theory of sense-data and its links to his logical atomism. From *Our Knowledge of the External World* (1914) onwards, Russell held that material objects, rather than substantial things, are collections of *sense data*. In turn, sense data are the physical events we have access to through psychological perceptions. In an effort to preserve realism, Russell's empiricist philosophy of the 1910s understood sense-data as the physical contents of psychological perceptions. This, in turn, informed his central distinction between direct and inferred knowledge (Salema 1971, 58). The knowledge of immediate things (which he called "acquaintance" until his 1940 *An Inquiry into Meaning and Truth*) was very different from the indirect knowledge gained by linguistic description (Russell 2008[1912]; 2007[1921]; 2009[1948]). Acquaintance forms the basis for the intelligibility of all language (Cassin 1968; Perkins 1973, 174–196; Nasim 2007, 153).

Everything but actual private sense-data, was for Russell either an inferred reality or a "logical construction". As Clack puts it: "Besides universals, only entities immediately presently in sense experienced can be genuinely known. All other entities, or supposed entities, are only 'inferred,' and for Russell inferred entities are not, strictly speaking, known" (Clack 1964, 135).

The distinction between inferred realities and logical constructions chez Russell is rather tricky. In *The Problems of Philosophy* (1912), Russell maintained that the existence of material objects can be inferred from sense data, not constructed out of them. Nevertheless, only two years later, in *Our Knowledge of the External World* (1914), Russell presented mind-independent external processes as inferred realities, but matter as a logical construction.

Russell's "logical constructions" and "inferred" realities share important similarities: both are opposed to direct knowledge from our private perceptions. Nevertheless, they also present important ontological and epistemological differences. In his key essay "Logical Atomism" of 1924, the British philosopher analyzes his previous main ontological and epistemological ideas since his abandonment of neo-Hegelian idealism. In that context, and for the first time, Russell described some of his former analysis and definitions as "logical constructions". Russell's examples ranged from mathematics (numbers as classes) and philosophy of language (his theory of definite descriptions) to general ontology and epistemology (the construction of matter, mind, and time from sense-data). Classes are logical constructions; and matter, mind, and time are classes of sense-data. Russell's epistemological and ontological atomism, therefore, did not renounce to epistemological operations of synthesis. Through classifications, definitions and other epistemological operations, we need classes to understand the world and ourselves, even if such classes are not absolute features of how reality is in itself but rather human constructions, logical constructions. When we analyze the world that surround us, we see that it is composed of individuals or particulars, which our cognitive processes arrange according to certain properties or patterns. This is how we form logical constructions. According to Russell, the logical constructions built from particulars are constitutive of human knowledge. Without them, the universe would appear as an unintelligible chaos.

Inferred realities, by contrast, can exist without human beings. They are not immediate. We can only directly know the data from our immediate sensory experience; everything else, is *inferred*. The external world itself is inferred. Therefore, inferred realities have an ontological privilege over logical constructions. For Russell, it is very probable that the external world exists independently from us; but this consideration cannot be applied neither to mind nor matter.

The metaphysical distinction between logical constructions and inferred realities was central to Russell's conception of realism. According to him, "the supreme maxim in scientific philosophizing" is that "Whenever possible, logical constructions are to be substituted for inferred entities" (Russell 1914, 155). This maxim persisted in Russell's philosophy even after he abandoned the sense data theory in favor of neutral monism—see below. He continued to consider mind and matter as logical constructions. But these constructions were no longer formed from ontologically different collections of events (mental and material). Mind and matter became for Russell logical constructions formed from the *same* (neutral) reality, just following different patterns of epistemological arrangement.

The central problem that thus organized Russell's approach to the theory of knowledge was the neat distinction between physical objects and psychological perceptions of those objects. There were two interrelated problems: that of preserving physical objects from their psychological reduction and that of salvaging perceived objects from their mere status as external things. Trying to avoid subjectivism as much as possible, Russell later identified the constitutive components of material entities with *sensibilia*, understood in Kantian terms as potential objects of sensation. When sensibilia are perceived, they then become *sense data* for the perceiver. Which means that sensibilia, *as sensibilia*, are inferred. And yet, both terms refer to the same kind of thing: objective physical entities or properties not reducible to psychological contents of the mind.

The notion of inferred sensibilia put Russell into dialogue both with traditional empiricism and with his contemporary "Edwardian controversy", a heated philosophical debate concerning the relationship between sense data and matter which took place in the ideologically convulse times of King Edward's rule (Nasim 2008). Well-known voices in such debate included T. P. Nunn (1910), Samuel Alexander (1910), G. E. Moore (1914), and G. F. Stout (1914). The most important issue under discussion was how to prove, against Berkeley's metaphysics, that the direct objects of perception, along with their sensory qualities, were extramental. Besides the rejection of idealism, contenders shared a mistrust of naïve realism: both physical matter and the very concept of matter, were the result of what was broadly described as a psychological or logical construction. "Matter" goes beyond what is directly perceived; and we do not mean here just the invisible material processes studied by quantum mechanics or astrophysics; "matter" itself, as a whole, is an idea grouping a class of things, and therefore an epistemological fiction constructed from both data directly available to our senses and inferred (from my subjective data) events.

In Russellian (early) terms: matter is known "by description," not "by acquaintance" (i.e., directly).² But, again, we should not confuse matter (logically constructed) with the external reality (inferred).

That the existence of the external world was a matter of belief and probability brought Russell closer to Hume's radical empiricism (McKeever 1973). This does not mean that for Russell the external world is *induced* from our private perceptions; just that, in a similar way as for Hume, there is no epistemological and ontological necessity for the existence of the external world. On this point, both Hume and Russell fit squarely with a long spiritualist tradition. Descartes asserted that we know that the external world exists because we believe that God, in His goodness, would not deceive us. Along the same lines, Malebranche held that our knowledge of the external world stems from our belief in what the Bible says (once again, in the Word of God) which tells us that His Most High created the world in six days. Drawing on the medieval and scholastic distinction between *essence* and *existence* (from Alfarabi to Thomas Aquinas) John Locke criticized the knowledge of the essence of substances, but not the thesis of their existence. Existence was ensured through the traditional principle of causality. Thus, while the cause of external perceptions would be the extramental world, the cause of internal sensations would be the soul. In turn, the cause of the extramental world and the soul would be God. Going beyond Locke, Hume did not count on the notions of causality or God. For him nothing really guaranteed the existence of things other than subjective perception and associations. In the 18th century, Thomas Reid appealed to "common sense" to demonstrate the existence of the external world. For Kant, in an argument Russell accepted, this was a pseudo-solution to Hume's problem by referring to the uncritical popular opinion (Reid 2005, 19).

Russell was not content with this rather weak rebuttal of idealism. If the external world was but a probable inference, it became harder to distinguish hallucinations from perceptions of actual objects (Nasim 2007, 157–158).³ More pressing for Russell was the problem of private knowledge and solipsism (Darlington 1978, 138). Our main source of knowledge stems from empirical sensations and everything else is inferred therethrough. Accordingly, since I do not experience the sensations of subjects other than myself, such sensations are also inferred. It thus follows that *my own sensations alone* are the main source of knowledge and that everything else is inferred through them. Even if we have strong rational reasons for believing in the existence of other minds, this belief is the result of a probable inference. The realm of objective reality—neither inferred nor logically constructed by the subject— was narrowing more and more (Copleston 1994, 440–441).

Neutral monism was an available option out of the subjective idealism to which empiricism seemed to take Russell. Having read the works of William James and Ernst Mach, in his unpublished 1913 manuscript *Theory of Knowledge* neutral monism appears as an attractive option from the point of view of the principle of parsimony, a worthy principle for Russell the logician. But, despite its simplicity, Russell saw no further reasons to accept such strange worldview. In his 1914 *Our Knowledge of the External World* Russell dismissed the approaches of James and Mach on the grounds of what he then thought to be the unavoidable distinction between the thing perceived and its perception.

But only a few years later, during his first lectures on logical atomism in 1918, Russell's objections to neutral monism appear clearly attenuated (Pears 1972, 135, 175; Brown 1974, 120–146). Instead of the classical epistemological structure of cognitive subject, object of cognition, and a relationship between the two, neutral monism required less entities to juggle. Russell's full embracement of neutral monism, however, had to wait for the publication in 1921 of *The Analysis of Mind.* Perceptions and percepts are in that book expressions of a common and prior reality. This meant a significant departure from his theory of sense-data (some authors have wrongly downplayed the incompatibility between sense-data and neutral monism. For an example of this mistake, see Stewart 1961, 10).

For Russell, pure sense-data uncontaminated by the psychological realm were no longer tenable. The very distinction between awareness of an object and the object itself crumbled—this took Russell to reject both Brentano's theory of intentionality and Husserl's phenomenology (Copleston 1994, 450).

Russell admitted that abandoning the theory of sense-data forced him to restructure his theory of knowledge almost entirely, but also that he did not immediately become aware of this necessity (Russell 1975, 101). Ideas such as acquaintance, experience, knowledge, and consciousness had then to be redefined. Furthermore, the traditional lack of rigorous analysis and definitions of these terms was for Russell the reason why empiricist premises ended up leading to idealist conclusions:

> Under the influence of Idealist philosophers the importance of "experience" has, it seems to me, been enormously exaggerated. It has even come to be thought that there can be nothing which is not experienced or experience. I cannot see that there is any ground whatever for this opinion, nor even for the view that we cannot know that there are things we do not know. I do not think that the opinion which I am combating could have flourished if people had taken the trouble to find out what the word "experience" is capable of meaning. (Russell 1975[1959], 107)

Unfortunately, Russell himself lacked a rigorous and systematic definition of these terms: "'consciousness' consists in the knowledge that something is happening to me or has happened to me. What is meant by 'knowledge' in this definition remains to be investigated" (Russell 1975[1959], 107). As is evident, Russell defines consciousness in relation to knowledge, thus giving the impression that he has untangled the gnoseological meaning of this term in the face of his adversaries. However, he acknowledged forthwith that he lacked a concrete definition for the term "knowledge", which he left for future investigations (a rather wishful project to announce at the age of 87). He pursued a similar strategy with regards of the term "acquaintance", which had been so central to his *The Problems of Philosophy* (1912): "In the *Inquiry into Meaning and Truth*, (. . .) I replaced 'acquaintance' by 'noticing', which I accepted as an undefined term" (Russell 1975[1959], 104).

These terms, like those of "imagination" and "memory," seemed to refer to mental activities without a clear physical correlate. This posed an enormous challenge to Russell's neutral monism (Pérez-Jara 2014). Worst still, the problem of the existence of the external world worsened within Russell's new theory (Nasim 2007, 150). For all changes in terminology, Russell never quite abandoned the distinction between direct (or immediate) knowledge and inferred knowledge (Salema 1971, 58). The material world and other minds remained something the subject construed (Gruender 1953, 33). He was fully aware of this, writing in *My Philosophical Development*:

> Everything that happens in me when I see something could, so far as its logical structure is concerned, quite well occur without there being anything outside me for me to see. This change in my opinions greatly increased the difficulty of problems involved in connecting experience with the outer world. (Russell 1975[1959], 10–11)

External reality had still to be inferred, thus falling back again into the very problem that had separated Russell from classical empiricism (Clack 1964, 135–153). In Russell's version of neutral monism, both "mind" and "matter" are inferred and logically constructed. Their difference is how they are constructed. Physical events and the contents of the mind were nothing more than expressions of a common neutral reality—expressions whose boundaries were conventional or logical, rather than ontological. And yet there was a preeminence of the psychological:

> Physics and psychology are not distinguished by their material. Mind and matter alike are logical constructions; the particulars out of which they are constructed, or from which they are inferred, have various relations, some of which are studied by physics, others by psychology. Broadly speaking, physics group

particulars by their active places, psychology by their passive places. (. . .) All our data, both in physics and psychology, are subject to psychological causal laws; but physical causal laws, at least in traditional physics, can only be stated in terms of matter, which is both inferred and constructed, never a datum. In this respect psychology is nearer to what actually exists. (Russell 2005[1921], 262)

The confusion between logical construction and inference in this text can be clarified if we keep in mind that the particulars through which mind and matter are logically constructed necessarily imply inferred events, such as subatomic particles and so on. What matters to us here is that the hubris of psychology in Russell's philosophy, like in much of the empiricist tradition, is an inevitable result of its own epistemological premises: because its point of departure are *internal* entities, it finds it troublesome to reconstrue from them the external realities those entities refer to. Of course, this tradition reached it utmost formulation in Berkeley's idealism. Russell confessed himself closer to this position than one would expect from a realist and science-informed philosopher:

The whole of what we perceive without inference belongs to our private world. In this respect, I agree with Berkeley. The starry heaven that we know in visual sensation is inside us. The external starry heaven that we believe in is inferred. (Russell 1975[1959], 20)

Neutral monism did not enable Russell to escape from this problem, which marked decisively the way he approached the epistemological status of science. The empiricism of Locke and Hume is often presented as an ally of modern science. And yet, basing the entire edifice of knowledge on subjective perceptions presented incompatibilities with the knowledge on physics and physiology that was already being developed in the time of these two philosophers. That Hume questioned the necessity of the sun raising every morning in Newton's time demonstrates the mismatch between empiricism and modern science (Romero, Pérez-Jara, and Camprubí 2022). Russell very consciously attempted to overcome this difficulty, trying to avoid virulent skepticism as much as he could (Griffin 2003).

Russell also insisted on an important shortcoming of empiricism, which opened also questions to his own neutral monist alternative It concerned the dual physical and psychological nature of *sense-data*. In 1935 he published "The Limits of Empiricism," a work he presented to Cambridge professional philosophers. The main point was that connections between objects are not objects, and yet they are part of our perception—take, for instance, the distance between two trees or the relation of someone's cry and their pain. Particular percepts are not enough to account for the non-chaotic world of our perceptions, which seems to already contain universals in some way. A draft prior to the one finally published even approached the Kantian solution: "knowledge is not derived solely from pure logic and pure sense, but also from synthetic knowledge concerning universals" (quoted in Monk 2001, 202). In Russell's analysis of connection, neutral monism seemed once again to lean towards the preeminence of psychology over physics.

In 1943, Russell wrote an outline of what would be some of the main problems analyzed in *Human Knowledge* (1948). It was entitled "Project of Future Work" and in it Russell raised what he considered to be epistemology's "main question": "In what circumstances does scientific method allow us to infer the existence of something unobserved from what is observed?" With this question, Russell was trying to go beyond radical empiricism. Russell recognized that, despite such an inference being never legitimate in deductive or demonstrative logic, it is ever-present in both scientific knowledge and everyday life. In *Human Knowledge*, more than in any other previous work, Russell is completely aware of the limitations of pure empiricism in both epistemology and ontology.

> The desire to escape from subjectivity in the description of the world (which I share) has led some modern philosophers astray—at least so it seems to me—in relation to theory of knowledge. Finding its problems distasteful, they have tried to deny that these problems exist. That data are private and individual is a thesis which has been familiar since the time of Protagoras. This thesis has been denied because it has been thought, as Protagoras thought, that, if admitted, it must lead to the conclusion that all knowledge is private and individual. For my part, while I admit the thesis, I deny the conclusion. (Russell 2009[1948], 2)

Russell presented a more complete theory of "percepts" in *Human Knowledge*. In his empiricist vein, percepts are events *internal* to a perceiver, and as such they can be analyzed through psychology's laws. Nevertheless, Russell thinks, there are good reasons to suppose that percepts are caused by gases, electromagnetic and mechanical waves from *external* regions of spacetime. A crucial epistemological consequence of the analysis of the percepts is that they bestow knowledge about the general structure of the perceived events, but not about their intrinsic quality. Or said in classical terms: about their *form*, but not about their *matter*. Since mathematical logic does not transcend tautological knowledge, and our knowledge of the external world is based on percepts, such knowledge (from ordinary life to the highest forms of natural science) ends up mainly being knowledge of structure. Like in Locke's epistemology, the ultimate contents of absolute reality remain necessarily unknown. For Locke, while accidents are empirical, substances are not, and hence they become epistemologically and ontologically problematic when the claims of metaphysical knowledge are abandoned. But Russell's goal was to distance himself from this kind of skepticism:

> Skepticism, while logically impeccable, is psychologically impossible, and there is an element of frivolous insincerity in any philosophy which pretends to accept it. Moreover, if skepticism is to be theoretically defensible it must reject all inferences from what is experienced; a partial skepticism, such as the denial of physical events experienced by no one, or a solipsism which allows events in my future or in my unremembered past, has no logical justification, since it must admit principles of inference which lead to beliefs that it rejects. (Russell 2009[1948], 1)

In order to avoid the most radical subjectivist conclusions of pure empiricism, incompatible with scientific knowledge and daily experience, *Human Knowledge* introduces five non-empirical postulates (i.e., they lack demonstration) of empirical non-deductive inference. Such postulates, according to Russell, justified scientific inferences from private experience. They enabled the leap from my private percepts to the (if not universal, at least social) scientific knowledge of physics, psychology and physiology. These postulates were Russell's last serious attempt to justify his confidence on the ability of science to produce firm concepts, hypotheses, theories, and general laws. At the same time, however, they showed that, from Russell's empiricists ontological and epistemological premises, the whole building of science is structurally inexact, partial and limited: it stands on feet of clay. Of course, some scientific theories are more certain and exact than others; formal languages, clarity of definitions to avoid vagueness, good experimentation and logical habits, move us away from the pre-scientific knowledge of everyday life's common sense. But this only means that some pieces of clay are more reliable than others.

THE PHILOSOPHY OF MATTER AND PHYSICS

Russell's epistemological and ontological investigations on matter and mind directly informed his evolving views on physics. After rejecting neo-Hegelian idealism, the main principles of logical atomism accompanied him for the rest of his career: radical ontological plurality, mutability, contingentism (since "external relations" are not necessary connections), inferred character of the existence and main characteristics of matter, and impossibility of knowing the ultimate nature of external realities in themselves. In keeping with his methodological insistence on scientific philosophy, Russell was certain that a correct (epistemo)logical analysis of modern physical theories led to these main ontological principles.

Russell's famous article "The Ultimate Constituents of Matter" (1915) is a very good example of how Russell endeavored to coordinate modern physical theories and logical atomism. Russell outlines his theory of particulars as the ultimate structures of matter that result from scientific analysis. In his ontological theory of matter, Russell argues that the world can be conceived as a set consisting of multiple entities arranged according to a certain pattern. He called these entities individuals or particulars. The patterns of their arrangement results from the (external) relationships between them—and recall that classes are series of individuals arranged to a certain property or pattern by a logical construction.

Particulars, Russell warns, should not be conceived in analogy with the bricks of a building; rather, we should understand them in analogy with the notes of a symphony, that is, as the "ultimate constituents" of a symphony. Each note lasts only for a short period of time, and, in a similar way as we can put all the notes together played by a single instrument, we can do with successive particulars that extend over time according to a certain pattern. The union of these successive particulars through time constitutes what common sense knows as a thing or entity. According to Russell, therefore, the things and entities around us, from dogs, houses and stars, have no more substantiality than being a contingent and mutable aggregate of particulars. It is therefore an epistemological illusion to consider the sun, or in general any other perceptual object, as a simple entity, endowed with a indissoluble ontological unity and nature. On the contrary, we must consider all the objects that surround us, among which are those that we see and touch, as pure aggregates or sets of these ephemeral units which Russell called particulars. Only through the right logical analysis we can be aware of this.

With this theory, Russell, aside of the influence of Moore's ontological pluralism, was following Hume's well-known "bundle theory".[4] Keeping with his dual view of perceptions and objects perceived, Russell argued that particulars can be grouped as "things" from the point of view of physics or as "perspectives" form that of psychology. Both approaches are generally correct, as long as none of them try to present itself as exclusive.

Going beyond Hume, Russell argued that particulars have "biographies". By this, he understood the total sum of all the particulars either occur in a direct simultaneous relationship with a given particular, or occur before or after this (i.e., successively). Trying to avoid subjective idealism, Russell held that these "biographies" do not need human beings to exist. Russell called these biographies that are not perceived by anyone "official biographies" (Russell 1915).

Russell extended his radical pluralism as well as the epistemological duality to spacetime. The material world is made up of multiple three-dimensional spaces, which can be divided, in a first analysis, in those spaces three-dimensional structures centered around an observer, and in those spaces that they are not focused on any observer. This plurality of spaces tends to be seen as a single three-dimensional space through correlation and succession of the different three-dimensional spaces that are taken, each time, as reference. But for Russell, the successive organization of multiple three-dimensional spaces in the same space, should lead us to the conclusion that this encompassing space is not itself composed of three dimensions, but on the contrary of six. This means that scientists should need at least six coordinates to fully map the position of a particular. On the one hand, three coordinates are needed to map the position of a given particular in its own space three-dimensional, while on the other hand three other coordinates are necessary to assign the position of that space among the other spaces around it.

Causal relationships, or, in general, correlations between some events and others, are established at the level of these tiny space-time units called particulars. Russell tried to account for modern physics' discoveries from a soft conception of causality very much inspired (again) by Hume. According to this, causality, instead of being a constitutive mechanism of our universe that structures certain necessary relationships between entities or events, is more an epistemological construct. Through this construct, the knowing subject tries to psychologically unite two or more events that show, when we observe them, a spatial or temporal contiguity according to a certain regularity (for an exposition of Russell's positions on this problem between 1912 and 1915, see Darlington 1978, 122–165).

For Russell's radical pluralist ontology, causality moves on the surface of phenomena. The causal relationships that we know are the result of inductive inference processes, and, as such, could therefore be subject to important errors. We do not really know if the epistemological causal relations that physics, or natural science in general, studies are the reflection of intrinsic relations of reality itself. This empiricist and skeptical theory of causality leads to a philosophy of absolute contingency: *necessity* seems a mere attribute of logical and mathematical propositions, rather than a real ontological dimension of our universe. That is: there is no necessity outside language. If everything is contingent, we should not rely excessively on causality relationships, since they do not provide us with necessary knowledge: just merely probabilistic or statistical knowledge, however important this may be against ignorance, blind dogmatisms and superstitions.

Russell's general epistemological and ontological take on matter informed his approach to specific physical theories being developed in his time, particularly quantum mechanics and relativity. Shortly after the publication of *The Analysis of Mind*, Russell set to work on two books aimed to present modern physics to a popular audience: *The ABC of Atoms* (1923) and *The ABC of Relativity* (1925). Both sold well and Russell had the opportunity of updating them through several successive editions, incorporating new scientific discoveries and theories on cosmology and quantum mechanics.

The first edition of *The ABC of Atoms* was published when quantum mechanics was still in the process of being formulated. Thus, Russell knew Heisenberg's version of quantum mechanics, but not Schrodinger's. As a consequence, Russell analyzes the "uncertainty principle" but not wave functions. Similarly, *The ABC of Atoms* takes protons and electrons into account, but not neutrons, which were discovered three years after the publication of the first edition. Importantly for this book, Russell stresses the role of technology for modern science: without electrical and chemical measuring devices, quantum mechanics and atomic theory would be indistinguishable from pure speculative metaphysics. Also important for this chapter is that, despite being a work of popularization, *The ABC of Atoms* introduces the ontological premises of his neutral monism. Russell suggests that the radical plurality of events that compose the external world resemble, in their very nature, mental events more than the "traditional billiard-balls" of many scientific and popular representations. Following the most rigorous methods of natural science, we can infer some basic properties of subatomic matter; but in truth, such inferences are tentative projections on an external reality that is mainly unknown *in itself*.

This made Russell rather cautious regarding scientific advances. He warned about the inadequacies of conventional language, based on pictorial and concrete images, to describe subatomic processes. Physics' non-mathematical language often betrays physics' scientific rigor, making people believe that an electron is some kind of little hard lump of matter with a specific size. Instead, he tried to stick to conditional and explicitly metaphorical language which constantly reminded readers of the inferred nature of subatomic knowledge. For instance, discussing electron orbits he left the door open to their interpretation as circles or ellipses as well as referred to their discontinuous movement:[5]

> One of the most astonishing things about the processes that take place in atoms is that they seem to be liable to sudden discontinuities, sudden jumps from one state of continuous motion to another. The motion of an electron round its nucleus seems to be like that of a flea, which crawls for a while, and then hops (. . .) The hops are a new phenomenon. [. . .] When an electron jumps from one orbit to another, this is supposed to happen instantaneously, not merely in a very short time. It is supposed that for a time it is moving in one orbit, and then instantaneously it is moving in the other, without having passed over the intermediate

space. (. . .) An electron is like a man who, when he is insulted, listens at first apparently unmoved, and then suddenly hits out. (. . .) The process by which an electron passes from one orbit to another is at present quite unintelligible, and to all appearance contrary to everything that has hitherto been believed about the nature of physical occurrences. (Russell 1923, 15, 63)

The ABC of Atoms was Russell's first effort for scientific popularization. In the same way, *The ABC of Relativity* also aimed to reach large markets and offered Russell's philosophical interpretation of a science in the making. The book's first edition (1925) was published when Einstein's general relativity was still linked to the static model of the universe. It was precisely in 1925 when Edwin Hubble challenged Einstein's previous idea about the size of the universe, showing that the universe was much larger than previously thought. In 1929, Hubble made an even more important discovery: the universe is expanding, getting larger and larger all the time. Following Hubble's 1929 discovery of a linear relation between the redshifts of the galaxies and their distance, Einstein abandoned his first model of the universe, proposing new revolutionary models, such as the so-called Friedmann-Einstein universe and the Einstein–de Sitter universe. In both models, Einstein's previous "cosmological constant" was set to zero. Fortunately, Russell was very prudent in his presentation of cosmology in the first edition of the book. He explained that the principles defended by Einstein were not logically necessary and could change with future scientific discoveries and analyses: "I propose, therefore, to continue to adopt Einstein's view as to the best way of interpreting the principles of physics, without suggesting that no other way is logically possible" (Russell 1992[1927], 80).

Russell stressed that the relativity principle stated that everything in the universe is in motion not in absolute terms, but relative to everything else. He interpreted this against much of the old science and philosophy: there is no privileged cosmic point of reference. This forced a complete revision of our theories of matter. But it also posed the challenge of unifying general relativity and quantum mechanics. For him, such a revolutionary theory resulted from the combination of two diverse elements, "new experimental data and a new logical method" (Russell 1992[1927], 100).

Beyond these two works of popularization, Russell intended his 1927 book *The Analysis of Matter* (1927) to be an academic work of reference on epistemology of physics and ontology of matter. The result of a decade of work, the book presented an ontology of matter and an epistemology of physics. Advances in the sciences accepted a variety of philosophical interpretations, not all of them equally valid. In particular, Russell opposed interpretations put forward by scientists themselves whom, with their mathematical abstractness, separated the world of physics from the world of perception:

> Hence IF modern physics invalidates perception as a source of knowledge about the external world, and yet depends upon perception, that is a valid argument against modern physics. I do not say that physics in fact has this defect, but I do say that considerable labor of interpretation is necessary in order to show that it can be absolved in this respect. And it is because of the abstractness of physics, as developed by mathematicians, that this labor is required. (Russell 1992[1927], 137–138)

As in previous works, Russell's point of departure was perceptions. This, in turn, encouraged him to define matter against substance metaphysics:

> The physical object to be inferred from perception is a group of events, rather than a single "thing." Percepts are always events, and common sense is always rash when it refers them to "things" with changing states. There is therefore every reason, from the standpoint of perception, to desire an interpretation of physics which dispenses with permanent substance. As we have seen that such an interpretation is possible, we shall henceforth adopt it. (Russell 1992[1927], 247)

In *The Analysis of Matter*, Russell elaborated on his contingentist conception of causality. Like all other scientific postulates, "the belief in general laws is rooted in the properties of nervous tissue—the same properties which make us believe in induction and enable us to learn from experience." At the same time, Russell holds the epistemological premise that natural science is necessarily linked to causality. And, although Russell embraces Hume's bundle theory against substance metaphysics, he thinks that causality is needed in order to introduce some kind of identity scheme of substantial identity through causality. E. Darlington (1978) synthesized this idea by stating that Russell introduces causal lines to define the "identity" of a physical object at different times, since he has rejected the concept of substances. Without such causal lines, the world would be a phantasmagoric chaos.[6]

Nevertheless, Russell recognizes that there are, at least, two main problems with his causality doctrine. On the one hand, if causality is an epistemological construct rather than an intrinsic quality of material reality itself, it means that physics (or natural science in general) is introducing a significative degree of distortion. On the other hand, quantum mechanics seems to show that causal relationships do not work at a subatomic level. Some elementary particles, for instance, decay without any external influence that can work as a "cause". In Russell's own words:

> We shall assume that there are causal laws, and try to discover them; but if none are found in a given region, that merely means that science cannot conquer that region. There are at present important regions of this kind. We do not know why a radioactive atom disintegrates at one moment rather than another. We cannot

be sure that these occurrences severally are governed by laws; but if they are not, science cannot deal with them individually, and is confined to statistical averages. Whether this will prove to be the case, we cannot yet say. (Russell 1992[1927], 168)

Once philosophically interpreted, physics could in return contribute to gauging alternative philosophical positions. According to Russell modern physics debunked traditional idealists and materialists philosophies. Relativity was not to be interpreted from the point of view of idealism. Even though the theory of relativity continually made reference to the *relativity* of certain physical notions with respect to such and such points of view, these points of view need not be understood as mental subjectivities, but rather as physical perspectives made possible by the new theories of space, time, movement and gravitation. With regard to 19th-century materialism (as represented by Büchner, Ostwald, Haeckel, and Engels), the new theories of matter and energy made it untenable. By contrast, Russell barely commented upon the much-discussed idealist or realist consequences of quantum mechanics, although he showed a great interest in the problems of causality and of remote action at the quantum level.

As to the ontological status of physical laws and theoretical entities such as electrons, *The Analysis of Matter* seems to restate the Platonism Russell had abandoned decades before. The material structures studied by physics can be reduced to pure mathematical "structures" that "can be expressed by mathematical logic". This seems to place Russell in the long tradition of objective idealism, stemming from Pythagoras and Plato, all the way to early modern theological philosophy ("God has created the world in mathematical characters"). The idea that the realm of pure essences is separate from matter and the human mind, however, was not something Russell was willing to entertain once he had come to understand mathematics as tautologies created by scientists according to certain rules of formal construction. The contradiction is partially solved if we recall that Russell is not discussing the ultimate intrinsic nature of reality. Matter, along with space and time, is a logical construction. And logical constructions—key is to remember it—are not part of the absolute furniture of the world. They are just extremely useful epistemological artifacts. And yet, mathematical properties acquire here a status that goes beyond their mere tautological nature:

> There is nothing in physics to prove that the physical world is radically different in character from the mental world. I do not myself believe that the philosophical arguments for the view that all reality must be mental are valid. But I also do not believe that any valid arguments against this view are to be derived from physics. The only legitimate attitude about the physical world seems to be complete agnosticism as regards all but its mathematical properties. However,

something can be done in the way of constructing possible physical worlds which fulfill the equations of physics and yet resemble rather more closely the world of perception than does the world ordinarily presented in physics. (Russell 1992[1927], 270–271)

Because we lack direct access to the microscopic world, all that we really know are the numbers that result from our measurements of exchanges of energy. If two theories can account for these results equally well, there is no way of deciding among them. This explained, according to Russell, the undecidability between waves and corpuscles or the discussions on the ontological existence of photons. The extent to which matter and physics refer to an external reality is actually one of the main themes of *The Analysis of Matter*. As a continuation of his 1921 *The Analysis of Mind*, the 1927 book realizes the program of neutral monism:

> Physics must be interpreted in a way which tends towards idealism, and perception in a way which tends towards materialism. I believe that matter is less material, and mind less mental, than is commonly supposed. [. . .] From the standpoint of philosophy the distinction between physical and mental is superficial and unreal. (Russell 1992[1927], 7, 402)

Russell took pains to navigate his allegiances to both neutral monism and the results of the science of his day. In particular, a large part of the book was devoted to what he called the casual theory of perception. In order to justify the inferences that, according to him, the subject needed to perform from precepts to the law of physics, Russell gathered the latest physiological results accounting for the way photons impact the retina or mechanical waves move the inner ear. It is physical stimulus that change our mental states.

Russell had been interested in physiology as a possible way to solve his epistemological conundrums since the 1910s. Indeed, physiology seems to solve the problems of subjective idealism through its studies of the human brain and organs. Russell saw it as the intermediate link between physics and psychology. And yet, the demon of idealism haunted Russell's interpretation of physiology through the so-called "physiologist's paradox": while it is true, Russell notes, that the external and empirical world is completely conditioned by our organs and brain, the knowledge we have of them is in turn contributed by own sensory organs and our brain. That is, if from the knowledge of physiology what we perceive (such as colors, shapes, sounds) cannot be interpreted as an absolute reality, neither could we maintain that the brain or our sensory organs are the reality in itself that is ontologically behind the complete configuration of the empirical world, since the brain and organs are also empirical themselves. In Russell's words:

This physiologist's argument is exposed to the rejoinder, more specious than solid, that our knowledge of the existence of the sense organs and nerves is obtained by that very process which the physiologist has been engaged in discrediting, since the existence of the nerves and sense organs is only known through the evidence of the senses themselves. This argument may prove that some reinterpretation of the results of physiology is necessary before they can acquire metaphysical validity. But it does not upset the physiological argument in so far as this constitutes merely a reductio ad absurdum of naïve realism. (Russell 2009[1918])

How to coordinate the thesis of mathematical equivalence of theories with the physiological causal theory of perception was one of the book's main challenges, and a problem which captivated both its contemporary defenders and his critics. Among the firsts was the physicist Eddington, who saw in Russell's book a confirmation of his own view of physics as a subjective enterprise—not incompatible with a certain Platonism of numbers, as Russell himself criticized in the short story quoted in our Chapter 1. Among the latter were the philosopher M. H. Newman, who pointed out that Russell's claims about numerical properties and mathematical structures as the only certain knowledge of physics directly contradicted the book's confident expositions of how the world affects the brain. The latter show that we know much more about the world than Russell's rather skeptical theory of knowledge allows us to know. Russell responded to Newman's criticism admitting that he was right in the inability of neutral monism to account philosophically for the success of science in describing reality, however partially (Monk 2001, 71–73). As we saw in the previous section, it was not until the 1940s that Russell presented a serious attempt at solving this central problem.

THE PHILOSOPHY OF MIND AND PSYCHOLOGY

From the point of view of Russell's 1921 *The Analysis of Mind,* the traditional boundary between physics and psychology is hardly justified. Mind and matter are logical constructions underneath which lies a neutral reality. For neutral monism, blurring the classical distinction between mind and matter implied questioning the epistemological demarcation between physics and psychology. Both study the same plural reality, but they do so from two main different epistemological (rather than ontological) points of view: psychological and physical.[7] In logical terms: these different points of view have more to do with the *intension* than with the *extension*. And yet, for post-logicist Russell, these are the two fundamental sciences, in the sense that the natural sciences could be reduced to physics, and the human sciences to psychology.

Russell never quite justified these choices. It is not clear in which senses he thought that biology, geology, and chemistry, for instance, could just be discussed together with physics without further specifications. Similarly, he never tried to argue how he considered that history, anthropology, ethology, sociology, and human geography could be reduced to the coordinates of psychology. As we mentioned in the previous chapter, from World War I onwards he tended to approach all political and historical problems through the lenses of psychology, but he hardly thought this merited much justification. He also did not attempt to coordinate his reductionist impulses with his own pluralist theory of truth, according to which an isolated truth can be completely true without counting with other truths or premises.

Russell did elaborate much more profoundly on the relationships between physics and psychology. If mind and matter are nothing but two dimensions of a common neutral reality, then the difference between physics and psychology was to be located in their respective perspectives and approaches (Russell 2007[1921]). In particular, if physics and psychology are relatively autonomous sciences it is because they differ in their methods for correlating the ontologically neutral events that constitute reality (Copleston 1994, 450–451). For instance, physics focuses on spatio-temporal determinations of particulars and psychology on the concatenations of mental images through memory (Russell 1975[1959], 19).

Despite these differences in approach, it should be expected that psychology and physics would be unified into a single unified global science (Russell 1948). But recall that sensations come first. It is from them that we infer matter. Therefore, in integrating both sciences the psychological dimension predominates over the physical one. The laws of physics are always approximate and contingent, because their evidence for them is empirical and rests, in the last analysis, on perceptions. The world of physics is thus epistemologically continuous with the world of our perceptions. It is the latter which supplies the evidence for the laws of physics.

And it would be a mistake to consider perceptions as transparent reflections of the outside world. Perception depends on bodily filters and unconscious associations and interpretations. Contrarily to naïve empiricism, the mind does not receive data from the outside world in a passive mode. Russell is here in agreement with those continental philosophers, from Nietzsche to Gadamer, who have insisted that there are no pure facts or phenomena. The empirical world, as presented to us, is completely conditioned by both our senses and our brain and its mental processes:

> The physiologists point out that what we see depends upon the eye, that what we hear depends upon the ear, and that all our senses are liable to be affected by anything which affects the brain, like alcohol or hasheesh. Psychologists point

out how much of what we think we see is supplied by association or unconscious inference, how much is mental interpretation, and how doubtful is the residuum which can be regarded as crude datum. From these facts it is argued by the psychologists that the notion of a datum passively received by the mind is a delusion, and it is argued by the physiologists that even if a pure datum of sense could be obtained by the analysis of experience, still this datum could not belong, as common sense supposes, to the outer world, since its whole nature is conditioned by our nerves and sense organs, changing as they change in ways which it is thought impossible to connect with any change in the matter supposed to be perceived. (Russell 2009[1918])

Distinguishing between the act of perceiving and the perceived content reminds us that what we perceived is not self-evident independent from us. This all means that, for Russell, psychology is the fundamental science. Its correct interpretation, in turn, depends on the philosophical theory of mind—which, as always, is informed by scientific results.

Russell's main ontological critique to traditional concepts of the mind mobilizes the existing psychological approaches of his time, includin, in particular, physiological explanations, behaviorism, and psychoanalysis. Exactly as there is an anti-materialist tendency in physics, which he both diagnosed and prescribed, there is a materialist tendency in psychology. After his neo-Hegelian youth, Russell tried to avoid any trace of idealism in studying the mind (Bikson 1967). We could say that he is de-mentalizing the mind by breaking the traditional "soul" down into sets of active and passive mental processes. This analytical method is explicit from the title of his major contribution to the subject, *The Analysis of Mind,* published in 1921. The most important result of this methodology is the critique of consciousness as an entity.

There are, Russell explains, several different ways in which conventional psychology defines "being conscious". One is through perception: we are aware of anything we perceive. The second is memory. While memory presupposes perception, it makes us aware of things that no longer exist. The next figure of consciousness immediately related to memory are ideas—not in the Platonic sense, Russell warns us, but in the empiricist sense of Locke, Hume or Berkeley for which ideas are psychic contents that differ from impressions. Russell finalizes his rhapsody of the fundamental figures of the consciousness with *belief*. By belief, Russell understands a way of being aware that can be true or false.

And yet, none of these inceptions of consciousness point towards an underlying substance. The critique of substantialism of the mind, although a common idea in Buddhism through the concepts of *sunyata* and *anatta*, is harder to find in the Western tradition before Hume. Right before Hume, Locke, for all his critique of traditional metaphysics, defended a *sui generis* substantialism of the mind.[8] Aside of Hume, William James's philosophy was an important source for *The Analysis of Mind* critique of consciousness as an entity. There, Russell uses two types of argument, which he admits to have borrowed from these authors. On the one hand, the analysis of mental life provides "direct reasons" to think of consciousness as a bundle of different and often contradictory processes. On the other, we can derive "indirect reasons" from experimental observation of animals (mainly studied by comparative psychology) and of insane and hysterical individuals (mainly studied by psychoanalysis).

Hume's bundle theory, as applied to the mind, became a fundamental tenet of Russell's approach to the human psyche. It took him as far as to question the reality of the ego—again, a hypothesis well-known in certain Asian traditions. In *An Inquiry into Meaning and Truth* (1940) Russell holds that propositions like "I am" could be translated to "this is" without losing their meaning. Traditional egological categories, including the so-called "egocentric particulars," can be removed. This kind of "taboo of ego" can be traced back to Comte's 19th-century positivism and was shared as well by Wittgenstein both in the *Tractatus* and in the critique of "private diaries" contained in the *Philosophical Investigations* (Pérez-Jara 2014). In the case of Russell, erasing the ego meant the final blow to the ego-centered metaphysics of Modernity, from Descartes and Fichte to the British idealists that he so well knew.

Russell's critique of consciousness included results from psychoanalysis. Mental activity is not exhausted by consciousness. Trying to avoid the usual love or leave it binary in philosophical approaches to psychoanalysis, Russell's take on it was far from simplistic. He acknowledged that psychoanalysis had wrapped itself up a halo of mythical mystery, distancing itself from scientific knowledge. But he admired it for having discovered the unconscious.[9] What began as a study of pathology, ended up transforming our vision of the mind, reason, and passions: "a man's actions and beliefs may be wholly dominated by a desire of which he is quite unconscious, and which he indignantly repudiates when it is suggested to him" (Russell 1921). Thus, psychoanalysis was at least partially true:

> What have been called "unconscious" desires have been brought very much to the fore in recent years by psycho-analysis. Psycho-analysis, as everyone knows, is primarily a method of understanding hysteria and certain forms of insanity; but it has been found that there is much in the lives of ordinary men and women which bears a humiliating resemblance to the delusions of the insane. The connection of dreams, irrational beliefs and foolish actions with unconscious wishes has been brought to light, though with some exaggeration, by Freud and Jung and their followers. As regards the nature of these unconscious wishes, it seems to me—though as a layman I speak with diffidence—that many psycho-analysts are unduly narrow; no doubt the wishes they emphasize exist,

but others, e.g. for honour and power, are equally operative and equally liable to concealment. This, however, does not affect the value of their general theories from the point of view of theoretic psychology, and it is from this point of view that their results are important for the analysis of mind. (Russell 2005[1921], 22)

The merit of psychoanalysis lied in redefining the psyche as composed of by various streams of mind, often in conflict with one another and also often unconscious. While most people are not aware that their behavior is driven by unconscious desires and motivations, psychoanalysis has shown this is the case. It has, nonetheless, failed to define unconscious desire and relegated it to a mysterious underlying force which emerges only to curve our reasonable respectability. Rather, scientific psychological investigations ought to enquire which are the mechanisms governing human behavior beyond both pure reason and allegedly mysterious dark forces (Russell 2005[1921]).

With that goal in mind, Russell found a promising approach in behaviorism. Unlike psychoanalysis, behavioral psychology limits its studies to external observation of behavior, projecting the empirical analysis of animal behavior onto humans. Behaviorist psychologists declared unknowable consciousness and internal mental processes and set out to find phenomenic laws. Many of this Russell rejected as incompatible with his own philosophy of mind. For Russell internal processes such as beliefs and wishes are key to understanding the psyche. Desiring is for Russell the most characteristic activity of the human mind. The acts of all men are governed by purposes, and purposes can be reduced to states of the will rather than to intellectual reasons. Nonetheless, he hoped that behaviorism would provide the basic understanding of how desires are formed—and, central for us, could be created or transformed.

In 1913 Russell's "The Place of Science in Liberal Education" was full of enlightened hopes on the reforming possibilities of human reason. If given the chance, people would understand the sacred virtues of science and rationality would pervade in their moral, social, and political choices. This view grew grimmer from the first days of World War I, when Russell was confronted with the joy with which both the uneducated masses and his more refined friends and colleagues received the news of Britain's declaration of war on Germany. Putting primal instincts at the center of the political life, Russell gradually abandoned his confidence that civilization could do much to tame those instincts. And yet, in his 1916 "Principles of Social Reconstruction" Russell still thought that "creative" impulses, including love, could be promoted through social commentary (like his own) and through education. Soon after, he found an ally to that effort in behaviorism.

Russell had started to study behavioral psychology in 1918, and he had read most of John B. Watson's works by the publication of *The Analysis of Mind*. Shortly after this book appeared, Watson and his wife published "Studies in Infant Psychology". Ray Monk has documented how important this was for Russell's views on education as well as for his experiments with his first son, John, who was born in that same year (Monk 2001, 9–13). In 1926, Russell's best-selling book *On Education* displays his full confidence on the scientifically informed possibilities of "moral training," which he hoped could create a generation of self-less citizens. While in his 1924 "Icarus" the science of psychology is likely to become an instrument of tyranny, in *On Education* Russell seeks for ways to enlist it for his own fight against egoism and fear which should ensure the betterment of society.

Shortly after the publication of his book, Russell and his then wife Dora decided to open a school and enable them to realize their theories on education with their own children and a few other fortunate pioneers. It was around this time that Russell wrote *Why Am I Not a Christian* (1927) and *Marriage and Morals* (1929).[10] Together with Dora, he felt the time had come to change traditional morality from below: its infants (Park 2013). As his paper "The Application of Science to Education" (1928) made clear, this reformist project was to be scientifically informed and also aimed at equipping new generations with scientific rationality.

The school opened in September of 1927 and closed three years later. But its failure was already quite evident in its first year, when Russell's marriage to Dora also irreversibly deteriorated (Monk 2001, 78–136). In his 1929 *The Scientific Outlook* the pessimism of "Icarus" is back in full swing. It was written against Eddington's attempt to fuse science with religion, and it repeated many of his well-known attacks to mysticism in favor of scientific rationality. But the science Russell defended in this book was explicitly not that of the mechanical modern world, linked to the technological control of nature. The latter brought with it an apocalyptic world. *The Scientific Outlook* is a direct precedent of Aldous Huxley's 1932 *Brave New World*: science, including in particular scientific psychology, will bring about an inhuman society by manipulating irrational and unconscious desires that make up the bundle of the human mind. The grim social picture of *The Scientific Outlook* had its epistemological correlate: Berkeley was right in questioning the foundations of all knowledge as based on subjective experience—and Russell could not even share Berkeley's optimistic believe that there is a God that guarantees the existence of the external world.

CONCLUSION

This chapter has tracked the genuine and strenuous effort by Bertrand Russell to make sense of the fabric of the world in a way that both draws from science and points to the limitations of scientific knowledge. Despite Russell's attempts to separate these philosophical themes from his social and political commentary, the chapter has shown that Russell's epistemological views were deeply intertwined with his changing perceptions of the role of science in society.

The supreme duty of the philosopher, Russell wrote in his 1959 *My Philosophical Development,* is to interpret scientific results and offer an epistemological and ontological picture more general and critical than the specific results of the main sciences—mathematical logic, physics, psychology and, as a bridge between the last two, physiology. Needless to say, and in keeping with our book's cultural sociological approach, his philosophical interpretation of science and its history was not the only available one. Russell confronted competing interpretations of physics and psychology put forward by scientists and philosophers (for instance by Einstein, Freud, Husserl, and Bergson). As with other historical events relevant for this book, we understand that quantum mechanics or psychoanalysis have little intrinsic value without their cultural interpretations, including philosophical ones. There is no science without philosophy and no philosophy without science. Scientific results underdetermine philosophical theories.

Russell's philosophical framework evolved as sciences yielded new results but also as he encountered new philosophical difficulties or was forced to recast old ones. There were also important continuities in Russell's post-1898 thought: ontological pluralism, event ontology, deep empirical and skeptical roots, and a tortuous relationship with epistemological realism. The latter was a result of the empiricist premise of taking perceptions at the point of departure. The specter of Berkeleyan idealism haunted Russell whenever his confidence on science was at its ebb. In order to avoid some of the pitfalls of empiricism, Russell followed Mach and James to present his own version of neutral monism. Matter was less material and mind less mental than hitherto thought. This would enable philosophy to overcome the traditional dualism between matter and mind and the associated binary between materialism and idealism. Both emerge as blind reductionisms. While referring to a neutral substance of which mind and matter would be but logical and inferred constructions, psychological categories permeated deeper. Because material processes are for Russell inferred from perceptions, psychology gained preeminence over physics. Psychology is closer to ontological reality, the existence of mental processes is more certain than that of the external world.

Psychologism became a woodworm silently devouring the building of epistemological realism (Romero, Pérez-Jara, and Camprubí 2021). After rejecting Locke's substance metaphysics for a bundle and event ontology, Russell had much less theoretical tools than Locke against subjective idealism and the claim that there is no external reality. In a more radical way than Locke, Hume had posed in all its crudeness the Cartesian problem of passing from our sensory perceptions to the alleged external reality that would be founding them. Berkeley radicalized the problem even more and hypothesized that there were no rational reasons to suppose that the so-called primary qualities were less dependent on our psychological perception than Locke's secondary qualities.

Russell's post-1898 rejection of idealism was completely vulnerable on this flank. For philosophers who consider the existence of external realities a structural *factum* without which the existence of psychic events is epistemologically unintelligible and ontologically impossible. This is important, because the "problem of the external world" was a pseudo-problem for other philosophers of the 20th century, including those who are generally considered to be much closer to the tradition of idealism than Russell was—take for instance Heidegger's *Being and Time* (1927). For Russell, on the contrary, solipsism was a logical possibility and the reality of the external world a matter of mere probability. "I am conscious," Russell stated in a 1964 interview, "of no major change in my opinions since the adoption of neutral monism" (Eames 1969, 108). And yet we have seen that in 1948 he tried to save scientific objectivity from the premises of neutral monism and that in 1959 he timidly reintroduced dualism to account for entities of seemingly exclusive mental nature. Like the ancient minotaur from which Icarus and Daedalus escaped, the demon of idealism always lurked in the shadows of Russell's tortuous mazes of mind and matter.

Russell's maze had deep effects on his changing views on the promises of science. His analysis of physics led him to conclude that our knowledge of the external world is always partial and tentative. Science can never get to the intrinsic qualities of the multiple processes that constitute the (postulated) external world. Humans do not have access to absolute reality, namely, reality as it really is. Even both mind and matter have to be interpreted as logical constructions. What we might be able to access are structural properties of reality, including in particular mathematical structures. At certain points in his works, Russell embraces a structural realism in contrast to a *correlationism* of contents.[11] Reality's structural properties include radical plurality, mutability, and contingency. But reality's absolute contents remain unknowable for our limited and finite nature.

The analysis of psychology was no more cheerful. The self is but a problematic inference from a bundle of contingent (and mostly ephemeral) mental processes. When some of these events are connected through memory-chains, the illusion of a substance is created. We can still talk about the identity of things, including ourselves, through causal chains, but in a quite contingent and precarious way. Following the classical distinction between *vis cognitiva* (cognitive faculties) and *vis apetitiva* (volitional faculties), Russell divides mental events into beliefs and wishes. The former is much more dominant than rational and certain knowledge, which always presupposes believed assumptions. The latter are often dominated by unconscious processes and impulses. Human nature is overwhelmingly irrational, contradictory, whimsical, and easily manipulable. At several points along his life, Russell hoped that scientifically informed education and education in scientific values provided a way out of this brutal and blind nature. Time and again he found reasons to despair from these hopes. The Janus face of science as harbinger of utopia or apocalypse accompanied Russell into the rapidly accelerating world of World War II and the Cold War.

NOTES

1. In Russell's words: "The value of philosophy is, in fact, to be sought largely in its very uncertainty. The man who has no tincture of philosophy goes through life imprisoned in the prejudices derived from common sense, from the habitual beliefs of his age or his nation, and from convictions which have grown up in his mind without the co-operation or consent of his deliberate reason. To such a man the world tends to become definite, finite, obvious; common objects rouse no questions, and unfamiliar possibilities are contemptuously rejected. As soon as we begin to philosophize, on the contrary, we find (. . .) that even the most everyday things lead to problems to which only very incomplete answers can be given. Philosophy, though unable to tell us with certainty what is the true answer to the doubts which it raises, is able to suggest many possibilities which enlarge our thoughts and free them from the tyranny of custom" (Russell 2001[1912], 91).

2. Prior to his conversion to neutral monism, Russell held acquaintance to play the metaphorical role that the pineal gland played in the Cartesian system, since acquaintance unites the physical and the mental, although Russell was not of course thinking then about a spirit independent of the brain (Brown 1974, 22).

3. Russell was quite dismissive of the problems posed by the ontological and epistemological status of hallucinations in his *Theory of Knowledge* and *Our Knowledge of the External World*, but this does not mean he had a convincing answer to it.

4. Let's remember Hume's words: "When we gradually follow an object in its successive changes, the smooth progress of the thought makes us ascribe an identity to the succession (. . .) When we compare its situation after a considerable change the progress of the thought is broken; and consequently we are presented with the idea of diversity: In order to reconcile which contradictions, the imagination is apt to feign something unknown and invisible, which it supposes to continue the same under all these variations; and this unintelligible something it calls a substance, or original and first matter" (Hume 1978[1739], 220). Hume's theory can be put into correspondence

with that defended by Buddhism thousand of years earlier through the concepts of *sunyata* and *anatta*.

5. Another example of Russell's caution is his discussion of the ether in the last chapter of *The ABC of Atoms*: although "the aether, which used to play a great part in physics, has sunk into the background, and has become as shadowy as Mrs Harris," such imaginary entity could have some kind of reality and come back in future physical theories, so modern physics could discover that "hydrogen nuclei are merely states of strain in the aether, or something of that sort". Russell's speculation of understanding an electron as being some kind of disturbance in the ether resemble current physical theories according to which elementary particles are not "entities", but properties or perturbations of quantum fields (Romero 2018).

6. Hume, trying to erase from his empiricist and skeptical philosophy any ontological substantial scheme, is led to the conclusion of contemplating the world of experience as a ghostly set of phenomena with no real causal connection between them, and without substantial identity schemes (and it is from this point of view that his criticism of personal identity has to be understood). We can only think in schemes of substantial identity and causality as practical beliefs to make everyday life possible. No doubt this extreme phenomenal idealism was that which led Hamilton to designate, as Jacobi had previously done with Fichte, Hume's philosophy as a form of ontological nihilism (see Pérez-Jara 2013).

7. In Russell's words: "We can now begin to understand one of the fundamental differences between physics and psychology. Physics treats as a unit the whole system of appearances of a piece of matter, whereas psychology is interested in certain of these appearances themselves" (Russell 2005[1921], 83–84).

8. Locke, in his *Essay*, puts it in this way: "The idea then we have, to which we give the general name substance, being nothing, but the supposed, but unknown support of those qualities, we find existing, which we imagine cannot subsist, sine re substante, without something to support them, we call that support substantia, which, according to the true import of the word, is in plain English, standing under or upholding" (Locke 1979[1695], xxii).

9. Although, in truth, it was already analyzed by several well-known philosophers, such as F. W. J. Schelling, Arthur Schopenhauer, and K. R. E. von Hartmann.

10. This book, often read in the lights of progressive Russell, is actually a defense of monogamy for the sake of children, if it accepts some degree of sexual freedom in order to make that goal more realistic. It also contained, beyond controversial commentaries on the intelligence of blacks and women, a chapter on eugenics in which Russell called for sterilizing women with mental disorders or deficiencies. While he had warned from "Icarus" onwards against the possibilities that eugenics posed for states to suppress individual freedoms and rights, he was willing to accept that risk in order to get rid of society's most polluted individuals (Monk 2001, 105).

11. By "correlationism" we mean the theory that all we can say about objects is in relation to subjects. Different versions of it have been discussed (from Husserl to Meillassoux) in the context of the Kantian problem of the relationship between phenomena and noumena.

Chapter Four

Lights and Shadows of Nuclear Death

"America", Russell claimed fervently in 1945, "should make war on Russia during the next two years, and establish a world empire by means of the atomic bomb" (1945). The previous chapters have explored the core of Bertrand Russell's philosophical thinking and some of its major transformations over time, particularly vis-á-vis science and its role in society. From World War I onwards Russell devoted less energy to academic philosophy than to becoming a public intellectual, advocating social reform and pacifism. Russell himself drew a thick line between both activities. And yet, as Chapter 3 has shown, his purest philosophical thinking shared with his political writings a preoccupation with the future of humanity in a technological and scientific age with equal potential of evolving towards a utopian paradise as towards apocalyptic annihilation.

This preoccupation became decisive for Russell's personal and public life in the years around and after the Second World War. Russell in his late 60s tried to regain his academic prestige and career as well as to preserve his family from the horrors of the war by fleeing to America. But he also advocated for surrender as the best way to stop Nazi domination, turned into a convinced belligerent against the German invaders, and went as far as advocating a nuclear preventative war against the Soviet Union before launching an international campaign against nuclear weapons. Is there a way to make sense of these transformations without accusing Russell of being lightheartedly opinionated, an opportunist, or just plainly inconsistent?

Russell biographers and critics have long debated this question, which as we will see can easily be extended to later periods of his life (see in particular Ryan 1988 and Monk 2001). Here we mobilize once again the tools of cultural sociological analysis to highlight the mechanisms that took Bertrand

Russell to modify his position in such central matters as war, the role of the US in the world, and the meaning of the atomic bomb.

Despite being, in absolute terms, the biggest, most brutal, and bloodiest war ever fought in the history of humankind, Russell interpreted the Second World War in a very different light as the one he employed on the First World War. During the 1930s, Russell had mainly maintained pacifist stances, arguing for surrender on the grounds that avoiding a full-scale world war was more important than defeating Hitler. By 1940 he had concluded that if Hitler (classified now as the embodiment of evil) took over all of Europe, then, democracy (classified as the embodiment of good) would be fatally wounded. In 1943, Russell incorporated this positioning into his theoretical approach to war, defining his view as "relative political pacifism". According to this doctrine, "war was always a great evil, but in some particularly extreme circumstances, it may be the lesser of two evils" (quoted in Monk 2001).

Ever a prophet of apocalypse, Russell's understanding of the perils of atomic power took him to defend extreme positions as to how to savage humanity from an assured destruction. These positions, in turn, rested directly on binaries of light and shadows which Russell applied with more or less nuances to nations and political agents which he understood as central actors in the world drama. After all, as Russell himself expressed, it would be madness to hold the same opinion in the face of different situations (Russell 1975[1959], 90).

And yet, what we want to argue is that Russell's interpretations of those situations (as everyone else's) were in no way self-evident or immediate, but required complex processes of resignification. For instance, while in absolute terms World War II was much more devastating in terms of human and material losses than World War I, we will see that for Russell it became somewhat a lesser evil. Furthermore, as historian Michael Gordin and others have argued, competing interpretations of the nuclear bombing of Hiroshima and Nagasaki became so strong in the following decades as to retrospectively obscure the meanings available at the time of the bombing (Gordin 2007). The symbolic attributions around nuclear weapons were relatively autonomous from the intrinsic impact of the two nuclear bombs ever deployed in combat.

In the first section, we look at the evolution of Russell's ideas on war at the brink of the Second World War. We argue that they stem at least in part from his changing perceptions of Hitler and Germany relative to other menaces faced by British society and liberal democracies more generally. The second section turns to Russell's experience in the US, interpreting the so-called "Bertrand Russell case" as part of Russell's perception of the role America ought to play regarding "civilization", since according to him no less was at stake in the belligerent scenario. Despite his confirmation of illiberal and mechanistic tendencies in the US, Russell came to identify the Nazis, Japan, and the Soviet Union as unbearable evils to be eradicated by all means, eventually including nuclear war. Section three investigates the transition from this position onto one of public anti-nuclear campaigning, which consolidated Russell's fame as a public intellectual. His approach to science as both a neutral ground in which experts could agree in the midst of the Cold War and a threat to human existence shows that Russell's duality towards science—utopia and apocalypse—could indeed lead to simultaneous seemingly opposing interpretations of the relationships between science and politics. The fourth and final section links Russell's anti-nuclear campaign to his growing mistrust towards the United States. Russell's ideas on the "role of science in society" (in his own formula), acquired a height in terms of social diffusion, if often in unexpected ways and at the prize of logical coherence and former alliances.

FROM CAPITULATION TO BELLIGERENCE

The world in 1936 was certainly different from that of 1914. And yet, when a 64-years-old Russell published *Which Way to Peace?,* he reinstated his former pacifism with little modification. Only that now he was calling for passive resistance in the face of the rise of Nazi Germany. This position resonated at the time with important parts of the British public opinion, with memories of war still too fresh to think on embarking in yet another fight with Germany. But, as always, Russell found arguments of his own which enabled him to connect to this receptive audience. These arguments, moreover, point to continuities as well as changes regarding his political positioning on war and on the place of Germany in Western civilization.

Regarding continuities, in *Which Way to Peace?* Russell encouraged once again the idea of a stable world government as the purest and most sacred solution for humankind's main problems. Accordingly, and as he had also done before, he made an exception in his condemnation of war as a universal polluting force of evil: war was to be defended, and even desired, against the potential rebels of the hypothetical World Government. While he would make this exception the backbone of his anti-Soviet belligerence in the mid-1940s, Russell did not think it applied against Nazi Germany. Because such global government was still far from sight, Russell's *Which Way to Peace?* defended passive resistance and even what we could call preventive surrender: if the Germans found no violent opposition to their aggressive expansion, they would soon find themselves with no motivation for aggression.

This was certainly a stretch of his former pacifist views, and one that has surprised commentators ever since. According to Alan Ryan, this type of argument is characteristic of the "all or nothing" Russell, who responded at least in part to an impoverished journalistic environment in which elite thinkers were deprived of venues to debate their political views. The consequence was a diffuse audience which Russel (and others) thought they could afford to take as fools (Ryan 1988, 128). Ray Monk also underlies the scandal of Russell's seemingly clumsy attempt of keeping coherent with his former pacifism despite the completely different environment. As Monk (2001, 184–185) reminds us, in some parts of *Which Way to Peace?* the Germans appear as a civilized people who would not act against a disarmed England and Germany while, in other parts of the same book, they emerge as ruthless bullies who would take advantage of other nations' weaknesses.

Russell himself was forced to do quite a good deal of retrospective justification once he changed his mind about the Nazis. Referring to *Which Way to Peace?*, Russell's *Autobiography* explains that, while he publicly urged conscientious objection, that became more and more insincere as he became aware of Nazi cruelty and untenable as he realized that Germany could actually defeat the UK (Russell 2010[1975], 410).

It is true that Russell's 1936 book already contains a view of the Nazis as both cruel and stupid. But in the book and his private correspondence of the date this view coexisted with one in which the Nazis were not yet interpreted as pure evil. War was. Thus, Russell saw Nazi domination as a lesser evil than war. Despite the later reconstructions by Russell himself and by some of his biographers, this was not at the time such a crazy idea, and Russell was not alone in defending it. Ever since Hitler's ascend to power in 1933 there was a debate in Great Britain regarding both rearming and appeasement with views that went from direct admiration of Nazi Germany to appeasement to buy time enough for rearming in view of a future war (Neville 2005). And Russell was not entirely off in suggesting that German animosity against Britain had to do with the aggressive and expansive character of the British Empire itself as well as that the sufferings of a second world war could become at least comparable to those of Nazi domination over Europe.

This last point is particularly important since Russell did not oppose war in absolute terms but because of its consequences in terms of human suffering. But, this is our point, there are no absolute parameters to compare the foreseeable suffering that two possible courses of events might cause. Even as late as 1937, Russell wrote in a private letter: "If the Germans succeed in sending an invading army to England we should do best to treat them as visitors, give them quarters and invite the commander and chief to dine with the prime minister."[1] What we have then is an argument which, however idealistic, attached an absolute negative value to war while acknowledging lights and shadows in the British Empire as well as in the Third Reich, which at least in part was mirroring itself in British and American expansionism (Blackbourne 2006). This nuance is partly lost in Russell's next big book, *Power: A New Social Analysis*, published in 1938 and considered by both Russell himself and most commentators as Russell's most sophisticated piece of political thought. Russell's *Power* was indeed ambitious. It presented an analysis of power as the primary category in the social sciences as well as a set of practical instructions to tame arbitrary and irrational forms of power. According to its author, all topics in the social sciences can be epistemologically reduced to analysis of different forms of power, namely economic, military, cultural, and civil.[2] This clarifies one key idea of Russell's philosophy: that the "laws of social dynamics" should be translated to the laws of power dynamics. These laws explain how some forms of power change into others (Russell 1938, 4–6). Russell is very clear in moving away from what he (simplistically) thinks is Marx's philosophy of power, namely, an economic determinism that would act as a single-cause behind all social phenomena (Russell 1938, 5, 95).

Russell's *Power* is divided among big thematic sections that try to cover exhaustively power's main dimensions: its nature, its forms, its structure of organizations, and its ethics. Russell's point of departure is a quite simple definition of power as the ability to achieve goals.[3] From this humble theoretical beginning, Russell aims at developing a whole theory on human nature and social systems and interactions in general. The picture that emerges is rather pessimistic. From Russell's point of view, the desire to empower oneself is unique to human beings. For the rest of the animals (Russell argues from a sheer ignorance in ethology and animal psychology), do not try to accumulate more goods than those strictly necessary to meet their needs. Humans, on the contrary, have an "impulse to power". This is the root of all kinds of polluting social behaviors.

This enables Russell to move away from naive analyses of power. He argues, for instance, that "the 'social contract', in the only sense in which is not completely mythical, is a contract among conquerors, which loses its *raison d'être* if they are deprived of the benefits of conquest" (Russell 1938, 149). Russell is no anarchist. As such, he does not see "power" as a universally polluting force. There are forms of power that can produce positive outcomes, from daily life affairs to the highest political and economic spheres. Positive forms of power need to fulfill the following conditions: first, moral power must be pursued only as a means to some end, and not as an end in itself; second, the ultimate goal of moral power should be the satisfaction of the desires of other human beings; third, the means by which an individual pursues his or her goal must not be egregious or malign (such that they outweigh the value of the end: Russell puts forward the example of a hypothetical situation in which the gassing of children could empower a future democracy); fourth, and finally, moral doctrines that should tame power should aim toward "truth and honesty," not the manipulation of others (Russell 1938, 201–218).

It is easy to translate Russell's theory of power to our cultural-sociological terms: despite Russell's distinctions and attempts to move away from simplistic thinking, the truth is that Russell ends up distinguishing two main forms of power: sacred/pure power and profane/polluted power. Once again, an apparently complex taxonomy can be reduced to a simplistic binary in line with millennial structures of political and social meaning. This is especially true regarding the topic of interest of our book: Russell's prophetic and apocalyptic narration of the power of science and technology. Actually, in *Power* Russell attempts to theoretically substantiate *Icarus'* pessimism by presenting power as the ontological fabric of social reality. Russell had expanded on *Icarus'* dark views of the techno-scientific sphere in his 1931 often dystopian book *The Scientific Outlook*. Whereas education and social reform could make future generations to direct science and technology towards constructing an earthly utopia, *The Scientific Outlook* announced a much grimmer future. It did so in plain apocalyptic terms which were then replicated in his *Power*. "In former days," Russell insisted, "men sold themselves to the Devil to acquire magical powers. Nowadays they acquire those powers from science, and find themselves compelled to become devils" (Russell 1938, 22). This mythical language, like the one used during the Great War, is more than a poetic device; it illustrates Russell's too-often simplistic binary structures of meaning.

It is therefore perhaps not surprising that, while Russell considered *Power* to be one of his chief contributions to political philosophy for his life, he was also shocked by its lack of academic success (Russell 2010[1975], 412). Despite its ambitious pretensions within the field of the social sciences, Russell's *Power* was mostly ignored by social theorists. It was also not popular within the general public, being much more abstract than his best-selling pieces of the previous decades. The book, though, did receive some positive reviews from important intellectuals, such as Edward Hallet Carr (2001, 131) and George Orwell (1998[1937]). Orwell's opinion is of particular interest since in his masterpiece *1948* there is a moment in which the Party declares its secret: although the Big Brother does not exist, there is indeed only one true god: Power (Orwell 2014[1948]). Orwell reviewed Russell's *Power* in *The Adelphi* magazine.[4] In his review, Orwell had a bittersweet opinion about Russell's book; on the one hand, he praised *Power*'s first half, stating that the most interesting part of Russell's book was the earlier chapters in which Russell analyses the various types of power, namely: priestly, oligarchical, dictatorial, and so forth. However, Orwell was not convinced by Russell's arguments in the second part of the book; he thought that Russell did not provide any kind of convincing and realistic argument for creating a society based on tolerance and justice. Russell only (Orwell claimed) put forward "a pious hope that the present state of things will not endure". In this context, Orwell suggested an idea that would be key for the writing of his future *1984*: "[Russell's argumentation] does not prove that the slave society at which the dictators are aiming will be unstable." Orwell's criticism is in point, since Russell's *Power* exploits the by now usual Janus-face duality between utopia and apocalypse. Education, one of his big obsessions of the interwar period (his *On Education* was published in 1926) is now presented as a chief tamer of power. This hope was, as before, based in education's supposed capacities to spread skeptical, anti-fanatical and scientific perspectives. There is also the usual suggestion of a world government composed of "sovereign" nation-states and whose primary goal would be dissuading nations from engaging in war—at the same time that it promotes war against the dissidents (Russell 1938, 197, 230–31). Finally, speaking of social reform, Russell resurrected his former defense of "guild socialism" (in contrast with the authoritarian socialism of actual communist countries) as the best global economic system (Sledd 1994).

Russell's *Power* is actually two books in one. There is the descriptive and theoretical goal of analyzing every social interaction in terms of the dynamics of power. But the book has also (perhaps even dominantly) a prescriptive side, offering a set of receipts to stop the growth of "arbitrary rulership". Here, importantly for this section, the main target became the Nazis, the Italian fascists, and the Soviet Union.

Against the totalitarian regimes embodied by Nazi Germany, fascist Italy, and communist Russia, Russell defended democracy as the most sacred form of government. Nevertheless, Russell was aware that, because of the gears of power, democracy could pollute itself, either collapsing into the tyranny of the majority or facilitating the ascent of demagogic tyrants such as Stalin, Mussolini or Hitler.[5] For that reason, Russell defends that the beginning of all ameliorative reforms to government must presuppose democracy as a rule, at the same time that such democratic rule has to be watched to prevent it from corrupting. But the dangers are always there: to begin with, Russell acknowledged that democracies are not particularly very good at dealing with issues that demand quick decisions (Russell 1938, 154–159). In times of turmoil and threat, such slowness can turn many politicians and citizens against democracy's apparent inefficiency. Moreover, added Russell in an echo of his pacifist stances, war-going democracies could easily slip into fascist-like organizations. To prevent democracy from corrupting itself, Russell concluded, citizens should be well aware of the separation between acquiescence to the collective will and respect for the discretion of the individual, the last bastion against holistic nightmares (Russell 1938, 227).

Russell had thus by 1938 already classified both Hitler and Stalin as plain and dangerous lunatics who had created polluting "autocracies" based on a "creed."[6] And yet, this binary was still on at least equal terms to the one between war and peace which had preoccupied Russell for so many years. In the months to follow, Russell would eventually join the shift in most of British opinion to fully support war against the Nazis. This required him to move one step further from *Power* and classify the Nazis as the perfect embodiment of evil. Russell did not take this step immediately after the outbreak of the war. In a letter of 11 February, 1940 addressed to his friend Robert Trevelyan, Russell wrote that it was becoming harder to remain a pacifist in face of the rise of Hitler and Stalin (Russell 2010[1975], 461). In keeping with radical binaries, to change positions he needed to abandon his previous views of Germans as a civilized people. In another letter to Trevelyan on 19 May he took this path all the way to the fall of the Roman Empire: "I don't think anything so important has happened since the fifth century, the previous occasion on which the Germans reduced the world to barbarism" (quoted in Monk 2001, 241). However, Russell did not completely abandon his appeasement approach to German expansion till the mid-1940s, when he publicly announced his change of mind in the *New Statesman,* conveniently coinciding with much of the British public (Monk 2001, 186). His previous stance "against the war," Russell explained, came from "believing that its evils were greater than any Hitler was likely to inflict upon the world." Now, however, war had become preferable to Nazi ruling. While in World War I, he reconstructed, British defeat was hardly an imaginable prospect, it became an imminent danger with the 1940 threat of invasion (Russell 2010[1975], 410).

According to Russell's later reconstruction, his pacifist stances before and at the beginning of the Second World War were the consequence of being "blinded by the theory" (Russell 2010[1975], 411). Hindsight might be equally blind, however, since throughout the war, pacifism was an option in the US, if one defended only by minority groups within Christians and isolationist socialists (Wittner 1984, 62). It is true that Russell was no isolationist and that he did not oppose war in absolute terms of principle like the radical pacifist Christians who advocated to just turn the other cheek. For Russell it was a matter of minimizing suffering. Once Russell abandoned his early pacifism, however, he took pains to justify what now he saw as his former error. His change of mind, he insisted, was not revolution but "only a quantitative change and a shift of emphasis". Nevertheless, Russell recognized that, despite the differences between the two contexts, it took him a great effort to abandon his former pacifist stance (Russell 2010[1975], 411).

Russell, in his *Autobiography* many years later, tried to soften this change of mind about defending a brutal war by stressing that he was never a complete adherent of the doctrine of non-resistance. Aside of the necessary wars that would be needed to establish his desired world government, Russell had always recognized the necessity of the police and the criminal law within every nation. What's more, Russell claimed, even during the First World War he had thought "some" forms of war were justifiable, although of course methods of non-resistance were always preferable. Further still, argued Russell rather naively, the archetypal example of Gandhi and India against the British Empire would show that Gandhi was triumphant because of the British ethics, who showed a restraint that was not to be expected from the Germans (Russell 2010[1975], 411).When Indians lay down on railways, and challenged the authorities to crush them under trains, the British found such cruelty intolerable. But the Nazis had no scruples in analogous situations. The doctrine which Tolstoy preached with great persuasive force, that the holders of power could be morally regenerated if met by non-resistance, was obviously untrue in Germany after 1933. Clearly Tolstoy was right only when the holders of power were not ruthless beyond a point, and clearly the Nazis went beyond this point.

Russell's narrative fit squarely within the Manichean ideological landscape of the Second World War. It would soon become popular and eventually turn Russell into a figure well regarded by the British political establishment, very much unlike during World War I. Of course, the cultural success of Russell's symbolic attributions came at a cost. Specifically, Russell's comparison between the British Empire's ethics and Nazi Germany's utter evilness required him to downplay, or just plainly ignore, the atrocities committed by the British during the Second World War. The factual brutality of British actions (for instance the Bengal famine of 1943, widely known by the time Russell wrote his *Autobiography*) left small room for the "scruples" Russell was so sure to see in British handling of the Indians (Davis 2000).[7] Equally important, Russell's symbolically powerful attribution of not only the brutal but also the foolish and irrational essence of the Nazis left unexplained the need of an incredible human, military, and economic effort to confront them. Whether Russell was aware of his contradictions is an issue of less importance (at least from a cultural-sociological point of view) than analyzing the symbolic impact of his social performances on his audiences. Russell's whitening of the British Empire had indeed powerful symbolic effects: to bluntly justify the (in absolute terms) most brutal war ever fought in the history of humankind.

This is not to say that Russell remained blind to the faults of the democratic countries within the allies. He never invested too much energy in constructing a cultural trauma around air raids, but he could not ignore the intrinsic power of destruction of the war, particularly brutal when directed to the annihilation of civilians. As he recalled in his *Autobiography*, the English and Russian destruction of Berlin or Dresden seemed to him monstruous (Russell 2010[1975], 491). I had known Berlin well in the old days, and the hideous destruction that I saw at this time shocked me. From my window I could barely see one house standing. I could not discover where the Germans were living. This complete destruction was due partly to the English and partly to the Russians, and it seemed to me monstrous. Contemplation of the less accountable razing of Dresden by my own countrymen sickened me. I felt that when the Germans were obviously about to surrender that was enough, and that to destroy not only 135,000 Germans but also all their houses and countless treasures was barbarous (Russell 2010[1975], 491).

Thus, although here and there we can find some Russell's fragmentary condemnation of some of the war crimes committed by the Allies, he fully supported the Nuremberg Trials without denouncing their double standard when dealing with war crimes (Russell 2010[1975], 694, 497). From 1940 onwards, Russell's demonization of the Nazis remained constant. In contrast, as the next sections describe, his views of the Allied countries, both the democratic and communist, did undergo subsequent changes. Even during the war, Russell did not idealize the Allies, often classifying them as incompetent and even foolish. And, as he had done since the 1920s and most fervently since *Power* onwards, he continued to classify the Soviet Union as a power of dread and oppression. This would shape his striking views regarding nuclear war. Before turning to them, however, the next section deepens in Russell's view of the US place in world politics through his World War II American experience.

THE BERTRAND RUSSELL CASE(S): RETHINKING THE UNITED STATES

Russell spent most of the Second World War in the United States with his new family, formed by the young Marjorie Helen Spence ("Peter" Russell) and their son Conrad, later to be joined by John and Kate (the son and daughter, already in their teens, that he had had with his second wife Dora Grace). He had his main reasons for moving there in the fall of 1938. First, his intentions of resuming an academic career (implausible in the US but just impossible in Europe for a man of his age). Second, and equally important, his search of protection from the foreseeable European war. Russell's arguments for and against pacifism thus came from a shelter well protected from enemy air raids and scarcity of food, water, medicines or electricity. These two reasons, together with his second thoughts about the war, meant that Russell's activism around World War II was to be much more limited than that which made him famous in World War I. To be clear, Russell did not at all ignore the war. While physically away from the war horrors, he became obsessed by it. Every day, he would wait for the news of the destruction of London (Russell 2010[1975], 441).

War also occupied an important part of his public intellectual activity through numerous talks, interviews, and newspaper contributions (all of which came to the rescue of his feeble finances). Between March and April of 1940, he went from calling for American neutrality to urge Roosevelt to mobilize American power against the Nazis (Monk 2001, 228). His argument for America not to enter the war had been that it ought rather to preserve its democracy in the purest form possible (unadulterated by war) in order to fulfill its civilizing mission after the war. This had seemed a tenable position given America's physical removal from the first stages of the war. Russell's shift towards belligerence indicated an increasing anxiety about Germany's capabilities and the unique role of the US in making its defeat possible. In spite of this combination of efforts to regain academic prestige with public exposure on the war issue, Russell's positioning about it was not strong or unique enough to gain any relevant traction. His public fame during this period came from elsewhere; a rather unexpected source: a controversy related to Russell's famous anti-Christian positioning of the 1920s. The outcome of this controversy became a part of Russell's complex interpretation of the United States and its place in world affairs.

In 1938, the same year of the publication of *Power*, Russell was hired at the University of Chicago to teach a seminar on words and facts, which was attended by Rudolf Carnap and Charles W. Morris (Feinberg and Kasrils 2012). The Russell family gladly sold Telegraph house in England and set sail for America. Although Russell enjoyed his teaching in Chicago, he disliked the rest, from the city and its weather to the university's President Hutchins. Hutchins who encouraged neo-Thomism, mistrusted Russell's radical anti-Christian positioning. The consequence of this animosity was that Russell's one-year contract was not renewed. Russell abandoned the "bleak hideousness" of Chicago and moved to Los Angeles to lecture at the University of California, Los Angeles, where he had got a new contract as lecturer.

During the summer of 1939, when the war was about to begin in Europe, Russell rented a house at Santa Barbara, where he seriously injured his back. As a consequence of his prescribed rest, Russell did not have enough time to prepare his lectures for the coming academic year, which he called "inadequate" (Russell 2010[1975], 439). Russell also despised UCLA's president, accusing him of being too conservative and of dismissing liberal professors without good justification. His dissatisfaction with his lectures and with the oppressive Christian climate of the university, took Russell to look for new positions. Towards the end of the academic year 1939–1940, he was hired by the City College of New York as a professor of philosophy of mathematics, logic, and metaphysics of science. But Russell soon met another difficulty which would impede him to teach in New York but increased his fame as an agitator.

Dr. William Thomas Manning, the Episcopal Bishop of New York City, strongly opposed Russell's anti-Christian views on sexuality. Manning thought that Russell's heated critiques of traditional Christian values constituted an important social danger. Given his power and influence, Manning publicly denounced Russell as a man unworthy of teaching at the City College of New York. Russell, Manning contended, encouraged sinful and scandalous sexual practices, included gay and lesbian behavior among students. Manning's denunciation sparked a wave of Christian conservatives who lobbied New York City's government institutions to strongly reject Bertrand Russell's position as professor (Monk 2001, 231–241).

The main target of Russell's critics was his book *Marriage and Morals* (1929). This scandal shows the cultural paradoxes in the change and metamorphosis of social meanings. In *Marriage and Morals*, Russell had declared opinions on race that would be more-than controversial for our current standards. They were not the target of Russell's Christian critics. On the other hand, Russell had at the same time contended opinions about sexuality that could even sound too conservative for many of our current standards. An example of this is his advice of avoiding divorcing when the couple has little children. But before the end of the Second World War, Russell's early racist views were mainly unnoticed; after all, we only have to remember the official American views on groups such as blacks and the Japanese during the 1930s and 1940s.

But if racism was culturally acceptable in the United States, Russell's opinions on sexuality were considered highly scandalous and dangerous for a significant part of the American civil sphere. Nevertheless, despite the pressure of these Christian conservatives, Russell was confirmed by the New York Board of Higher Education as professor at the City College of New York (Russell 1967[1957]).[8] Predictably, the Christian lobbies that wanted Russell to be expelled from American academia, were very disappointed by this decision. The next step to expel Russell was given by Jean Kay, a private citizen who took the matter to the New York Supreme Court. Kay claimed that Russell's profane philosophy would pollute her pure daughter, despite the fact that Russell was not teaching ethics in that moment and Kay's daughter was not a student at the City College of New York (among other things because in those times the institution only accepted male students). But Kay's narrative resonated with a significant part of the conservative population of New York.

Russell, perceived as a perpetrator, was a foreigner who embodied the threat of spreading evil and polluting influences in the United States, a country chosen and blessed by God that should resist such pernicious influences. In the imaginary collective of many New Yorker conservatives, Kay's daughter perfectly embodied the archetype of the victim of Russell's profane attacks. Russell recalled the beginning of this scandal in this way:

> The Government of New York City was virtually a satellite of the Vatican, but the professors at the City College strove ardently to keep up some semblance of academic freedom. It was no doubt in pursuit of this aim that they had recommended me. An Anglican bishop was incited to protest against me, and priests lectured the police, who were practically all Irish Catholics, on my responsibility for the local criminals. A lady, whose daughter attended some section of the City College with which I should never be brought in contact, was induced to bring a suit, saying that my presence in that institution would be dangerous to her daughter's virtue. This was not a suit against me, but against the Municipality of New York. (Russell 2010[1975], 440)

The judge in charge of the Russell Case was John E. McGeehan, a conservative Catholic from Irish ancestry. As expected, McGeehan ruled against Russell's appointment as professor. John Dewey, likely the most famous American philosopher living at the time, summarized this in his 1941 book, published together with Horace M. Kallen, *The Bertrand Russell Case*. The book was a collection of articles defending Russell's right to teach at College of the City of New York and presenting McGeehan's ruling as punitive, unjust, and libelous. Dewey's influence made many important Western intellectuals to protest against Russell's treatment. Among them, Albert Einstein's famously held that "great spirits have always encountered violent opposition from mediocre minds". Einstein expressed this opinion in an open letter (dated 19 March 1940) to Morris Raphael Cohen, who was a professor emeritus at College of the City of New York and supported Russell's appointment. That Dewey embarked in this defense of Russell despite the fact that Russell had repeatedly (and, at the time, recently—see Monk 2001, 223) despised Dewey's philosophy in both popular and academic writings is telling of the significance of this controversy for American cultural wars of the time.

According to Dewey's recollection, McGeehan based his decision on three criteria: first, he argued that since Russell was not a citizen of the United States, he should not be allowed to teach at the City College of New York: The New York law prohibited foreigners from teaching in public schools. Second, McGeehan contended that Russell had started to teach without a previous competitive examination of his teaching and research merits for the position to which he was appointed (despite the fact that Russell was already very famous during those times). Thirdly, McGeehan came to the point that had originated the controversy: according to him, it was very well proven that Russell held immoral views on sexuality. McGeehan cited four of Russell's popular books as textual evidence: *What I Believe* (1925), *On Education* (1926), *Marriage and Morals* (1929), and *Education and the Modern World* (1932). Of all these books, *Marriage and Morals*, McGeehan held, was the most dangerous. According to the accusation, Russell's opinions regarding sexual relations between college-aged students amounted to an endorsement of abduction, rendering him morally unfit to teach philosophy and an advocate of lawlessness (Kennedy and White 1941; Dewey 1941). In the line of Manning's accusations, McGeehan contended that Russell's very dangerous writings encouraged sex before marriage, homosexuality, temporary marriages, and the privatization of marriage, among other scandalous things for those times.

Various reasons were put forward to prevent Russell from appearing in court. Underlying all of them was the fear of granting Russell's ideas even more unwanted publicity and of exposing the whole process to the witty sarcasm of the British philosopher. The Russell Case worsened when an appeal by the American Civil Liberties Union was denied in several courts. According to an article published by the editors of the *University of Chicago Law Review* in 1940, the City of New York's lawyers told the Board of Higher Education that the verdict would not be appealed. A few days later after this resolution, New York's Mayor La Guardia removed the funds for the position from the budget.

Russell did not shy away from commenting on Judge McGeehan. "As an Irish Catholic", Russell wrote, "his views were perhaps prejudiced." He went on to construe an analogy between his own case and Socrates' famous trial: "precisely the same accusations were brought—atheism and corrupting the young" (quoted in Feinberg and Kasrils 2013). Russell compared this to a witch hunt in a country of fanatics (Russell 2010[1975], 440).

At the midst of this public scandal, Russell was invited by Harvard University to give some special lectures on epistemology. Despite his public lynching, the contract had been already signed before the scandal (Russell 2010[1975], 442). That same year, those lectures were published in Russell's book *An Inquiry into Meaning and Truth*. There, in the British version of the book, Russell ironically added in his presentation "Judicially pronounced unworthy to be Professor of Philosophy at the College of the City of New York" to the listing of distinctions and academic honors on the title page.

Following his dismissal from the College of the City of New York, Russell was hired by Albert C. Barnes to teach at the Barnes Foundation, near Philadelphia. Barnes, the famous inventor of Argyrol, was devoted to liberal education of workers and artists. He sympathized with Russell's anti-establishment image. Barnes was well aware of the effects Russell's positionings could have in the US society: he had helped finance the publication of Dewey's *The Bertrand Russell Case,* for which Barnes himself had written a prologue. Barnes offered Russell a five-year appointment to lecture on philosophy at his foundation. This relieved Russell of a great anxiety, since he had important economic problems: two of his children had visited him and were unable to come back to England after the beginning of the Second World War. And the cost of living for the Russells was not cheap.

The public support that Russell received from Dewey and other influential figures worked as a set of social performances that counter-narrate Russell's enemies: Christian conservationism was narrated as a polluting force of intolerance and fanaticism; against such evil force, Russell was saved by Barnes, who embodied rational thinking, science, and Enlightenment.

Russell's duties with Barnes began at the New Year of 1941. Despite the symbolic power of the counter-narrative allowed by this, Russell was dismissed from the Barnes Foundation in December 1942. Personal animosity explains this breaking of the initial five-years contract and the subsequent legal turmoil (Monk 2001, 245–265). Barnes thought that Russell had a distaste for lecturing and an impolite attitude towards students that violated the core values of democracy and education Russell and Dewey had much campaigned for (Barnes 1944). Barnes's questioning of Russell's teaching seems particularly odd because it was precisely this course at the Barnes Foundation which served as the basis for what would become Russell's most popular and best-selling book: *A History of Western Philosophy*, published in 1945 and written with the help of his wife Peter. Beyond the personal quarrels, what interests us is that Barnes quickly presented Russell as a new threat to the sacred values of democratic education. Barnes even published a sequel to the book he had helped Dewey in publishing just two years before, which he significantly titled *The Case of Bertrand Russell vs Democracy and Education.* Towards the end of Russell's American journey, it had become clear that a significant part of both American Christian conservatives and democratic liberals considered Russell "morally unfit" to teach at their respective institutions.

Finally, Russell spent his last days in the United States at Princeton. There, he came to know Einstein "fairly well," discussing with him, Gödel, and Pauli on several occasions—encounters that Russell found disappointing on several grounds (Russell 2010[1975], 444).[9] After his several misadventures in the United States, the University of Cambridge's Trinity College had invited Russell to a five-year lectureship. Russell gladly accepted the invitation. He returned to the United Kingdom ready to fulfill his goal of reentering the academic life, and no less that at the institution which had put an end to it as a consequence of his political activism during World War I. Russell's controversial stay in the US, however, had conferred a strong public presence to his views, including those on pacifism and war, which would occupy an increasing space in his writings in the next decades. More importantly for our argument, Russell's American experience had also confirmed his previous mixed feelings about that country. While in his *Autobiography* he would compare his dismissal as a professor to McCarthy's "witch-hunts" of the late 1940s, at the time of this scandal he had a different analogy at hand: "All this fuss frightens me. It makes me fear that, within a few years, all the intellect of America will be in concentration camps" (quoted in Monk 2001, 238). Russell's fears that Western liberal democracies were corrupting themselves into fascist dictatorships through war and fanaticism were, at least at this time, weaker than his hopes in the United States as a savior of Western liberal democratic values. This helps explain Russell's early positioning relating nuclear weapons, but also sets the stage for the radical changes this stance would undergo in the years to follow.

NUCLEAR UTOPIAS

On 18 August 1945, Russell published his short but influential piece "The Bomb and Civilization" in the *Glasgow Forward*. Crucially for our argument, the article opened and ended with a reference to science and its role as harbinger of apocalypse or utopia. The first two sentences contrasted scientific successes to moral failures:

> It is impossible to imagine a more dramatic and horrifying combination of scientific triumph with political and moral failure than has been shown to the world in the destruction of Hiroshima. From the scientific point of view, the atomic bomb embodies the results of a combination of genius and patience as remarkable as any in the history of mankind. (Russell 1945, 1, 3)

The last three plead to tame the power of science though political organization:

> Science is capable of conferring enormous boons: it can lighten labour, abolish poverty, and enormously diminish disease. But if science is to bring benefits instead of death, we must bring to bear upon social, and especially international, organization, intelligence of the same high order that has enabled us to discover the structure of the atom. To do this effectively we must free ourselves from the domination of ancient shibboleths, and think freely, fearlessly and rationally about the new and appalling problems with which the human race is confronted by its conquest of scientific power. (Russell 1945, 1, 3)

The dichotomy—peace or annihilation—was not new to Russell. In other chapters we have seen him making similar arguments about other industrial and technological weapons. What is new here is precisely the significance that Russell now ascribes to nuclear weapons to the detriment of all others:

> In an instant, by means of one small bomb, every vestige of life throughout four square miles of a populous city has been exterminated. As I write, I learn that a second bomb has been dropped on Nagasaki. The prospect for the human race is somber beyond all precedent. Mankind are faced with a clear-cut alternative: either we shall all perish, or we shall have to acquire some slight degree of common sense. A great deal of new political thinking will be necessary if utter disaster is to be averted. For the moment, fortunately, only the United States is in a position to manufacture atomic bombs. (Russell 1945, 1, 3)

Note that, at this point in time, what makes the nuclear bomb unique for Russell is not radioactive contamination, but the possibility of doing with just one bomb the job formerly done by many. And yet, this quantitative change is enough for Russell to declare a new fearsome era for humankind. What is surprising here is that all the industrial weapons that Russell had condemned for so long appear now as negligible in view of this new threat to live on earth. This is all the more surprising because at the time the only country with nuclear capability had a rather small arsenal, absolutely incapable of the obliteration of all life on earth.

As surprising as it may be, Russell's reaction was actually fairly common in the immediate weeks after the deployment of Little Boy over Hiroshima and Fat Man over Nagasaki. There are precedents to this narrative before 1945. H. G. Wells's *The World Set Free* (1914), for instance, described an uncontrollable weapon based on atomic energy. Wells, who appeared in earlier chapters advocating for world government with Russell, knew well the atomic theories and views of nuclear energy of scientists like William Ramsay, Ernest Rutherford, and Frederick Soddy. In turn, physicist like Leó Szilárd read his book and might have found inspiration in it.[10] Russell himself had, in his 1923 *The ABC of Atoms,* spoken of the possibility of nuclear energy producing unprecedented deadly explosives. But this narrative, while popular among physicists, coexisted with others in which nuclear weapons were just one more step in a continuous military escalation. Its triumph in August 1945 was to a great extent a result of America's war propaganda machine and in part a result of Japan's rapid surrender on 15 August, just six days after Nagasaki (but also seven days after the Soviet Union's declaration of war on Japan, which is what the Soviet propaganda machine identified as the cause of Japan's surrendering). As Gordin (2007) has shown, US military strategists saw the nuclear bombing of Hiroshima and Nagasaki as an additional support to the fire raid campaign being launched against Japan. They did not expect to end the war immediately. Actually, fire-bombing continued after Nagasaki and a third nuclear bomb was about to be launched when Japan announced unconditional surrender. But the Truman Administration, particularly through science journalist William L. Laurence at the *New York Times*, was announcing nuclear bombs as an epoch-changing scientific wonder already since early August (Gordin 2007, 110–113). When Japan surrendered, the official line became that the two nuclear bombs had made victory possible (and thus that it had been necessary to drop them). Public opinion followed, thus forgiving the many other efforts involved in the process. This same official mythologizing of the bomb included the prospect of the annihilation of all life on earth at a time when this was still a distant possibility. In Gordin's own words:

> The image formed in those days of late August 1945, shaped by William Laurence and proselytized by scientists, journalists, and politicians, is still very much with us. The point is not whether nuclearism has shaped how individuals the world over view these weapons, but how it has done so. In both the United States and Japan, in particular, the sudden end of World War II inscribed nuclear weapons as the symbols of our modern age and as the key to unlocking both past and future. That this was not inevitably built into the hardware of the weapons does not make its power any less real. (Gordin 2007, 124)

Thus, as we have seen throughout this book, it is crucial to distinguish between the intrinsic effects of historic events and the symbolic power that public opinion, and public opinion makers, assign to them. Russell's adoption of the American narrative about the uniqueness of the atomic bomb, combined with his (back then also fairly orthodox in the West) despise of Japan and of Soviet Russia, along with this squarely defense of Western democracies, had two immediate symbolic effects in his early thinking about nuclear weapons.

The first effect of this retrospective reading of the bombing of Hiroshima and Nagasaki as unique was downplaying the damage that regular bombing had caused during World War II as well as the effects of regular fighting in deciding its ending. Russell did condemn the brutality of massive civilian killing by the Western Allies in Trieste and Tokyo, but this was not at all his priority and never spent much ink on it. His negative view of the dropping of the two atomic bombs was indeed not because of the loss of Japanese life, but because of a concern with the entrance into world politics of a greatly destructive weapon. In "The Bomb and Civilization" he rather casually pointed that "the immediate result [of the successful nuclear bombings] must be a rapid end to the Japanese war, whether by surrender or by extermination." That this was published three days after Japanese unconditional surrender might show that it was written before (as Russell himself explained) or just that there were still many doubts about the certainty of such capitulation.

What interests us in Russell's sentence is the casualness with which he spoke of the extermination of the Japanese. This was likely a result of Russell's negative view of Japan and of its role in the world war. This was of course in line with American and British anti-Japanese propaganda before, during, and after the war, which often got the point of dehumanization.[11] But even before the war Japanese society embodied for Russell all kinds of political, cultural, social, and psychological vices. This was partly related to Victorian orientalism, supported on the ancient binary between West (usually classified as transparent, rational and free) and East (usually classified as mysterious, tyrannical and irrational). But Russell's orientalism was much softer with the case of China.[12] In Russell's imaginary, China's main issue was how to face, adopt, and adapt to Western industrialism. As if the Western techno-scientific sphere were the mythic Prometheus, Russell wondered whether the benefits of science, technology and industry could be given to an Eastern society without it also importing the aggressive militarism that characterizes Western nations. This would matter to all humanity because of China's huge population. But, aside of that, Russell (1922) held that China is a nation whose "virtues are chiefly useful to others and vices chiefly harm to [itself]." Furthermore, "the Chinese are gentle, urbane, seeking only justice and freedom (. . .) They have a civilisation superior to ours in all that makes for human happiness (. . .) I think they are the only people in the world who quite genuinely believe that wisdom is more precious than rubies" (Russell 2000[1922], 331). This did not compare to Japan's wickedness. Russell classified Japan as a brutal imperialist society composed of unpleasant, cruel, and sexist individuals destitute of good manners. Russell claimed to have liked only one Japanese person during his twelve-day-trip in 1921—a Japanese woman married to an anarchist who despised Japan.[13] In 1938, Russell compared Japan's imperialism with the British and French, acknowledging that it necessitated a highly industrialized society:

> Japan, by purely military means, has acquired in China raw materials which are essential to great military strength, and in like manner England and France have acquired oil in the Near East, but both would have been impossible without a considerable degree of previous industrial development. (Russell 1938, 107)

But one lacking any traces of the civilization which adorned the Western imperialist powers. For Russell, Japanese traditional dual political and religious system of the Shogun and the Mikado was almost "savage". (Russell 1938, 56). Modern Japanese people, Russell allowed, could be considered "civilized people", but mainly thanks to Western influence. (Russell

2010[1975], 172). Given Russell's general dislike towards Japan, we can better understand the lack of empathy towards victims of fire or nuclear bombing that his "The Bomb and Civilization" publicly exhibited. What Russell was really concerned about was the possibility of a nuclear war of global scale. The second effect of the narrative of nuclear weapons as awesome and unprecedented epoch-making devices was the entire reorganization of geopolitical thinking around them. Russell quickly translated his pacifist and world government ideals to what he perceived as the new nuclear era. In "The Bomb and Civilization" he advocated a world government, as he had done before. Only that now this idea was conditioned by the fact that "for the moment, fortunately, only the United States is in a position to manufacture atomic bombs." There were thus two options for organizing a world authority centered around nuclear weapons. The first was creating an international authority to control all uranium resources as well as all bombs and manufacturing plants. This Russell thought ideal but unlikely, since the US would not give its monopoly away to anyone. Even though the USSR had no weapons and that the Cold War had not yet officially started, Russell argued that "each will insist on retaining the means of exterminating the other, on the ground that the other is not to be trusted".

The second solution Russell proposed in "The Bomb and Civilization" was certainly "less Utopian and less desirable, but still preferable to the total obliteration of civilized life": The United States becoming more "imperialistic" and imposing disarmament everywhere else: "If one or two wars were necessary," Russell argued, "they would be brief, and would soon end in decisive American victory. In this way", Russell continued, "a new League of Nations could be formed under American leadership, and the peace of the world could be securely established. But I fear that respect for international justice will prevent Washington from adopting this policy" (Russell 1945, 1, 3).

Again Russell's words are more surprising that many commentators have noticed; we are talking about a time in which nuclear weapons did not still give the US any significant advantage in a potential war against the Soviet Union. The arsenal was too small and the technology to deploy the existing weapons not sufficient to reach the heart of the Russian territory. Moreover, Russell once again betrayed his former pacifism, only that now the rapidly-created nuclear myth made him minimize the potential destruction of non-nuclear warfare and exaggerate the strategic advantage of the US as the only nuclear power.

As in many other occasions, however, Russell was not alone in defending these new ideals. On the one hand, the world government movement gained immense traction rapidly after the Hiroshima's and Nagasaki's nuclear blast, particularly in the US (but also in Britain, in large part through Russell himself [Wittner 1993, 92]). This movement was now recrafted as the alternative between world peace or total nuclear annihilation. On the other hand, American strategists were very rapidly imaging scenarios in which the Soviet Union had access to nuclear weapons and the arsenals were enough to destroy all life on earth (Gordin 2007, 128). They were also rather publicly debating how to stop the USSR from getting the bomb or from using it once it had it. The three alternative scenarios presented by Russell came up very early after Japan's surrender and in the years to come: obliteration of life on earth, global authority controlling nuclear weapons, or US military enforcement of disbarment of all countries, including the Soviet Union.

Russell's view of nuclear weapons was very much in line with the official line in August 1945 and in the years to follow. American strategists and scientists were also publicly discussing the possible implications of a nuclear escalation with the creation of the hydrogen bomb, based on nuclei fusion instead of fission. Some of Russell's biographers do not seem to realize this when they state, following Russell's own account, that he predicted this development a few months after Hiroshima in a speech delivered to the House of Commons. His point was that enormous destructive power of nuclear weapons was bound to exterminate humans if immediate action was not taken. While his speech was well received, it did not move to action as he had expected (Russell 2010[1975], 489). Russell was outraged. Despite his auto-proclaimed status of universal moral legislator, his speech was only able to produce a certain amount of talk, but without any clear action to take. In his view, the reason was post-war euphoria:

> In spite of hundreds of thousands of Japanese deaths, nobody grasped that Britain had escaped only by luck and that in the next war she might be less fortunate. Nobody viewed it as an international danger which could only be warded off by agreement among the Great Powers. (Russell 2010[1975], 489)

Russell had a point. Scientists and intellectuals warning of the prospect of a coming nuclear war were often considered to be unjustified harbingers of apocalypse in a moment when the collective imaginary was occupied with American and British triumphant narratives. The Nazis, the Fascist, and the Japanese Empire had been defeated by the brave forces of democracy, justice and freedom; what was the point then of worrying about gloomy views of the future? Western Allies had defeated the forces of evil, the future was full of hope and glory! Sure, there were threats to be faced; after all, this narrative had to coexist with the growing view of communist countries as totalitarian threats to the glorious peace achieved at the end of the war. But such threats could not come from the very means through which the Second World War was over: the nuclear bomb. An artifact that had been, according to President

Truman, providentially guided by God Himself to put an end to the totalitarianism, cruelty and irrationality embodied by the Japanese Empire. Nevertheless, Russell was by no means alone in dissenting with the general euphoric mood. For American and British politicians, scientists, strategists, the question was already how to face a Soviet nuclear threat.

And thus did Russell come to advocate for a preventive war against the Soviet Union. Of the two possible solutions that Russell had presented as necessary to avoid mutual destruction, the US attempted the first one through the so-called Baruch Plan, presented to the UN in 1946. It was a call for an international organization to regulate atomic energy. Stalin politely refused, on the grounds that it would serve the US to maintain its monopoly of nuclear weapons. The atomic race was on and, as various countries were trying to find and secure uranium, the US was stepping in where it could to regain control (Adamson, Camprubí, and Turchetti 2014). But the Soviet Union was out of reach. According to Russell and other nuclear catastrophists, the only solution left was forcing the USSR to abandon its nuclear plans, even if that implied using force. In September 1945, he wrote to Gamel Brenan: "there is one thing and one thing only which could save the world, and that is a thing which I should not dream of advocating. It is that America should make war on Russia during the next two years, and establish a world empire by means of the atomic bomb" (quoted in Monk 2001, 298). In the following months and years, an increasingly bellicose Russell went on to advocate just that. In a speech on December 3, 1947, Russell claimed that:

> If the whole world outside of Russia were to insist upon international control of atomic energy to the point of going to war on this issue, it is highly probable that the Soviet government would give way on this issue. If it did not, then if the issue were forced in the next year or two, only one side would have atomic bombs, and the war might be so short as not to involve utter ruin. (Quoted in Schwerin 2002, 5)

On the same day, Russell told his audience at the Royal Empire Society:

> I think you could get so powerful an alliance that you could turn to Russia and say, "It is open to you to join this alliance if you will agree to the terms; if you will not join us we shall go to war with you." I am inclined to think that Russia would acquiesce; if not, provided this is done soon, the world might survive the resulting war and emerge with a single government such as the world needs. (Russell 1948, 18–21)

In May 1948, Russell positioned himself in an even more explicit way in a private letter to Walter W. Marseille. "Communism must be wiped out, and world government must be established. (. . .) I do not think the Russians will yield without war" (Russell 1954a).[14] Marseille was a famous psychiatrist who also corresponded with Einstein. And, like Einstein and Russell, he also was a promoter of a world government as a supreme panacea for humankind's problems. Russell was feverishly anti-communist. In this letter, it is clear that communist countries led by the Soviet Union just got in the way of his world government dream. To Einstein, he wrote that his views on how Great Britain should face the Soviet threat were opposite to what he had recommended in the 1930s to do against the Nazis: "I favored appeasement before 1939, wrongly as I now think; I do not want to repeat the same mistake" (quoted in Monk 2001, 300). Russell's negative views of the Soviet Union played a crucial role both in his thinking about a nuclear preventive attack and in his orthodox positioning within the British establishment. This alignment granted Russell a new international recognition as a public intellectual. According to Ray Monk, Russell compensated the lack of attention from Cambridge young philosophers with a much more rewarding feeling that the wider public and the British government were listening to his voice: he felt welcome at home and exhibited a fervent nationalism (Monk 2001, 280). As Russell later acknowledged, the contrast with his ostracism from official circles during and after World War I could not be starker (Russell 2010[1975], 492). Still during the war, and for many years after, the British government asked Russell to lecture to the Forces (Russell 2010[1975] 491). From 1945 onwards he became a regular opinion-maker in the BBC radio. In October 1948, the British ambassador to Norway invited Russell to travel there to promote anti-communism through a series of public lectures. A few weeks later the Foreign Office arranged a visit of Russell to Berlin to harangue soldiers to resist the Soviet blockade to the city.[15] In 1949 he received the utmost prestigious official honor, the Order of Merit. Russell was also recognized as a powerful ally by British partners in the Western block. In 1950, Russell attended the inaugural conference for the Congress for Cultural Freedom, a CIA-funded think-tank whose main purpose was the dissemination of anti-communist propaganda around the world. Russell was one of the best-known patrons of the congress, until he resigned in 1956. The culmination of Russell's glorification came in 1950 with the Nobel Prize for literature. Anti-communist politics was an explicit reason for this award, granted "in recognition of his varied and significant writings in which he champions humanitarian ideals and freedom of thought". While it is true that Russell later exaggerated his role as a diplomat, it is no less truth that he was well integrated in the early efforts at Cold War scientific and intellectual diplomacy that later came to be recognized as soft-power (Turchetti et al. 2020).

According to Monk, it was precisely Russell's good standing within the Labour government which made him change his mind about a nuclear preventive attack in late 1948 (Monk 2001, 303–305). After a widely reported speech at Westminster in November of that year, Russell's position received strong criticism by his own political allies, who accused him of calling for an unprecedented bloodshed. Russell's reaction was quick, and in a series of public lectures which he started the next month his tone had watered down considerably. From 1949 onwards, he distanced himself from his previous position not only negating it but denying to have ever supported it. These denials have proved to be especially troubling for both Russell and his many admirers because they have been taken by some of his critics as evidence of a long-term cover-up. The debate has been going on since Russell's letter to Marseille was published in 1955. In a famous interview at the BBC in 1959:

> FREEMAN: Is it true (. . .) that in recent years you advocated that a preventive war might be made against (. . .) Soviet Russia?
>
> RUSSELL: It's entirely true, and I don't repent of it. . . . [N]ot that I advocated a nuclear war, but I did think that great pressure should be put upon Russia to accept the Baruch proposal, and I did think that if they continued to refuse it might be necessary actually to go to war. (Russell 1959, 505)

This became Russell's line of defense: he had never advocated for war but just for the *threat* of it. As in other occasions, Russell's *Autobiography* offers a retrospective recasting of his own public identity. His argument then was that the goal at the time was to stop nuclear war, and that he only meant for the US to threaten with an attack, not to conduct one. More awkwardly, he justified giving his advice on the grounds that he knew if would not be followed and downplaying as much as possible the publicity he had given to his position—he went as far as claiming to have simply forgotten to have defended a nuclear attack (Russell 2010[1975], 489–490).

Russell's repositioning led to heated debates among Russell scholars and sympathizers (see, for instance, Schwerin 2002). Few of Russell's admirers were satisfied by the excuse that he had forgotten his own positions, particularly when he professed them in many more occasions than in the letter in question. Some tried to argue, however, that Russell really believed that the threat would be enough for the Soviet Union to agree to international control of atomic energy and weapons (Perkins 2002). Russell's explicit positioning in his letter to Marseille would thus just be a matter of heated rhetoric, rather than a display of his real positions. More common, and more in agreement with the sources, is the acceptance that Russell indeed had defended a preventive attack (Stone 1981; Lackey 1984 and 1996; Perkins 1996 and 2002; Blitz 2002a and 2020b).

As Alan Ryan points, what motivated the debate was the difficulty of shallowing Russell's defense of a policy that, according to his own account, would cause millions of deaths. And yet, Ryan continues, this was perfectly in line with Russell's consequentialist approach to war and peace, provided one also accepted his premises about nuclear warfare and strategy as well as about the wicked nature of Soviet Russia (Ryan 1988, 177–184). In our view, the terms of the debate are also interesting from the point of view of social trauma theory. There has been much less concern about Russell's positioning regarding German and Japanese loss of civilians lives than on his positioning about the loss of Soviet lives. The obvious difference is that, in the first case, war had already been declared, but Russell did fear Soviet expansionism and often compared it to the Nazi one. The perceived uniqueness of nuclear bombs, coupled with his horror towards the USSR, made Russell prioritize world peace over the death of some million civilians.

THE KOREAN WAR, ETHICS, AND THE RUSSELL-EINSTEIN MANIFESTO

Russell changed his mind regarding a nuclear attack on Russia first in late 1948 when he feared that it could ruin his public persona and then when the Soviets announced to have successfully detonated a nuclear bomb in August 1949. American monopoly was over; there was, therefore, no point in defending it. The truth is that Soviet ability for nuclear war was still too limited in comparison to the American one. But for Russell, one Soviet bomb was enough to change his entire strategy on how to save the world from nuclear doom. He would soon become one of the most vocal anti-nuclear activists of his time. As we will see in this section, this change of view was also motivated for Russell's increasingly negative view of the US—in response to McCarthyism and the Korean War—and a slightly more moderate attitude towards the USSR, in response to Stalin's death.

Russell's mistrust of the US tendency towards illiberalism runs since the 1920s. The problems he had to face during his long stay there during World War II only confirmed these suspicions. And yet, we have seen, none of it tainted his defense of US imperialism against the Soviet Union to prevent both a nuclear Armageddon and the rise of Soviet dominion. This was to change in the last two decades of Russell's life. First slowly, then radically. Let us put it with Ray Monk: "Though it is rarely mentioned in the secondary literature, the Korean War marked a crucial turning point in Russell's political thinking, the point around he swung from the extreme and belligerent anti-Sovietism of the late 1940s to the equally extreme and belligerent anti-Americanism of the 1960s" (Monk 2001, 327).

Very much like Germany, Korea had been divided after World War II around parallel 38°: the Soviets to the North and the Americans to the South. In 1948 the two Koreas were left to administer themselves, and each started to claim rights to the other part. In June 1950, North Korean forces entered into the south, rapidly advancing and taking Seoul. In September 1950, a UN force led by General Douglas MacArthur and his American troops entered the war, retaking South Korea and entering the north. At this precise moment, Russell travelled to the US to give a series of lectures—and to find his soon-to-be fourth wife Edith Finch. His public utterances were consistently and belligerently anti-Soviet. A nuclear war might be, after all, necessary to stop the Soviets, and "in spite of some alarmists, it is hardly likely that our species will completely exterminate itself" (quoted in Monk 2001, 330). This odd attempt to minimize the nuclear annihilation he had been warning against for five years was short-lived. Russell seemed to have entertained the feeling that even nuclear war was preferable to Soviet domination. If so, he abandoned it rapidly as American troops advanced towards the Chinese border.

The Chinese communist revolution of 1949 did not fit with Russell's anti-Soviet expansionism narrative, simply because he was not willing to recast his beloved China as evil. In November 1950, as China was making public moves to enter Korea, he published "Fists for Russia and a Smile for Peking". The article appeared the same month that Russell's Noble Prize was announced. His lectures on "The Impact of Science and Society," where he repeated well known arguments, became crowded.[16] On 27 November, as Mao sent 200,000 men to North Korea to fight the American-led force, Russell was more worried of a possible nuclear attack by the US than of a possible US defeat. As usual, he was not alone in making this move. Clement Attlee, British Prime Minister and leader of the Labour Party, tried to convince Truman to recognize Mao's government and negotiate with China in order to avoid nuclear escalation. In December 1950, When Russell came back to England, he became vocal on criticizing American aggressiveness in Korea, arguing that the UN troops should have stopped in parallel 38 (Ryan 1988, 182). He also denounced the anti-communist witch-hunt initiated by Republican Senator Joseph R. McCarthy in February of that same year. As Monk underlies, in the following months Russell's condemnation of nuclear war did no longer distinguish between democratic America and communist Russia; that was now a mere matter of ideology to psychologically unite rival groups (Monk 2001, 336). In October 1951, when Russell returned to the US, he declared it would be his last visit. He met McCarthyist intolerance against his new positioning with increasingly angry provocations. That same year, Russell published *New Hopes for a Changing World*. In this book, Russell analyzed humankind's main conflicts, from the ones with nature, to the disputes with other human beings, and the human beings with themselves. As in many other writings, Russell held that modern technology had the power to almost eradicate poverty and other human problems. But that would be if science were on the hands of wise and kind men, which was far from being the case. Although modern science and its technology had the potential power to dramatically increase human well-being and happiness, nationalism, greed, and other forms of human stupidity and irrationality put science and its technology at the service of doom. Russell defended once again that the only solution to avoid a coming apocalypse and achieve humankind's utopian progress was through the establishment of a world government:

> If a world Government is to prevent serious wars, there are certain minimum powers that it must possess. First and foremost, it must have a monopoly of all the major weapons of war, and adequate armed forces for their employment. Whatever steps may be necessary must be taken to ensure that the armed forces will in all circumstances be loyal to the Central Government. The world government should proclaim certain rules for the employment of its armed forces. The most important of these should be that, in any dispute between two States, each must submit to the decision of the world Government. (Russell 2019[1951], 97–98)

To be clear, at this point of his intellectual career, Russell did not yet advocate mutual disarmament and still valued American democracy over Soviet autocracy. But his narrative no longer fitted the binary logic that opposed sacred democracy to polluted communism. His relations to the British military were not as rosy as they had been in the late 40s. After several years encouraging the troops by presenting war as a lesser evil at the Imperial Defence College, Russell gave a lecture in which he denounced the contradiction between the defense of war and Christianity. Knowing that his audience was composed mostly of Christians who believed that it is not possible to win a war without God's help, Russell read the Sermon on the Mount. In it, Russell ironically remarked no mentions to the H-bombs could be found. Naturally, after that lecture, Russell was not invited again.

Hydrogen bombs were indeed the real turning point for Russell. After the first successful American test of a hydrogen device in November 1952, Russell (and everyone else) became convinced that the Soviets would soon enough get their own and that doomsday had become many times more likely. While he understood the escalation, he still advocated world government as the only way to enforce peace. In that same year of 1952, Russell published *The Impact of Science on Society*. It reproduced much of his Australian and American lectures of 1951. Again, it followed *Icarus* and other former writings, although updated to the techno-scientific and cultural situation of the early Cold War. *The Impact of Science on Society*, therefore, emphasized the darkest aspects of scientific innovation. Only by following some metascientific recipes, humanity can avoid science of bringing an eternal night of darkness. Such recipes are well-known for Russell's audience: even distribution of ultimate power, limitation of the growth of population and, above everything else, abolition of nuclear war. Russell again connected the state's power with its weaponry's power. From this point of view, the modern power of the state started in the late 15th century as a consequence of the massive use of gunpowder. From that day to this, Russell claimed, the authority of states has increased, and throughout it has been mainly improvement in weapons of war that has made the increase possible. The problem, of course, Russell thought, was that now, in the early 1950s, it is not gunpowder, but nuclear weapons of mass destruction what backed state's power. That was frightening.

In the vein of his *Icarus*, Russell speculated with a probable nightmarish way of domination of world populations through science:

> Diet, injections, and injunctions will combine, from a very early age, to produce the sort of character and sorts of beliefs that the authorities consider desirable, and any serious criticism of the powers that be will become psychologically impossible. Even if all are miserable, all will believe themselves happy because the government will tell them that they are so. (...) A totalitarian government with a scientific bent might do things that to us would seem horrifying. The Nazis were more scientific than the present rulers of Russia, and were more inclined towards the sort of atrocities that I have in mind. (Russell 1968[1952], 50)

In 1953 the Korean War came to an end. It did so after enormous damage, but for Russell none of it was so traumatic as the possibility of a nuclear escalation. Monk is right to point out that the secondary literature has largely ignored the significance of Korea for Russell's nuclear thought. But the reason is that Russell himself did not spent much time talking about its inherent brutality (as he would do a decade later with Vietnam). Russell was not alone in his concern that the Korean War would trigger world-wide nuclear catastrophe—many strategists were of the same opinion (Hamblin 2013). Stalin's death in March 1953 further softened Russell's anti-communist stance. And in that same year Republican Eisenhower won the American elections, which increased Russell's suspicions towards the US.

His warrior ardor of the immediate post-war years gone, Russell reduced his public statements considerably during 1952 and 1953. He directed his energies towards writing literature (like *Nightmares of Eminent Persons*, mentioned in previous chapters) and to complete *Human Society in Ethics and Politics*, which appeared in 1954 and mostly compiled former texts.[17] The

Autobiography aside, this book represents Russell's last full account of his moral and political philosophy. Russell defended once again that ethics and politics should constitute a unity. Such unity is necessary to every society to control and balance the structural conflict between intelligence and impulse. He would later acknowledge that the book's theoretical ethics did not quite ground the political part. More specifically, Russell was unable to justify an ethics that was not subjective but at the same time was convinced that his political stances were the only ethically sound ones (Russell 1975[1959]; Ryan 1988, 47–48). In December of that same year, Russell delivered his radio broadcast "Man's Peril". There, he coined a very successful motto: "remember your humanity, and forget the rest". In this effective speech, Russell called for a neutral commission that would inform leaders and populations in both sides of the iron curtain of the fatally destructive effects of an H-Bomb war. The goal was to promote a universal agreement to end war (Russell 2008). After knowing of Russell's broadcast, Frédéric Joliot-Curie, the famous French Nobel Prize physicist, wrote Russell informing him of a very similar plea made by the World Federation of Scientific Workers, which Joliot-Curie presided. Both Joliot-Curie and the World Federation of Scientific Workers had known communist allegiances—Joliot-Curie had been in charge of the French nuclear energy program from 1945 until his dismissal in 1951 for being a member of the communist party (Hecht 2009, 68–69). While Russell explicitly sought neutral experts, having allies whose voices could be heard by the Soviets was important, and they decided to gather a dozen of world-top scientists to sign what would soon be known as the Russell-Einstein Manifesto.

After Russell discussed the idea with Einstein, he set to work on what was conceived as a letter addressed to nuclear powers. Besides Einstein, who agreed to sign the letter a few days before his death, Russell, and Juliot-Curie, a late comer into the group of signatories was Joseph Rotblat.[18] Rotblat had been the only scientist to abandon the Manhattan Project for ethical and political reasons. Once Germany was defeated, he thought certain that the real objective was the Soviet Union. From Los Alamos he moved to the UK and continued working on nuclear subjects, specializing in the early 1950s in nuclear fallout and its effects. This made him redouble his efforts to curb nuclear proliferation, which brought him to collaborate with Einstein and Russell himself. According to Rotblat's own account, his several conversations with Russell in 1954 had convinced the philosopher of the real scope of the dangers of radioactivity beyond the blast (Butcher 2005). The manifesto was officially released on 9 July 1955 at a hugely attended press conference in London's Caxton Hall. It was purposely scheduled before the UN Geneva Atoms for Peace conference, where the US took the leadership of world nuclear commerce and nuclear programs. Rotblat, who chaired the meeting, recalled Russell's opening words: "I am bringing the warning pronounced by the signatories to the notice of all the powerful Governments of the world in the earnest hope that they may agree to allow their citizens to survive".[19]

After presenting nuclear weapons as harbingers of apocalypse, the Manifesto went on to recast many of the main points of "Man's Peril". In both the broadcast and the Manifesto Russell kept out his idea of a world government, judging that it would decrease the appeal of the main message. He was, as others in the peace movement, moving away from world government and towards verifiable disarmament (Wittner 1993). Instead, the Manifesto called for world leaders to seek peaceful resolutions to international conflict. Again, it proposed a conference where well-respected and politically neutral scientists would impartially judge the catastrophic threats posed to humanity by nuclear weapons. The Manifesto, perhaps predictably, failed to achieve its first goal of having leaders agree towards world peace. But it was an important step towards the second, i.e., organizing a conference of international experts. Shortly after the Manifesto was released, philanthropist Cyrus S. Eaton offered to sponsor a conference of neutral anti-nuclear scientists in Pugwash, Canada. The Russell–Einstein Manifesto became the Pugwash Conferences' founding charter. The first of many Pugwash Conferences on Science and World Affairs was held in July 1957 under Rotblat's presidency. Under the umbrella of scientific internationalism, these conferences actually served as venues for semi-official science diplomacy bringing together scientists from both sides of the Iron Curtain to negotiate a test ban treaty (Wolfe 2018, 113–134).

The Manifesto's success put Russell back again at the center of the international peace movement. It repeated (and multiplied the echo of) the motto "remember your humanity, and forget the rest". But, for better or worse, there is no such thing as a global civil sphere. While addressed to all nations and people, it was obvious that its main target was the United States. For instance, the Manifesto included a paragraph about forbidding thermonuclear hydrogen bombs which directly favored Soviet interests, because they did not yet possess one at the time of its release. This paragraph was not in "Man's Peril" and was added after Russell's conversations with Joliot-Curie and other members of the communist-leaning World Federation of Scientific Workers (Monk 2001, 376). But Russell's own insistence on neutrality was a far cry from his former defense of American imperialism as the only possible salvation from apocalypse. In the years to follow, Russell's coloration of the US would turn even darker.

CHICKEN! CUBAN MAD, AND THE BRITISH ANTI-NUCLEAR MOVEMENT

Through "Man's Peril" and the Manifesto, Russell became used to addressing humanity as a whole. His self-invested role as representative of the future humanity guided much of his nuclear activism in the following years, when nuclear escalation boosted the anti-nuclear movement. At the time of the release of the Russell-Einstein Manifesto, the Soviet Union did not yet have a hydrogen bomb. It got it in November of that same year. Moreover, in the years around the Manifesto the technology and strategy of nuclear weapons was rapidly improving. In the early 1950s, the United States and the Soviet Union, although equipped with powerful nuclear weapons, lacked the technological means to effectively use nuclear devices against each other. The development of American and Soviet aircraft and soon nuclear-equipped submarines gave both sides the power to drop nuclear weapons into the interior of the opposing country. In response to this new situation, in 1954 Secretary of State John Foster Dulles coined the term "massive retaliation", which became part of the US nuclear strategy. It called for expanding the nuclear arsenal to ensure deterrence of any Soviet aggressive move. In the years to follow, both the US and the Soviet Union tested hundreds of nuclear weapons, and other countries joined the nuclear club—Great Britain in 1952, France in 1960, and China in 1964. As a response, nuclear annihilation entered the popular imagination, and the peace movement gained millions of adepts. Russell managed to surf that wave for the years to come, making sure that his individual voice stood out from the chorus.

In 1957, the year of the first of the Pugwash conferences, Russell became less interested in his original idea of a committee of experts and pursued instead his own role as world savior. In November, he wrote an open letter in the *New Statesman* addressed to President Dwight D. Eisenhower and Soviet Premier Nikita Khrushchev. The article urged them to celebrate a summit to consider "the conditions of co-existence" to avoid mutual nuclear destruction. Khrushchev sent his response to the *New Statesman,* agreeing that such a meeting could indeed assure world peace and going further than Russell and proposing the elimination of nuclear weapons. In turn, US Secretary of State John Foster Dulles replied for Eisenhower, defending American foreign policy and signaling the Soviet Union as inherently aggressive. Not surprisingly, Russell liked Khrushchev's response better, even if he did not advocate, as Soviet propaganda did, for the prohibition of all nuclear weapons.

In January 1958, Russell elaborated his views on such a meeting in *The Observer*. The only way of avoiding an imminent apocalypse, Russell claimed, was the cessation of all nuclear weapons production. In Russell's proposed plan, the United Kingdom would take the first step by unilaterally suspending its own national production of nuclear weapons. In this plan, Germany should also be "freed from all alien armed forces and pledged to neutrality in any conflict between East and West". Thanks to this article and its responses, *The New Republic*, a liberal American magazine, asked Russell to further elaborate his views on world peace. Russell published an article in which he urged that, in order to avoid the apocalypse, all nuclear weapons testing and flights armed with nuclear weapons should be halted immediately. Furthermore, Russell defended the necessity of opening international negotiations for the destruction of all hydrogen bombs. Only a limited number of conventional nuclear devices should be allowed in order to ensure a balance of power that served as a deterrent for war. Russell also bestowed himself of enough political and ethical authority to propose specific measures for Europe. First, Germany ought to reunify, accepting the Oder-Neisse line as its border. Second, a neutral zone ought to be established in Central Europe encompassing, at a minimum, Germany, Poland, Hungary, and Czechoslovakia. These countries ought to be free of foreign troops, prohibiting them to form alliances with other nations outside the neutral zone.

On 15 May 1957, Great Britain successfully tested its first H-Bomb. A series of articles appeared in the *New Statesman* calling for British disarmament, coinciding with Russell's public correspondence published in that paper (Ryan 1988, 192). This created the conversation which would lead to the creation, early in 1958, of the Campaign for Nuclear Disarmament (CND). Russell became its first president, sharing its leadership with Christian anti-nuclear activist Canon Collins, who was appointed chair. Russell's consequentialists ethics differed from those of Collin, based on principles. Thus, the CND motto was "Ban the Bomb," a step which Russell had until then considered "futile". But Russell's and Collin's goals did meet regarding the British bomb. Other members of the CND included anarchists from Direct Action, communists, and members of the Labour Party. Their goal was double: British unilateral disarmament and British unilateral abandonment of NATO to embrace neutrality in the Cold War. These theses were gaining acceptance within the Labour Party and the CND lobbied to promote them into government action.

In 1959, Russell published *Common Sense and Nuclear Warfare*. It was seen by many as a CND pamphlet, which did much to increase its public impact. And yet, *Common Sense* argued for British disarmament only in passing and focused instead on world politics, a nuclear international authority, and the usual dilemma between annihilation or paradise through a simple choice: to end all wars. This was not the CND's goal.[20] Written after *Sputnik*, Russell warns that weaponization has now jumped to the space, an extreme example of the excesses of escalation. In *Common Sense* Russell coined what would become a hugely successful metaphor: the Nuclear World War was like playing *Chicken!*: two cars run against each other at full speed and the one who backs first loses. "As played by youthful plutocrats", Russell added with characteristic wit, "the game is considered decadent and immoral, though only the lives of the players are risked. But when the game is played by eminent statesmen, who risk not only their own lives but those of many hundreds of millions of human beings, it is thought on both sides that the statesmen on one side are displaying a high degree of wisdom and courage, and only the statesmen on the other side are reprehensible". The book was read widely, reaching much beyond the CND's target audience. Duncan Sandys, the conservative Minister of Defense, summoned Russell to discuss it—and then did nothing about it (Russell 2010[1975], 578). While Russell complained later by the lack of action which followed the book's general praise, its influence was felt in an unlikely place as the Rand corporation. No other than the most famous nuclear strategist, the author of the hugely influential *On Thermonuclear War*, published in 1960. Herman Kahn took Russell to epitomize the disarmament movement and used him jokingly to stress the contradiction it would mean for Western powers to plea for deterrence and disarmament simultaneously (Ghamari-Tabrizi 2005, 218). To soft-handed diplomacy, Kahn opposed what one of his collaborators popularized in 1962 as "Mutual Assured Destruction" (MAD).[21] Kahn's point was that, from a purely rational cost-benefit analysis perspective, it was pointless to start a nuclear attack on a nation equipped with nuclear weaponry. Kahn epitomized what the authors of *How Reason Almost Lost its Mind* describe as "the strange career of Cold War rationality" (Erickson et al. 2013). Given that only two players were needed for massive retaliation to work, Russell used Kahn's *On Thermonuclear War* as an ally for the argument for British neutrality (Ghamari-Tabrizi 2005, 21). Everything else he despised. In 1961 Russell published *Has Man a Future?* While it repeated many of the arguments of *Common Sense,* it responded to Kahn by emphasizing the mathematical aspects of his argument regarding the increasing probability of error and vulnerability with increased numbers of weapons as well as with increased members to the nuclear club.[22] Also in contrast to Kahn's rational choice theory, Russell emphasized irrational psychological aspects that increased the possibilities of launching nuclear weapons (Russell 1961b, 109). Finally, Russell ridiculed what Kubrick's 1964 film *Dr. Strangelove* would establish as Kahn's most enduring legacy: the doomsday machine (Russell 1961b, 36). In turn, Kahn contributed a good to the spread of Russell's *Chicken* analogy. He did so by refuting it in his also widely read *On Escalation: Metaphors and Scenarios* (1965):

"Chicken" would be a better analogy to escalation if it were played with two cars starting an unknown distance apart, traveling toward each other at unknown speeds, and on roads with several forks so that the opposing sides are not certain that they are even on the same road. Both drivers should be giving and receiving threats and promises while they approach each other, and tearful mothers and stern fathers should be lining the sides of the roads urging, respectively, caution and manliness. (Quoted in Erickson et al. 2013, 88)

Kahn preferred the metaphors provided by game theory. Together Thomas Schelling, he was the chief theoretician of the doctrine of MAD, as a purely rational way to avoid the actual use of the bomb. While Russell and his peers at anti-nuclear movements contributed to the diffusion in the collective imaginary of the cultural trauma around a nuclear holocaust to come, Kahn assured that no nuclear war was the most likely outcome of nuclear escalation, provided that information on the mutual retaliatory capabilities was sufficiently available (Erickson et al. 2013).

Russell's and Kahn's contrasting theories were put to the test in 1962 with the Cuban Missile Crisis. Predictably, both parties interpreted the outcome of this crisis in their own terms, and thus claimed victory to their respective approaches to nuclear warfare. For Kahn, it showed that deterrence worked. For Russell, it showed that he, as an individual, had a role to play in averting nuclear doom. In 1961 the US-financed Bay of Pigs Invasion had failed, but it was clear that the US was not ready to tolerate a Soviet-friendly island facing Florida. In October 1962, after gathering evidence that the Soviet Union was installing nuclear missiles in Cuba, US President John F. Kennedy declared a blockade around the island and promised to stop and search incoming Soviet ships. Nikita Khrushchev, in turn, warned that this violated international law and declared the Soviet right to defend its naval and commercial ships. Nuclear war became a real possibility, with the two powers literally running towards one another at full speed.

Russell took it upon himself to stop the escalation and, once again, wrote to the presidents of the two superpowers. Only this time not an open letter but urgent telegrams. Doubting the truthfulness of the US accusation that the Soviets were installing nuclear missiles (something the Soviets did actually not deny), he put the blame on Kennedy; and thus, Russell's telegram to Kennedy read:

YOUR ACTION DESPERATE. THREAT TO HUMAN SURVIVAL. NO CONCEIVABLE JUSTIFICATION. CIVILIZED MAN CONDEMNS IT. WE WILL NOT HAVE MASS MURDER. ULTIMATUM MEANS WAR . . . END THIS MADNESS. (Quoted in Davis 1984, 437)

To Khrushchev he wrote a milder telegram, urging him not to launch a nuclear attack. The Soviet president, as he had done before, replied publicly and assuring that his government would not be reckless (Seckel 1984). Facing accusations that he was being more belligerent with the United States than with the Soviet Union, he insisted that US imperialism in Latin America was responsible for the crisis because the American government considered that it had the supreme right "to dictate what form of government should prevail in every country of the Western Hemisphere" (Russell 1963a, 22). On the other hand, Khrushchev was to thank for having lowered the tension:

> President Khrushchev is personally responsible for the avoidance of a war of nuclear devastation. He has acted with the greatest restraint in a crisis of the first magnitude. (. . .) The [American] blockade violates international law. It is illegal. It is immoral (. . .) If nuclear bases are intolerable in Cuba, they are intolerable everywhere. This is the heart of what I have been saying to the British people for the length of our campaign for nuclear disarmament. Nuclear bases threaten the peace of all. (Russell 1963a, 41)

As Monk and others have pointed out, at this time Russell's strong collaboration with Ralph Schoenman (see below) marked his approach to Cuba, including signing articles defending the Cuban revolution and turning a blind eye on Fidel Castro's very aggressive tone during the crisis (Monk 2001, 439–452).[23] Shortly after the crisis, Russell published *Unarmed Victory* (1963). There he no longer proposed a world government, but he did warn against nationalism's dark side: the hatred of other countries.[24] And yet the book displayed dislike, when no hatred, of America and its imperialism. Nevertheless, the book's main point was to account his own "unarmed victory". He did so by narrating his personal involvement in both the Cuban and the Sino-Indian crises and by defending his own role in influencing world leaders and public opinion.[25] Russell justified the moral and political legitimacy of his social performances:

> Many people seem to have been surprised that I should intervene in such matters without having any official status, but I think events show that, even in our highly organized world, there are things that a private individual can do which are much more difficult for a Minister or an organization. In particular, it is much easier to agree with a powerless individual without loss of face than it is to agree with those whose arguments are backed by H-bombs of almost infinite destructive power. (Russell 1963a, 10)

Russell's self-invested role in world politics and his increasingly negative coloration of the US marked his nuclear activism in the early 1960s, in particular his abandonment of the CND to fund and support the Committee of

100. The CND's yearly Aldermaston marches were not enough for some of its members, particularly those closest to the anarchistic Direct Action. They were discontent with the CND legal methods and advocated for mass civil disobedience against governments which defended nuclear weapons. Among them was Ralph Schoenman, a young anarchist philosopher who took part in the early years of the British New Left Movement. He offered Russell to lead the step towards civil disobedience (Monk 2001, 404–411). After intense negotiations with CND's chair Collins, Russell resigned from the CND and became the first president of the Committee of 100, which was officially launched in London on 22 October 1960. The point was to have one hundred prominent persons arrested for carrying out anti-nuclear illegal campaigns (Carroll 2010). Russell explained his move in an article in the *New Statesman* (February 1961):

> The Campaign for Nuclear Disarmament has done and is doing valuable and very successful work to make known the facts, but the press is becoming used to its doings and beginning to doubt their news value. It has therefore seemed to some of us necessary to supplement its campaign by such actions as the press is sure to report. There is another, and perhaps more important reason for the practice of civil disobedience in this time of utmost peril. There is a very widespread feeling that however bad their policies may be, there is nothing that private people can do about it. This is a complete mistake. If all those who disapprove of government policy were to join massive demonstrations of civil disobedience they could render government folly impossible and compel the so-called statesmen to acquiesce in measures that would make human survival possible. Such a vast movement, inspired by outraged public opinion is possible, perhaps it is imminent. If you join it you will be doing something important to preserve your family, compatriots and the world. (Russell 1961a)

The goal was thus explicitly to reach the news. They succeeded. The Committee's main campaign tactic was to organize non-violent mass sit-down demonstrations with at least 2,000 volunteers. Despite his old age and worsening health, Russell was one of the very few 100 signatories who took active part in such demonstrations. Soon, the Committee of 100 was receiving more attention, as well as more funding and popular support, than the CND. This might have damaged the nuclear movement at a point in which the CND was actually gaining traction within the Labour Party (Taylor 1988; Monk 2001, 419–423). But to Russell convincing the British Labour Party was not enough (the Conservatives were still in power), the whole world population needed to tell their leaders that they were willing to risk legal action in order to prevent annihilation (Ryan 1988, 193). The CND's famous Aldermaston marches had been useful, but Russell was right that the press needed novelty.

The image of an old Russell sitting with young activists became an icon of the anti-nuclear movement and of the philosopher's cultural and political responsibility. On 15 April 1961, at his address to the first Annual Conference of the Midlands Region Youth Campaign for Nuclear Disarmament, Russell referred to world leaders in an increasingly simplistic rhetoric: "we cannot obey these murderers. They are wicked and abominable. They are the wickedest people that ever lived in the history of man and it is our duty to do what we can".[26] Russell's provocations worked, and he was jailed for seven days in Brixton Prison—he was well aware that this short sentence was a privilege granted to him (Russell 2010[1975], 589). On 17 September 1961, on the symbolically powerful Battle of Britain Day, the Committee carried out its most famous public demonstration. They blocked the pierheads at Holy Loch and the approaches to Trafalgar Square. A week before this successful demonstration, the Committee members were summoned to court without charge under the Justices of the Peace Act of 1361. According to the judge in charge, the Committee "incited members of the public to commit breaches of the peace". And what was even worse, the Committee had plans to continue to do so. As a consequence, the Committee was bound to a "promise of good behaviour" for twelve months. Thirty-two members, including Russell, refused and chose to go to prison instead. The accusation was "breach of peace" for taking part in a forbidden anti-nuclear demonstration. According to Russell's recollection, the magistrate offered to exempt him from jail if he pledged himself to "good behavior," to which Russell replied: "No, I won't".[27]

Prison increased Russell's legend, and it did not steal Russell any energy to continue with this activism. It enabled him, moreover, to return to one of the topics that had fascinated him since 1914: the relation of an individual to the State, conscientious objection, and civil disobedience. This theme had formed the core of his 1949 *Authority and the Individual*. Nuclear war, however, gave it new meanings. A nuclearized world meant greater public to states and demanded even greater efforts to preserve private liberty (Russell 2010[1975], 495).

In 1963, when he and Schoenman could no longer control it, Russell left the Committee of 100—it rapidly deteriorated, embracing libertarianism and abandoning its plea for non-violence, until its final dissolution in 1968 (Shelley 1965; Taylor 1988). True to his belief in individuality, Russell (and Schoenman) funded instead the Bertrand Russell Peace Foundation, to which the next chapter returns. But his time at the Committee of 100 was not in vain for Russell. Besides his renewed insistence on the role of the individual in world politics (and in particular of his own individual role), his activities at the Committee invigorated Russell's anti-American rhetoric. "We were impressed by the seriousness of Hitler's threat to Britain in 1940", Russell had written to the *New York Times Magazine* in 1960, "but it was not nearly as serious as the US threat to Britain at this present moment" (quoted in Monk 2001, 407). He still attacked the Soviets, but as his reaction to the Cuban crises showed, he thought the United States was being unnecessarily aggressive and thus running towards MAD. Schoenman organized Russell's anniversary as a propaganda event for non-alignment. An impressive list of leaders who opposed American imperialism but were also outside of the Soviet sphere sent words of praise for the occasion, including leaders from Zambia, Ghana, India, and the UN (Monk 2001, 433).

Importantly, his increasing anti-Americanism led him to revise some of his former value attributions regarding Great Britain, Germany, and Japan. Regarding the first two, in one of his 1961 speeches he declared that Kennedy and British conservative president Harold Macmillan to be "much more wicked than Hitler" (Russell 2010[1975], 618). Hitler, previously presented as the very embodiment of evil, was now recast as a lesser evil than the leaders who had fought him and imposed a nuclear order.

Regarding Japan, from 1962 onwards, Russell actively supported the Japanese anti-nuclear movement. As a consequence, the Bertrand Russell Society in Japan was established, conducting many successful meetings and publications. In his "Statement to Young Japanese from the President of the Committee of 100 in Britain", Russell humbly declared: "In Britain we have created a movement of mass resistance against nuclear war. I do not need to tell the people of Japan about the horrors of such warfare; nor do I need to tell you about the effectiveness of resistance, for I have been encouraged by what you have yourselves achieved already". The physicist and Nobel Prize recipient Hideki Yukawa, who had been among the eleven signatories of the Einstein-Russell manifesto, became active in promoting Russell and his ideas in his country.[28] Thanks to Russell's growing demonization of the United States, he could at last empathize with the Japanese civilians killed by American nuclear bombs. Russell, however, would not extend this symbolic attribution of solidarity to the Japanese victims of American fire bombings—what mattered for him were nuclear deaths.

CONCLUSION

Russell has been often accused of changing his mind too quickly and of defending each new position with the same dogmatic fervor as the old one. In this chapter we have seen him inviting the Nazis for tea, repudiating capitulation as blind, advocating a US all-out nuclear attack against the Soviet Union, campaigning for world peace, and advocating for the end of nuclear weapons.

It is true that Russell insisted that the circumstances themselves were changing, and it is also true that certain tenets of his political position remain constant, namely a consequentialist criterion by which minimizing suffering and preserving "civilization" were the main goals. Nonetheless, it is undeniable that Russell painted similar peoples and actions with very different colors as he construed or promoted new social narratives. What interests us here is not deciding whether Russell was an opportunist or a hypocrite. Rather, we want to be able to understand in which way his symbolic construction of certain tragic social events, and his abuse of simplistic binary logic to promote that construction, enabled his ideas and works to move across different audiences and discourses.

The cultural import of nuclear holocaust is the most sticking example. Russell stood out among the many social actors who helped to create a heavy culturally traumatic perception of nuclear weapons. This perception lead, in the collective imaginary of many countries, to growing fantasies in a coming nuclear apocalypse that would destroy human civilization on earth. As in the case of the traumatic perception of the First World War, there was a cultural feedback between Russell's apocalyptic views and other cultural references, from intellectuals' and politicians' speeches to popular movies and books. Science fiction novels and movies about technological Armageddon predated the nuclear age and shaped Cold War narratives (Seed 2013). Nuclear weapons soon became the center of catastrophic books, films, and other popular works of art, particularly in the West.[29]

Intellectuals are storytellers. When their stories make it through the gatekeepers of media and other means of symbolic production, they can become popular, creating powerful intellectual and emotional attachments among disparate groups of people. We have insisted on this thesis throughout this book, as a key element to account for Russell's rhetoric when discussing the role of science in society. This chapter has contributed to show how the stories of nuclear holocaust helped weave the cultural trauma around nuclear weapons. Russell participated in this collective imaginary, and, in turn, contributed to expand it. The gears of (culturally constructed) sorrow usually work in this "circular" way, a sort of spiral of social sorrow.

The traumatic perception around nuclear weapons was not directly generated by nuclear weapons' actual power of destruction. There has been no nuclear holocaust (to the day of this writing). And from 1940 onwards, many more civilians and cities were reduced to ashes in air raids, napalm bombing, and through chemical and biological warfare than in nuclear attacks. The air raids over Germany, Japan, Korea and other places during the Second World War and the Cold War were, there is no doubt, *biologically* and *psychologically* devastating for their survivors. But the truth remains that air raids on civilian populations did not become powerful cultural traumas. Even in Germany and Japan, nuclear bombs displaced the trauma of the incendiary bombs, torture, and rape (Heins and Langenohl 2011).[30] Equally important, the Cold War was a peaceful period only from the point of view of the anticipated nuclear holocaust that never came. But the period witnessed many wars which destroyed many millions of lives.

Sociotechnical imaginaries of the future shape the way the present is perceived (Jasanoff and Kim 2016). In the face of these cultural paradoxes, the success of nuclear apocalyptic narratives needs to be explained, and this explaining needs to go beyond ridiculing those positions as being just wrong (Maloney 2020). Why did public intellectuals as Russell downplay the power of destruction of incendiary bombs, while they magnified nuclear weaponry's dangers to nightmarish-apocalyptic dimensions? Why did Russell feel more concerned and empathetic for some killed innocent civilians than for others, depending on their nationality, political affiliation and race? Why were some of these situations reverted over time? The answers for these pressing questions can be provided neither by psychology ("guilt," "learning from mistakes," "to mature") nor by mechanistic sociological theories that ignore the relative independence of culture. The answers for these questions need a cultural-sociological explanation.

Using this approach, we have seen how the cultural perception of nuclear weapons changed in Russell's evolving narratives and positionings. Thus, nuclear weapons changed from something that could become safe tools in a world government's hands, to a "lesser evil" against the spreading impurity of Soviet communism (even at the cost of millions of innocent lives), to the purest embodiment of human stupidity, irrationality and inner darkness that should never ever be used under any pretext whatsoever. Again, it would be rather naive to think that these changes *only* obeyed the intrinsic changes in technology, economics and politics.

As we have seen, narratives must be emotionally compelling, and several of Russell's dramaturgical performances during his anti-nuclear activism were successful in that regard. Although he was already famous during the 1930s and 1940s, being awarded with the Nobel Prize in 1950 consecrated Russell's world fame both inside and outside academia. But to have a large audience is never enough for a public intellectual if she is unable to connect both intellectually and emotionally with the public who is watching her performances. Russell invested his best efforts in addressing powerful politicians and the general public alike. He mobilized several rhetorical devices, from comparing nuclear dangers with the Black Death, to apocalyptic narratives of an imminent collapse of humankind. Russell's critiques of nuclear weapons had a wide range, from "reasonable" technical reasons (the more-than-possible mechanical or technical mistakes given the growing number of nuclear devices) to apocalyptic-nightmarish tales about human nature's foolish darkness. Despite decades of social performances against nuclear weapons, Russell declared to be unsatisfied by the results. Targeting specific audiences, organizing marches of large numbers, and civil disobedience were all available methods, but no one completely useful to meet its purpose (Russell 2010[1975], 629–630). I tried alerting a particular group, but though this had a limited, it had little effect on the general public or Governments. I next tried the popular appeal of marches of large numbers. Everybody said, 'These marchers are a nuisance'. Then I tried methods of civil disobedience, but they, too, failed to succeed. All these methods continue to be used, and I support them all when possible, but none has proved more than partially efficacious (Russell 2010[1975], 629–630).

We have seen how Russell's role in the cultural construction of the nuclear-drama was more successful than he admitted. But his narrative was not overwhelmingly self-evident or without opposition. It was balanced by powerful counter narratives that presented nuclear weapons as peace makers, first in Japan and then in the Cold War through deterrence. Key actors like Kahn thus understood Russell to be a childish utopian ignorant or as an impostor who did not know (or pretended to not know) the elementary gears of *Realpolitik*. The world followed its course and Russell was unable to stop the arms race during the Cold War or to drastically change any important political event involving nuclear weapons, but from the so-called Russell-Einstein Manifesto to the Committee of 100, several social performances of Russell became reasonably popular and had a significant cultural impact. The Russell-Einstein Manifesto became a hugely important symbolic actor in the anti-nuclear movement. The Manifesto's popularity cannot be explained only because it was signed by important scientists; that is not enough to engage with significant parts of civil spheres, if other cultural factors are missing. The Manifesto became famous among so many people because Russell, Einstein and other signatories (perhaps most saliently Max Born) had already been culturally constructed as public intellectuals, "wise men" with the sacred right of addressing humankind in order to protect it from the increasing threats of darkness (Pais 1994). Significant parts of several civil spheres already identified that darkness with a coming nuclear apocalypse. They also identified science with neutrality and universalism (Somsen 2008). In this context, the Manifesto's role was similar to that of a totem with (in anthropological terms) apotropaic effects.

Even more than during the times of the First World War, Russell's imprisonment when he was in his 90s, along with the police brutality employed in several of the Committee of 100's non-violent demonstrations, also had powerful symbolic effects upon Russell's growing audiences. A significant part of British and other Western audiences identified themselves with the pacifist activists being beaten up by the police. This made perfect sense within a culture heavily influenced by Christianity, in which so many historical sacred fighters for justice and good were tortured and punished by evil authorities. In a different culture this strategy would not have been so effective—for instance, those cultures which, through the idea of *karma,* perceive torture and other evils as retribution for past sins.

Russell and his followers' social performances helped spread the narrative according to which the perpetrators were tyrannical governments that supported nuclear holocaust, while the victims were pacifist civil spheres that would be in the future the main victims of a nuclear apocalypse. It is not difficult to trace some similarities between these processes of symbolic identification in the anti-nuclear movement and in the American civil rights movement, as Alexander (2008) has studied.

Let's finish our conclusion returning to air raids. Although Russell had downplayed them for decades, at the end of his life he constructed a new apocalyptic narrative around their use in Vietnam. The last Russell narrated air raids, including the extensive use of napalm on Vietnamese cities, towns and villages in the grimiest imaginable apocalyptic terms: no other than the salvation of humankind was at stake in this proxy war, fought in the "far" Vietnam, and *without* nuclear weapons.[31] On 15 February 1965, Russell pronounced his famous speech "The Labour Party's Foreign Policy" at the London School of Economics:

> The American proposition that an independent Vietnam free of control is worse than a nuclear war is madness. If America is allowed to have its cruel way, the world will be the slave of the United States. Once more America summons mankind to the brink of world war. Once more America is willing to run the risk of destroying the human race rather than bow to the general will. Either America is stopped now or there will be crisis after crisis until, in utter weariness, the world decides for suicide. (Russell 2010[1975], 683)

The years in which Russell narrated the United States as a sacred force of good, democracy and freedom were far away. The dreams of a world government were broken. The next step in Russell's apocalyptic account of the 20th century was ready. Such a step would imply, in dramaturgical terms, what could be considered the biggest theatrical performance that Russell had ever delivered.

NOTES

1. This letter became famous in 2014, when many newspapers reported that the Museum of Tolerance had bought it. The museum, part of the Simon Wiesenthal Centre, paid USD 4,000 for the letter at an auction in England last month. Reporters around the world denounced Russell's remarks.

2. This thesis precedes the one Michel Foucault (1991) made famous for whom "'power is everywhere', diffused and embodied in discourse, knowledge and 'regimes of truth'".

3. From the perspective of what we could call a psychological reductionism, Russell (1938, 11) states that "the love of power" is probable motivated by a sense of entitlement which arises from exceptional and deep-rooted self-confidence.

4. *The Adelphi* or *New Adelphi* was a well-known English literary journal founded by John Middleton Murry and published between 1923 and 1955. The first issue appeared in June 1922, with issues published monthly thereafter.

5. "Hitler and Mussolini, no less than Stalin, owe their success to Robespierre and Napoleon" (Russell 1938, 91).

6. In Russell's words: "A collection of lunatics, each of whom thinks he is God, may learn to behave politely to one another. But the politeness will only last as long as each God finds his omnipotence not thwarted by any of the other divinities. If Mr A thinks he is God, he may tolerate the pretensions of others so long as their acts minister to his purposes. But if Mr B ventures to thwart him, and to provide evidence that he is not omnipotent, Mr A's wrath will be kindled, and he will perceive that Mr B is Satan or one of his ministers. Mr B, of course, will take the same view of Mr A. Each will form a party, and there will be war—theological war, bitter, cruel, and mad. For 'Mr A' read Hitler, for 'Mr B' read Stalin, and you have a picture of the modern world. 'I am Wotan!' says Hitler. 'I am Dialectical Materialism!' says Stalin. And since the claim of each is supported by vast resources in the way of armies, aeroplanes, poison gases, and innocent enthusiasts, the madness of both remains unnoticed. [. . .] Autocracy, in its modem forms, is always combined with a creed: that of Hitler, that of Mussolini, or that of Stalin" (Russell 1938, 213, 246).

7. In 1942 Russell spoke and wrote on the Indian question against what he perceived to be anti-English sentiment in America, arguing that independence would come after the war but also that Gandhi was actually hindering the prospects of an allied victory (Monk 2001, 260).

8. In 1957, Paul Edwards published Russell's classic *Why I Am Not a Christian*, incorporating texts about this scandal and its background.

9. Gödel would later recall the inaccuracies of Russell's memories: Gödel himself was not Jewish and he recalls only one of such meetings (see Monk 2001, 270).

10. Szilárd read Wells's book in 1932 and in 1933 he conceived the idea of neutron chain reaction, filing for patents on this new technology in 1934 (Rhodes 1986, 24).

11. American propaganda oscillated between the most brutal and dehumanizing one that called Japanese "yellow rats," "vermins," "subhumans" and called to exterminate Japanese civilians and play with the bones of Japanese soldiers' corpses, to mild pieces or propaganda such as Frank Capra's *Know Your Enemy: Japan* (1945).

The "mild" pieces of propaganda, although insensible to the mass killing of Japanese civilians or their imprisonment in American Internment Camps, did not at least openly dehumanize them. We could place Russell within this category.

12. William T. Ross (1994) has explored Russell's binary between China and Japan.

13. Although Russell's polluted view of Japan was certainly influenced by his leftist political ideas of the moment, other stereotypes that Russell attributed to the Japanese were very common during that time (Clifford 2001).

14. The letter was published, with Russell's consent, on 16th Oct of 1954 in *Saturday Review*.

15. Russell served gladly to the military, even though his view was that Berlin's partition by the Allies had been "almost incredibly foolish," having perpetuated a dangerous continuation of the strife between East and West and a competition between the two powers that would only end up making Germany dangerously powerful again (Russell 2010[1975], 659).

16. Monk notes that in these lectures Russell used as an example of sentimental irrationality . . . those who argued for appeasement to confront the Nazis! (Monk 2001, 333).

17. The first nine chapters of this book were written in 1945–1946, the rest in 1953, with the exception of the lecture, included in Chapter 2, that Russell gave in Stockholm when he was awarded with the Nobel Prize for Literature in 1950.

18. Namely, Bertrand Russell, Albert Einstein, Max Born, Percy W. Bridgman, Leopold Infeld, Frédéric Joliot-Curie Hermann, J. Muller, Linus Pauling, Cecil F. Powell, Joseph Rotblat, and Hideki Yukawa. It is important to note that, with only the exception of Infeld, all of the signatories of the Russell-Einstein Manifesto were Nobel Laureates (although Rotblat achieved his Nobel Award in 1995). Also, most of them had a (complex) history of political activism for world peace.

19. Rotblat described it in the following way: "It was thought that only a few of the Press would turn up and a small room was booked in Caxton Hall for the Press Conference. But it soon became clear that interest was increasing and the next larger room was booked. In the end the largest room was taken and on the day of the Conference this was packed to capacity with representatives of the press, radio and television from all over the world. After reading the Manifesto, Russell answered a barrage of questions from members of the press, some of whom were initially openly hostile to the ideas contained in the Manifesto. Gradually, however, they became convinced by the forcefulness of his arguments, as was evident in the excellent reporting in the Press, which in many cases gave front page coverage" (Rotblat 1982, 6).

20. For the complex relations of the British left and the CND to the military industrial complex, see Edgerton 2006, 237.

21. This term was coined by Donald Brennan in 1962, a strategist working at the Hudson Institute, which Kahn had created in 1961.

22. In this same sennse went Russell's famous phrase: "The human race may well become extinct before the end of the century. Speaking as a mathematician, I should say the odds are about three to one against survival" (Interview in *Playboy*, 10, No. 3, 42, March 1963).

23. Russell's friends and former allies in the Manifesto, like Rotblat and Born, wrote Russell warning that his close alliance to Schoenman was ruining his reputation (Monk 2001, 447).

24. By stating that "I do not mean to suggest that nationalism is wholly evil. It has two sides: love of one's own country, and hatred of other countries. One is good; the other is bad" (p. 117), Russell declared, in a binary way, that national identities can only be supported on hate towards other nations. This fits into Russell's rather pessimistic philosophical anthropology (Russell 2010[1975], 629).

25. For a sobering account of Russell's/Schoenman's involvement in the Sino-Indian crisis, see Monk 2001, 451–452.

26. Russell's claim became very famous and, of course, controversial. Many years later, Russell downplayed it as being taken out of context by the press (Russell 2010[1975], 619).

27. While in prison, Russell released a note addressed to humanity alerting that the populations of the East and West had been tricked into believing they were enemies when in reality they had a common enemy: their rulers, who threatened to destroy all life on earth (Russell 2010[1975], 620).

28. In 1972, Yukawa's lecture on Russell served as a landmark for the social impact of Russell's ideas in Japan. The impact of Russell's humanist thought on the Japanese academia became evident through the creation of the first research groups on his thought in the 1960s, in particular the Bertrand Russell Society of Japan and the Tokyo Branch of the Bertrand Russell Peace Foundation.

29. Among the popular books, one might list Pat Frank's *Alas, Babylon* (1959), Harlan Ellison's *A Boy and His Dog* (1969), to Buronson's and Tetsuo Hara's *Fist of the North Star* (1983–1988), and Katsuhiro Otomo's *Akira* (1982–1990). Other books did not become movies, though, and were mainly influential on other writers and intellectuals; a good example of this is represented by Aldous Huxley's *Ape and Essence* (1948). The list of movies set in a post-apocalyptic nuclear world is long, including from *Five* (1951), *Unknown World* (1951), *Invasion U.S.A.* (1952), *Captive Women* (1952), *Day the World Ended* (1955), *On the Beach* (1959), *The World, the Flesh and the Devil* (1959), *Alas, Babylon* (1960), *The Time Machine* (1960), *The Last War* (1961), *The Day the Earth Caught Fire* (1961), *The Creation of the Humanoids* (1962), *La jetée* (1962), *Panic in Year Zero!* (1962), *This is Not a Test* (1962), *Ladybug Ladybug* (1963), *Fail-Safe* (1964), *Dr. Strangelove* (1964), *The War Game* (1965), *Late August at the Hotel Ozone* (1966), *In the Year 2889* (1967), *Planet of the Apes* (1968), *The Bed Sitting Room* (1969), *Beneath the Planet of the Apes* (1970), *Glen and Randa* (1971), *Battle for the Planet of the Apes* (1973), *Zardoz* (1974), *A Boy and His Dog* (1975) . . . to *Mad Max 2* (1981), *The Terminator* (1984), *Fist of the North Star* (1984–1988), *Mad Max: Beyond Thunderdome* (1985), *When the Wind Blows* (1986), *and Akira* (1988).

30. In Japan there are indeed works of art and intellectual products which reflect the collective horrors about the fire-bombing destruction of cities, such as the movie *Grave of the Fireflies*, written and directed in 1988 by Isao Takahata, and which was based on a Akiyuki Nosaka's pseudo-autobiographical short story.

31. Although nuclear weapons were not deployed in Vietnam, they were both on board aircraft carriers and stockpiled in the region. What's more, the American army increased its numbers up through mid-1967. But they were kept as a last resort that was never used. Russell's nightmarish account of the American intervention in Vietnam did not include nuclear weapons, but war crimes committed by "conventional" ways, including a tremendous amount of air raids on both military targets and civil populations. Among the American bombs that were extensively used we can name the Douglas A-1 Skyraider, the Cessna A-37 Dragonfly, the F-100 Super Sabre, the Northrop F-5 Freedom Fighter, Douglas A-4 Skyhawk, Grumman A-6 Intruder, and Ling-Temco-Vought A-7 Corsair II. The American air campaign during the Vietnam War was, in absolute terms, the largest in military history. The United States dropped more bombs in Vietnam than during the Pacific War.

Chapter Five

The Vietnam War and the Judgment Day

By the time that the Vietnam War broke out, Russell had created in his mind a new meta-adversary: the United States. As we saw in the previous chapter, Russell's progressively alienated feelings towards the United States started during the Korean War, worsening during the nuclear arms race. Russell's demonization of the United Started reached its climax during the 1960s. Thus, he could dramatically ask: "Is there anything that can be done to prevent [United States'] universal empire of evil?" (Russell 1967, 73). In Russell's new compelling story, the United States was the embodiment of wickedness to be stopped at any cost if a world apocalypse wanted to be prevented. For that salvific purpose, Russell thought he needed a new and bigger social stage on which to address his audiences, aside of his usual ones represented by newspapers, speeches, articles, and books. That new stage was what became known as the Bertrand Russell Tribunal on the Vietnam War (1966–1967). Or just the Russell Tribunal.

Despite being planned as an unprecedented powerful means of symbolic production, the Russell Tribunal had a more limited power in reaching the Western public than Russell and his allies had anticipated—a limitation of power that, nonetheless, Russell never recognized. Nevertheless, and despite all the attempts of its dominant enemies to silence and cancel it, the Tribunal played a role in the cultural process of decline that the United States experienced in its political, military, and moral prestige from the mid-1960s onwards. This chapter identifies the main social processes through which Russell's interventions added to the cultural perception of the Vietnam War as one of the most traumatic events of the 20th century. Also known as the International War Crimes Tribunal and the Russell-Sartre Tribunal, it was formed by about twenty-five public intellectuals from around the world, the most prominent of which was, together with Russell himself, Jean-Paul Sartre.

Political activism enabled a philosophically unlikely alliance. Russell and his main allies, we intend to show, played a significant role in the symbolic inversion through which the American government and its military technology came to be perceived as forces of apocalyptic evil rather than salvific good.

The United States and its allies presented World War II in the terms of a sacred action in the pursuit of global justice and freedom. The US extended this narrative onto the Korean War. The cultural success of these narratives prevented war atrocities from reaching or affecting the Western public (Casey 2010). Outside East Asia, and for many years, no popular traumatic narrative reflected the wide scope of these wars, mass destruction and mass extermination of civilians. No social group had enough interest, resources, authority, or interpretive competence to successfully broadcast powerful traumatic claims over these violent events.

The situation with the Vietnam War was very different. Public awareness of war crimes in Vietnam fuelled domestic opposition to the war and even became a factor in its ending. By the end of the 1960s, only a third of the American population kept defending the United States' foreign policy in Indochina, and almost a third of the Americans were strongly against the war (Hunt 1999; Lewy 1978; Kerry et al. 1971). The situation worsened with the fatal shooting of four students at Kent State University in 1970, known as the Kent State Massacre. In 1973, after the Paris Peace Accords, the American government ordered the final withdrawal of the troops. In 1975, with the Fall of Saigon, the war was officially over.

The cultural construction of evil is a complex process involving a rich arena populated by many social actors and cultural factors. Ontological views of evil consider values a result from facts: when an event is intrinsically evil, it will likely be considered as such. On the contrary, here we consider the evil attributed to the Vietnam War as a cultural representation resulting from several processes of narration and signification. Depending on the nature of cultural representations of good and evil, a social or historical event may be regarded as absolutely evil, demanding continuous remembering and restitution. Alternatively, its evilness may be interpreted as contingent and relative, as something that can be ameliorated and overcome, when not even forgotten (Alexander 2003, 32). Being evil is thus a matter of *becoming* evil. But every culture distinguishes between several categories and degrees of evil. People not only interpret some events as evil; they also "weight" them. As Alexander points out, cultural processes of "weighting evil" have great social and political repercussions in terms of responsibility, punishment, remedial action, and future behavior (Alexander 2003, 33).

The question arises as to why the war crimes committed in the Vietnam War by the United States and its allies left such suppurating social wounds, instead of being incorporated in a more or less routine way, as it happened with other American massacres during World War II and the Cold War (Alexander 2001). For answers, this chapter explores the cultural role of Russell as a dramatic intellectual. Despite the lack of support from Western governments, Russell found ways to contribute to the social spread of persuasive and compelling narratives about the traumatic nature of the war.

We identify three interconnected aspects of the Tribunal, which organize the chapter's three sections. First, the ideological battle around Vietnam was about coding evil, and it was fought largely in the media. As in other moments of his life, Russell himself revised his own targets and standards. As we saw in previous chapters, Russell had abandoned his positivist and enlightened optimism for an increasing mistrust of science and technology as instruments for world evil in the hands of nationalist and tyrannical politicians. In World War I he supported Wilsonianism and in World War II and its immediate aftermath, as communism became his main target, Russell argued that the only way to overcome the profane interplay between nationalism and industrialism was the establishment of a US-led world government. Those days were long gone in the 1960s, when Russell pointed to the United States as the universal empire of evil whose possible victory in the Vietnam War would mean an unavoidable future of techno-scientifically produced apocalypse. In this picture, science and technology appear once again as instruments of evil.

The anti-American and pro-revolutionary rhetoric of what Monk has dubbed Russell's "Guevarist years" was so unlike Russell's earlier positionings that many at the time and since have preferred to assume that Schoenman had taken complete control of a senile man and his public statements. On the contrary, the evidence points towards an alliance between Russell and Castro-led anti-imperialism (Ryan 1988, 199–206; Monk 2001, 455). Russell was willing to put up with pro-communist thesis that contradicted much of his previous thought in order to combat what he at the time perceived to be the most urgent and dangerous evil: US foreign policy.

The second section analyzes some of the rhetorical devices deployed by the Tribunal. In particular, it explores the feedback loops between two different but interconnected layers of Russell's opposition to the war. One, the practical or ritualistic, consisted in mimicking a real court in the vein of the Nuremberg and Tokyo trials, though without the official state support these had actually received. From the point of view of cultural pragmatics, the Tribunal worked as a stage in which well-known leftist thinkers and activists played the role of universal judges. Without any kind of state power to enforce their verdict, the Tribunal condemned the US and its allies for the war crimes committed in Vietnam. "Our tribunal, it must be noted, commands no State power. It rests on no victorious army. It claims no other than a moral authority" (Russell

1967, 125). The Tribunal directly challenged legalism, the judicial monopoly of the state, and the economic global order, becoming an early instance of a non-legal and non-state-centric transitional justice (Zunino 2016). As with other "nongovernmental tribunals" (Blaser 1992), the legitimacy of Russell's tribunal lied elsewhere.

The other layer was mythical, i.e., the ideological justification of the actions of the Tribunal. Anthropologists have extended the distinction between rite and myth beyond religion and magic (Ackerman 2002). These categories are ubiquitous in cultural life. But the usual conceptions of "ritual" tend to be less flexible than the concept of *social performance* that we use (Alexander 2006b). A meaning-centered approach highlights Russell's intellectual interventions during the Vietnam War as cultural devices deployed in these inseparable layers, the mythical and the ritualistic-performative. In this performative sense, the Tribunal's cultural power comes to light.

Russell's Tribunal was indeed powerful. Borrowing from a sentence President Lyndon Johnson used often in the Vietnam War, we argue that wars are fought and won not only on the battlefield, but also "in the hearts and minds of citizens" (Alexander 2011). The third section shows that, despite US interest in ignoring it, Russell's Tribunal succeeded in mobilizing public opinion. Its meetings were reported around the world and its theses discussed in political and academic fora. A cultural feedback emerged between the Tribunal's performative activities and the popular traumatic perception of the war that Russell and his collaborators helped to build. The Tribunal contributed to increase the domestic opposition to the war. Thus, however indirectly, it helped to enforce shifts in America's fighting and propaganda strategies. As a result of this influence, after Russell's death in 1970, subsequent Russell Tribunals extended their "jurisdiction" to other parts of the world, from Chile's military coup d'état to the Israeli-Palestinian conflict (Nakazato 2016, xxiv).

RUSSELL AGAINST "THE FEAR OF COMMUNISM"

In the cultural construction of evil, the traumatic dimension of some events *is weighted* more than that of others, to a great extent independently from the intrinsic real impact of the event that is culturally recast as "devastating". From World War I onwards, Russell increasingly attributed growing levels of evil in his assessments of the interplay between the techno-scientific sphere and the political sphere. But readers of Chapter 4 will recall Russell's support of the Allies' intervention during World War II in spite of all their mass destruction technology, and even his encouragement of a post-war preemptive nuclear attack against the Soviet Union. As a public intellectual, Russell was willing to gauge similar events very differently, depending on sociocultural circumstances and audiences. As his targets moved, he adapted his arguments and measuring standards, often to the point of compromising logical coherence with former views.

As in other cases, Russell mobilized ancient radical binaries in his fight against the Vietnam War. Oppositions such as sacred/profane, salvation/apocalypse and universal justice/world evil are key in the formation and maintenance of collective identities and the emotional ties towards them. Russell was well aware of the intellectual limitations of such binaries, which tend to sacrifice logical coherence and philosophical depth in the holy altar of the social glue that keeps communities stronger in their mutual ideological and material struggles. And yet, the Russell Tribunal put binaries to the service of engaging with a significant part of the Western public.

The Cold War's ideological polarization was more than just a context. It provided the resources and motivations for Russell's rhetorical choices, but it was in turn partly shaped by the efforts of Russell and his companions at the Tribunal. During the Cold War, the American government consciously and consistently chose to narrate its own intervention in the Vietnam War as a justifiable lesser evil (Willbanks and Wert 2017). Russell pursued the opposite strategy. Despite his former anti-communism, he gradually chose to justify the Vietcong's violence against US that, in his view, had become the world's greatest criminal. For that, he played on the cultural trauma generated by the Vietnam War while simultaneously helping to create that trauma and to deepen the social wounds inflicted by the conflict.

By the end of the 1960s, war atrocities had made it to the US media and political debate through images and their interpretations (Alexander 2003).[1] The situation was different at the beginning of the decade. Russell's cultural influence on the Vietnam War set off in 1963, the same year of his creation, together with Schoenman, of the Bertrand Russell Peace Foundation. The occasion was brought by a controversy between Russell and the *New York Times* concerning the American intervention in Indochina. Russell believed that the Western press hinted only obliquely at the scope of the war's criminal brutality. In its justification of the war, the media included but systematically downplayed testimonies of carnages in villages completely destroyed by napalm bombs or of Viet Cong prisoners being summarily executed. For Russell, the main American newspapers were simply publishing isolated pieces of horrifying information while simultaneously avoiding drawing a coherent picture of the war (Russell 1967, 29–30). Russell saw himself as having the responsibility of putting the pieces together to show the war's true face to the public in order to stop the conflict.

Following this direction, Russell published a letter to the *New York Times* which had been previously declined by *The Washington Post* but published at two pro-North Vietnamese papers. In it, Russell denounced the horrors of the war and blamed the United States for them. It was published on 8 April 1963, alongside an editorial that accused Russell of being a biased puppet of communist propaganda. Russell's reply appeared on 22 April. He responded that the paragraph in which he talked about the use of dangerous chemicals to starve the population, thereby destroying crops and livestock, had been cut. Against the accusation of bias, Russell defended himself by stating that his main sources demonstrating war crimes in Vietnam came from the Western world, not from communist propaganda. He also stated that the accusation of speaking only half-truths and distorting the picture could be easily and more accurately turned against his opponents, since, for instance, *The New York Times*'s argument that Americans were only in Vietnam as advisors or trainers was obviously contradictory with the fact, published in the same journal, that they were bombing military targets. Russell also insisted that he criticized atrocities where he found them. As such, he concluded boasting authority as both an academic and an activist, being true to his philosophical convictions led now to accusations of communism exactly as they had led in Stalin's day to left-wing accusations of anti-communist when he denounced Russian crimes at that time.

When Russell discovered that his letter appeared redacted in the *New York Times*, which had suppressed his evidence regarding dangerous chemicals used to commit war crimes in Vietnam, he angrily wrote to them stating that he had not been treated in such a way either in *Izvestia* or *Pravda*. When he requested that the *New York Times* publish the evidence that was omitted by the newspaper, he got the dry answer that his letter was too long and needed to be shortened and that the paper reserved the right to cut without notice and would not allow Russell to monopolize the letters columns.

From this point on, an exchange of letters full of mutual reproaches took place between Russell and John B. Oakes, editor of the paper's editorial page. Russell remained convinced that the *New York Times*'s editorial policy was "a conscious fraud". The last letters of this exchange never appeared in the paper. Russell himself, however, published them three years later in his book *War Crimes in Vietnam* (Russell 1967, 37–41). This heated exchange was not an isolated event. Also in 1963, Russell had a similar quarrel with the editor of *Harper's Magazine*, whom he ended up comparing to the Nazi Adolf Eichmann—judged and executed in Israel in 1962, Eichmann had become the archetype of the collaborator with evil (Monk 2001, 458–459).

From 1963 to 1969, the Bertrand Russell Peace Foundation provided the scene for Russell's performances. Schoenman spent a good deal of that and the subsequent years travelling around the world to meet world leaders, presenting himself and Russell as mediators in world conflicts, and campaigning for funding for the Foundation. As Monk shows, besides Vietnam a strong focus of the Foundation was Latin America and, in particular, Cuba. This included Russell signing papers (sometimes penned by Schoenman) which echoed Che Guevara's own interventions. It also included supporting Cuba's foreign policy in Africa through meetings, trips, and speeches—like Russell's messages to the 1965 World Congress of Peace or the 1966 Tricontinental Conference, supporting anti-American guerrilla warfare throughout the world. In his bellicose ardor against US imperialism, Russell went as far as to telegram the Russian premier urging him to put the Soviet Union's air force at the service of Vietnam's National Liberation Front. The Foundation publicly supported Che's strategy of creating "one, two, many Vietnams". For that purpose, there is evidence that Schoenman helped finance Che's collaborators in Bolivia with money coming from the Foundation—which, at that time, drew in part from the selling of Russell's *Autobiography*. In 1969, after Schoenman's activities led to serious problems with the US and British authorities, Russell, his then-wife Edith Finch, and their collaborators, put an end to Schoenman's involvement in the Foundation and ensured to dissociate Russell's name from the Foundation's pro-guerrila activities (Monk 2001, 454–479).

Throughout this whole period, Russell very consciously insisted that the real menace to the world was no longer communism, but "the fear of Communism". To support his anti-imperialist theses, Russell did not hesitate to favor an apocalyptic narrative at the cost of deforming and silencing alternative more nuanced views. He even sacrificed the logical coherence with respect to his own previous social philosophy, based to a large extent on the liberal defense of individual freedoms. These shifts in strategy are key to explain the cultural repercussion of the Tribunal's activities. Because, among other factors (such as good access to influential means of cultural production), the Tribunal's social echo (or lack thereof) depended upon a range of rhetorical and dramaturgical devices through which their creators positioned themselves and their institution, along with their adversaries, within larger social, political, and intellectual contexts.

RITUAL AND MYTH IN THE RUSSELL WAR CRIMES TRIBUNAL ON VIETNAM

In the 1960s, the Russell Peace Foundation expanded efforts to denounce the American intervention in Vietnam, including sending Schoenman and other collaborators to Indochina to search for first-hand reports of the war crimes committed there (Russell 1967, 30). Russell started plans for the International War Crimes Tribunal. In 1966 Russell sent a letter to American President Lyndon Johnson notifying him about the Tribunal's formation and main goal: informing the general public about the atrocious war crimes committed by the United States in Vietnam (Duffet 1968, 18; Torell 2015, 112). Specifically, the Tribunal would seek to answer uncomfortable questions regarding the use by the United States of weapons forbidden by international law, the killing and torturing of civilians, the destruction of schools and hospitals as military targets, and the creation of labor camps and massive deportation of the civilian population (Coates 1971).

The Tribunal was founded at a meeting in London, on 13–16 November 1966. The original plan for the Tribunal had included prosecuting individuals, including the president of the United States. As that seemed unfeasible, the Tribunal was presented instead as a "Commission of Inquiry" which, following the "Nuremberg Principles," investigated possible war crimes committed by the United States in Vietnam (Nakazato 2016). According to Stefan Andersson, "this shift of emphasis, was the result of the French branch of the Tribunal with Jean-Paul Sartre, Simone de Beauvoir, Vladimir Dedijer, and Laurent Schwartz as the dominant figures" (Andersson 2017, xxiv).

The Tribunal held two sessions, both in 1967, before announcing its verdict of genocide. These meetings took place in Stockholm (Sweden) and Roskilde (Denmark). Funding came from a variety of sources, eventually including the North Vietnamese government controlled by Ho Chi Minh after Russell himself requested its support (Griffin 1992). More than thirty witnesses testified at the Tribunal's hearings, among them American military personnel.

Predictably, the Tribunal met strong opposition from the onset (Ryan 1988). Although it was originally set to take place in Paris, President de Gaulle made sure that did not happen. The United Kingdom was equally inhospitable for Russell and his collaborators. The last-minute solution of meeting in Sweden and Denmark, two countries that, to different degrees, often played the neutrality card in the Cold War, also encountered difficulties (Torell 2015, 115). After those two meetings, and after Sartre's and other prominent members of the Tribunal quarreled with Schoenman, the name Russell was removed from the Tribunal and the headquarters moved from London to Paris (Monk 2001, 471).

In his opening of the Roskild session in November 1967, Russell declared: "We are not judges. We are witnesses. Our task is to make mankind bear witness to these terrible crimes and to unite humanity on the side of justice in Vietnam" (quoted in Chomsky 1971). This sort of tribunal, he insisted, had no clear historical precedent and it responded to equally unprecedented challenges (Singh 1987, 228). In Russell's words:

I have lived through the Dreyfus Case and been party to the investigation of the crimes committed by King Leopold in the Congo. I can recall many wars. Much injustice has been recorded quietly during these decades. In my own experience I cannot discover a situation quite comparable. I cannot recall a people so tormented, yet so devoid of the failings of their tormentors. I do not know any other conflict in which the disparity in physical power was so vast. I have no memory of any people so enduring, or of any nation with a spirit of resistance so unquenchable. (Quoted in Coates 1971, 59)

In the scale of historical atrocities, Vietnam represented the maximum level. Russell positioned the Tribunal, both in the imitation of real courts and in the introductory speeches made about them, as a universal institution seeking the consummation of sacred ideals such as justice, world peace, and freedom (Ryan 1988; Coates 1971; Duffett 1968). Russell himself recognized that the Tribunal claimed no other legitimacy than a moral authority: "we do not represent any state power, nor can we compel the policy-makers responsible for crimes against the people of Vietnam to stand accused before us. We lack *force majeure*. The procedures of a trial are impossible to implement" (Singh 1987, 228). As such, the Tribunal could be considered to be a large-scale theatre, where Russell, Sartre, and the others were *playing* the roles of universal judges for a culturally traumatized audience.

This was noted by critics at the time, some of them sharing the Tribunal's goals but not its methods. Richard A. Falk, famous for studying the ideological aspects of the "American Human Rights Debate" during the Cold War, published on the legality of the Vietnam War and other military operations (Falk 1968; Falk and Melman 1968; Falk and Hanrieder 1968). In this context, and although he strongly opposed the war, he referred to the Russell Tribunal as a "juridical farce" (Andersson 2017, 24; Falk and Hanrieder 1968). But "juridically power," with all its importance, is just one of the multiple powers that populate cultural spheres. Setting the classical Weberian notion of power aside, the Tribunal's performative power is impossible to ignore. Power often results from social actors exercising their agency similarly to dramatic actors projecting their characters' power into a play (Alexander 2016; 2011, 3). Imitating a tribunal invested Russell and his allies with a ritualistic power unattainable otherwise (Pérez-Jara 2015).

What interests us here is the interplay between the Tribunal's ritualistic and mythical layers, i.e., the set of narratives, ideologies and rhetorical tools deployed by the Tribunal. The impact of anti-war ideas depended on the specific ritualistic and dramaturgical devices that Russell used to channel them. Like the two sides of a coin, the Tribunal's ideological layer is inseparable from the practical one. Nevertheless, although each layer existed only in connection with the other, they can be dissociated in sociological analysis—again, the situation is similar to the anthropological analytical distinction between ritual and myth.

The most obvious example is Russell's own *War Crimes in Vietnam* (1967). This publication acted as both the empirical and ideological grounding for the Tribunal. The book provided the Tribunal with its ideological justification and main ideas, and the Tribunal's moderate degree of social influence made the book more visible. For this feedback to be fully effective, the book referenced the Tribunal's "very considerable public support" (Russell 1967, 130) and introduced readers to it:

> Along with world famous figures, Nobel prizewinners, novelists, mathematicians, I am forming a War Crimes Tribunal in order to pass judgment, in most solemn terms and with the most respected international figures, upon the crimes being committed by the United States Government against the people of Vietnam. I appeal to you to end your participation in this barbarous and criminal war of conquest. (Russell 1967, 111)

That this theoretical layer can be considered mythical is not an exaggeration or just a metaphor; it is directly in tune with one of our book's main thesis as argued in the Introduction: that ancient mythical structures of good and evil persist in modern intellectual performances. Russell mobilized all the dramatical force of ancient binaries to present the United States as a universal evil corrupting everything it touches, a sort of backwards King Midas: a force for suffering, reaction and counter-revolution. Humanity ought to defeat that force, as the Greeks at Salamis vanquished the Persian juggernaut. The struggle in Vietnam was a struggle for human decency and emancipation (Russell 1967, 112–114). According to Russell, Americans had at last succeeded in "shocking the conscience of mankind. In the endeavour to exterminate the inhabitants of South Vietnam in the sacred name of freedom, they have adopted the use of what we are told is 'non-lethal' gas" (Russell 1967, 72). Employing highly Manichean rhetoric he depicted the US as a universal empire of evil which could only be stopped by helping the people of Vietnam "to win and preserve their freedom" (Russell 1967, 73).

Recall Russell's scale of evil as presented in his above-mentioned letter to President Johnson. "Within living memory," Russell added in the same letter, "only the Nazis could be said to have exceeded in brutality the war waged by your administration against the people of Vietnam" (Duffet 1968, 18). And yet, we already saw in the last chapter how Russell was ready to compare the absolute evil he attributed to the Nazis with what he perceived as equal or even worse evils of first the Soviet Union and, later, the United States. One of the main "axioms" of the usual narrative of the Holocaust, its *uniqueness* as radical evil in human history, was already well established in the 1960s

(Coates 1971, 59). And yet, Russell was prepared to deny it in his attempts to demonize the American intervention in Vietnam. Weighing evils implied recoding them. Following the *Reduction ad Hitlerum* strategy, Russell drew an analogy between the Vietnamese and the Jewish uprising in the Warsaw ghetto against the Gestapo (Russell 1967, 127). In the closing address to the Stockholm Session of the Tribunal, Russell affirmed that:

> The International War Crimes Tribunal must do for the peoples of Vietnam [. . .] what no tribunal did while Nazi crimes were committed and plotted. [. . .] Our social institutions, impregnated with racism, must be reconstructed. The Tribunal must begin a new morality in the West, in which cold mechanical slaughter will be automatically condemned. The Tribunal must inspire a new understanding that the heroic are the oppressed and the hateful are the arrogant rulers who would bleed them for generations or bomb them into the Stone Age. (Quoted in Coates 1971, 311)

Combining his Manicheism with an acutely apocalyptic rhetoric, Russell declared that the drift towards total disaster would be unavoidable if the situation in Vietnam was not brought to an end (Russell 1967, 81). This paved the way for his use of rhetorical devices typical of a military speech, very much like a captain addressing his troops: "The people of Vietnam are heroic, and their struggle is epic: a stirring and permanent reminder of the incredible spirit of which men are capable when they are dedicated to a noble ideal. Let us salute the people of Vietnam" (Russell 1967, 99). Meanwhile, he encouraged the American troops to ask themselves, when they returned from battle, who were those people they were killing, how many women and children died at their hands that day, and what would they feel if these things were happening in the United States to their wives, parents, and children (Russell 1967, 109).

Importantly for our book, *War Crimes in Vietnam* rendered science and technology as polluted. Russell extended his interpretation of the war in East Asia and the US media as evil to science and technology as the main US means to wage that war. In the same way as roads and ships had made possible prior empires, new technologies, including in particular the nuclear bomb, made it now thinkable that "a stable empire can be as large as the world" (Russell 1967, 75). Because there was more than one nuclear power, however, other weapons like "defoliants" or so-called "non-lethal gases" were being deployed by the US in Vietnam to avoid nuclear annihilation. But the effects of these chemicals upon the local population and nature, Russell held, was horrific (Russell 1967, 72). This of course connected with the mistrust of the social role of science that had intermittently accompanied Russell from the early 1920s. *War Crimes in Vietnam* pointed not only to physics but also to chemistry, biology and to what Eisenhower had dubbed in his 1961 farewell speech the military-industrial complex (Crim 2018). While physics was associated with the atomic bomb in the popular mind, it was the use of chemical and biological weapons in Vietnam, aimed against civilian populations and their crops, what changed the views of science of significant portions of society, often including scientists themselves (Moore 2008; Hamblin 2013, 179–198; Bridger 2015, 88–145). Russell's warnings against the perils of science were thus able to connect with larger groups of public opinion who were questioning research at the service of the military and of large corporations for their effects on both people and nature.

THE TRIBUNAL'S BINARY LOGIC

In order to gain the support of wide-ranging sectors of American public opinion, Russell praised American supporters of the Tribunal, explicitly acknowledging their support: "The Tribunal received from the beginning very considerable public support, not least from very many citizens of the United States" (Russell 1967, 130). The widespread media impact of particularly violent incidents contributed to the fame of Russell's reports, thus deepening the traumatic perception of the war. In 1968, for instance, the media covered the My Lai massacre in detail (Hunt 1999).

Mainly in response to this massacre, the Bertrand Russell Peace Foundation organized the Citizens Commissions of Inquiry (CCI) to continue investigating war crimes in Indochina. The institution's hearings, held in several American cities, would eventually lead to two widely broadcasted investigations carried within the US: the National Veterans Inquiry—sponsored by the CCI—and the Winter Soldier Investigation, sponsored by Vietnam Veterans Against the War (Hunt 1999; Lewy 1978; Kerry et al. 1971). These initiatives made it impossible for the American government and the mainstream media to continue silencing the existence of war crimes in Vietnam.

Admittedly, the Tribunal's social echo was targeted to very specific left-wing audiences. The left/right political distinction was key in the ideological definition of the Cold War. Communist regimes often considered this distinction bourgeois and used alternative binary codes such as socialism/capitalism (Bueno 2003). In the West, however, the "political left" referred to communist and non-racist socialist movements during the Cold War era. For decades, the distinction defined—often in starkly black-and-white terms—the polarized ideological context through which the Western public perceived the conflicts in Indochina. And the Vietnam War itself did much to deepen this division, further dividing the ideological spectrum between the right justifying American foreign policy against communism and the left, which in turn became ever more combatant against these policies as war crimes were being publicized.

Russell positioned himself alongside left-wing intellectuals opposing right-wing political stances. Prominent members of the Tribunal included left-wing politicians and intellectuals such as Jean-Paul Sartre, Ken Coates, Noam Chomsky, A. J. Ayer, and Julio Cortázar (Duffett 1968). Adopting these alliances (and their binaries) meant for Russell abandoning former binaries that he had previously held. While he had worked alongside the anti-war socialists in World War I and even supported guild socialism, he had also fiercely opposed the Soviet Union and, more generally, Marxist communism. He despised both its practice and the theoretical principles that supported it. This attitude did not change after Stalin's death:

> My objections to Marx are of two sorts: one, that he was muddleheaded; and the other, that his thinking was almost entirely inspired by hatred. [. . .] His belief that there is a cosmic force called Dialectical Materialism which governs human history independently of human volitions, is mere mythology. I have always disagreed with Marx. But my objections to modern Communism go deeper than my objections to Marx. It is the abandonment of democracy that I find particularly disastrous. (Russell 2009[1956], 457)

But the left/right divide made Russell downplay his anti-communist stances in favour of new binaries. Processes of construction of evil generally imply transforming existing narratives while maintaining others (Harding et al. 2016). And Russell was proud of not really fitting within clear-cut ideological labels (Russell 2010[1975], 246). It is thus not surprising that he modified the target of his criticisms. But what is particularly relevant for this book's analysis is that, at every stage of his political ideas, Russell supported his narratives on binary structures. That these coding structures were more oversimplified or more nuanced depended on the varying cultural contexts of Russell's public utterances. By the time of the Vietnam War and the Tribunal, Russell continually employed extremely simplistic binaries between the forces of the sacred/good (identified with the Vietnamese communist soldiers and their supporters) and the forces of the profane/evil (identified by the United States and its allies).

While this strategy increased the echo of Russell's ideas among certain audiences, it also alienated others. The Tribunal's enemies pointed to this strong binary logic as proof of left-wing bias. They even accused Russell of explicitly supporting communism, as the *New York Times* had done in 1963. This accusation gained further ground once the Tribunal started to work. And Russell never hid his pronounced support of the communist government in Vietnam:

Our Campaign for Solidarity, our War Crimes Tribunal, our films, our books, our meetings and our material help must have one aim: the victory of the Vietnamese over their tormentors. And I express the wish that this victory may herald similar victories of the oppressed everywhere until the day when our own people reclaim their government and transform it into an instrument of good. (Russell 1967, 115)

For those who denied, downplayed or overlooked US atrocities in Vietnam, the Tribunal was straightforward anti-American propaganda. They perceived the Tribunal as a cultural form of "evil". The accusation of bias against Russell and his collaborators spanned the entire political spectrum, although it was obviously much more widespread among right-wing commentators. In the conservative side, Norman Podhoretz, who denied the very existence of American war crimes in Vietnam, attacked: "What Guenter Lewy calls 'a veritable industry publicizing alleged war crimes' emerged both in the United States and abroad (in the form of the International War Crimes Tribunal organized by Bertrand Russell)" (Podhoretz 2004, 166). On the liberal side, even some of those who recognized the existence of war crimes committed by the United States accused the Russell Tribunal of using a double standard. For instance, Staughton Lynd, a Christian Quaker and a peace and social right activist who stood far from Podhoretz's conservative positions, refused an invitation to join the Tribunal. He argued that Russell focused only on the crimes committed by one side, ignoring those perpetrated by North Vietnam and the communist National Liberation Front. For Lynd, evidently, this was highly biased and unfair:

In conversation with the emissary who proffered the invitation, I urged that the alleged war crimes of any party to the conflict should come before the Tribunal. After all, I argued, a "crime" is an action that is wrong no matter who does it. Pressing my case, I asked, "What if it were shown that the National Liberation Front of South Vietnam tortures unarmed prisoners?" The answer, as I understood it, was, "Anything is justified that drives the imperialist aggressor into the sea". I declined the invitation to be a member of the Tribunal. (Lynd 1967)

Russell's view on this matter was that "no equation can be made between the oppression of the aggressor and the resistance of the victim" (Russell 1967, 127). This invited criticism, even from some of Russell's affiliates (Ryan 1988, 198). David Horowitz, a member of the Bertrand Russell Peace Foundation, distanced himself of the Russell Tribunal by attacking Sartre. He recognized that the Russell-Sartre Tribunal did not have the intention of investigating the more-than-likely heinous crimes committed by the communist side during the Vietnam War. In his political memoir *Radical Son: A Generational Odyssey*, Horowitz discussed Sartre's prejudices:

Sartre, a consummate sophist, attempted to solve the problem in advance by declaring that the Communists were by definition incapable of committing war crimes. "I refuse to place," said Sartre, "in the same category the actions of an organization of poor peasants . . . and those of an immense army backed by a highly organized country." (Horowitz 1998, 149)

But there was also a left-wing audience to Russell's Manichean approach to the war. The members of the Tribunal defended themselves against the accusation of bias. Particularly relevant in this context is John Gerassi, who served as an investigator for the Tribunal. By documenting that the American army was bombing, among other civilian targets, hospitals, schools and villages in Vietnam, Gerassi sought to show that the Tribunal was not a mere act of propaganda against the United States (Gerassi 1968). Other collaborators of the Tribunal used a different argument. They accepted the bias but sought to legitimize the Tribunal's one-sided investigations arguing that Western Cold War propaganda already flooded the public day and night with an equally biased message about the evils of communism and the benevolence and virtues of capitalist societies. As a result, they continued, countering this official view by focusing on the crimes committed by the "good" side was a necessary act of critical thinking. It was perhaps linguist and activist Noam Chomsky who pressed this point furthest. In his "Foreword to Bertrand Russell's *War Crimes Tribunal on Vietnam*," Chomsky wrote:

> Though not reported honestly, the Tribunal was sharply criticized. Many of the criticisms are answered, effectively I believe, in Part 1 of this book. There are two criticisms that retain a certain validity, however. The participants, the "jurors" and the witnesses, were undoubtedly biased. They made no attempt, in fact, to conceal this bias, this profound hatred of murder and wanton destruction carried out by a brutal foreign invader with unmatched technological resources. (Chomsky 1971)

Russell himself addressed the accusation of serving as pro-Viet Cong propagandist:

> I do not maintain that those who have been invited to serve as members of the Tribunal are without opinions about the war. On the contrary, it is precisely because of their passionate conviction that terrible crimes have been occurring that they feel the moral obligation to form themselves into a Tribunal of conscience. [. . .] I have not confused an open mind with an empty one. (Russell 1967, 126)

In his closing address to the Stockholm Session, Russell defended the Tribunal verdict: "the International War Crimes Tribunal has been subject to abuse from people who have much to hide. It has been said that the conclusions of this Tribunal were known in advance" (Coates 1971, 186). Against this accusation, Russell held that the conclusions of the Tribunal were built out of the empirical evidence. Nevertheless, Russell only addressed the accusation of not investigating the war crimes committed by the communist side of the war by coding them as necessary and justified defensive acts for the sacred pursuit of freedom and justice.

CONCLUSION

Several decades have passed since the collapse of the Soviet Union and the end of the Cold War. New sociological, historical, and philosophical works and approaches have appeared in recent years that have sought to change traditional opinions about this historical period (Mazower 2004; Kwon 2010; Scott 2013). Nevertheless, despite its historical transcendence, the Russell Tribunal is still a mainly unexplored territory. It is also a fascinating case study for current cultural sociology. Our analysis has accounted for its cultural impact, analyzing under which historical and social conditions Russell and his main collaborators helped to disseminate the idea that American political and military technology had become an instrument for world oppression and evil. Through its study, we have beheld a shocking clash of narratives: that of an independent Russell Tribunal driven by the highest ethical and humanitarian ideals, and its contrary, the Tribunal as a biased stunt or theatre; as a mere puppet of evil communist propaganda.

This plurality of competing narratives shows that the intrinsic impact of political or military crimes is far from the whole story when accounting for their cultural interpretation and relevance. As such, this chapter confirms this book's main theses. Cultural traumas require work, a complex machinery of ideas and practices. The Tribunal's gears of sorrow put US actions in Vietnam at the forefront, while downplaying other no less violent events of the period. In 2011, Ron Eyerman, Jeffrey C. Alexander and Elizabeth B. Breese sought out to answer uncomfortable questions in *Narrating Trauma: On the Impact of Collective Suffering* such as: "how do some events get coded as traumatic and others, which seem equally painful and dramatic not? Why do culpable groups often escape being categorized as perpetrators? Why are some horrendously injured parties not seen as victims? Why do some trauma constructions lead to moral restitution and justice, while others narrow solidarity and trigger future violence?" (2013). Through answering some of these questions, we hope to have contributed to both the Russell's and Vietnam War's scholarships.

Among the scholars that have referred to the Russell Tribunal, some consider its cultural relevance (for instance, Richard A. Falk) while others consider it a failure with little social transcendence (the case of David Torell's view). According to the deflationist view, the Tribunal was totally ignored, and Russell dubbed a communist puppet. This view remains long after Russell's death. John Podhoretz, the son of Norman Podhoretz, wrote some years ago in the conservative American journal *National Review*:

> Oh, Yeah, Bertrand Russell Was a Great Man . . . Who ended his life lending his prestige to an effort by barely closeted Stalinists to declare the United States the moral equal of Nazi Germany for its conduct during the war in Vietnam (. . .) Poland? The Low Countries? The counterinsurgency war in Algeria? The Japanese in Manchuria? Russell passed over these to claim the United States had done something uniquely evil in the course of human history. Russell ended his life a lamentable fool and a Communist dupe. David Horowitz goes into brilliant detail about the War Crimes Tribunal in his book *Radical Son*. No wonder Russell is little remembered and mourned even less. (Podhoretz 2006)

But reducing Russell to a "Communist dupe" is just a rhetorical strategy whose power starts to fade away outside the conservative side of the ideological spectrum. During the Vietnam War, this spectrum was, as still is today, very far from having any kind of ideological monopoly. On the other side of the political spectrum, however, the Tribunal's cultural role has also been downplayed. Thus, Chomsky recently maintained that the Tribunal "failed to enter History" because "it charged the US with crimes, [and] the US is self-immunized from prosecution" (Torell 2015, 119). But Chomsky's explanation would make it hard to account for the immense cultural impact of the Civil Rights Movements in the United States, which implied some degree of acknowledgment of US historical crimes (Alexander 2006a).

Luke J. Stewart has recently studied how the US government deployed both the national security state and the international diplomacy "in order to discredit and disrupt the proceedings of the Russell Tribunal and ultimately contain the embarrassing damage caused by this first major international antiwar initiative during the Vietnam War" (Stewart 2018). The Tribunal never achieved the social success Russell and his collaborators aimed for; the American government, along with other powerful Western nations, did their best to silence it from the very beginning. What is more, the Tribunal's media coverage was very modest, both within and outside the United States. Russell's pro-communist collaborators had very limited access to Western public opinion, and Western influential media gatekeepers did not consider that popularizing the Tribunal was particularly interesting for their goals. The Tribunal would have likely been more influential if it had performed after the

My Lai and Kent Massacres, when the traumatic cultural perception of the Vietnam War was much stronger both inside and outside the United States, and the mainstream media could no longer ignore or downplay the anti-war movement.

Despite all these handicaps, the Tribunal's small-scale social influence helped plant the ideological seeds through which the My Lai and Kent Massacres achieved such big cultural impact in a significant part of the American psyche, leaving long lasting scars. Although their presence in the media was limited, Russell's and his main collaborators' fame made a significant number of Western University students and intellectuals aware of what Russell, Sartre and other famous intellectuals were doing in opposition to the Vietnam War. For instance, a quick search shows that the Tribunal appeared often in the *New York Times* only during 1966 and 1967, despite Russell's heated controversy with the newspaper in 1963. There are also interesting cases beyond America's frontiers. In Spain, for instance, and despite the fact that the country was officially under a Catholic dictatorship with strong media censorship and a powerful anti-communist bias, the Russell Tribunal and its claims about war crimes concerning the American intervention in Vietnam were also present in the main newspapers, such as *La Vanguardia* and *El ABC*.

Governments do not have the monopoly of the means of symbolic production of a given cultural sphere. The Russell Tribunal had a peculiar sort of legitimacy and power, defined from a performative point of view. The narrative that the Tribunal was broadcasting resonated with a significant portion of the American and European public. This identification created powerful emotional ties against the US official interpretation of the war, playing a key role in the civil opposition of the American intervention in Vietnam. Although the traumatic perception of the war already existed before Russell's public performances, the Tribunal contributed to "engorge" the scope of the cultural trauma around the conflict and transformed American actions into universal symbols of wickedness.

American propaganda regarding the evils of communism was unable to stop the growing evidence that capitalist countries, especially the United States, were also prepared to commit heinous crimes in order to stop the spread of communism, even when this included torture, rape, mass killings of civilians and support of right-wing tyrants. Furthermore, hundreds of thousands of American parents were seeing how the government was sending their sons to distant Vietnam to be killed or mutilated or obliged to participate in the war crimes denounced by Russell and other intellectuals. The government could no longer ignore this opposition, as was made clear by the National Veterans Inquiry and the Winter Soldier Investigation.

The Tribunal's bias was thus not only difficult to avoid, but also likely very useful for the success of its political positioning. The usefulness of binaries is particularly salient in ideological struggles concerning more than one state and in ideologically polarized societies. In the case of the Russell Tribunal, Russell and his affiliates aligned themselves with an extremely simplistic binary code according to which the Viet Cong represented the forces of justice, liberty and good, while the American government embodied the forces of evil that would bring apocalypse to the world. This binary positioning was central, from a sociocultural point of view, to the promotion and diffusion of Russell's criticisms of the Vietnam War.

In the "Lamarckian ecology" (Harré 1993) constituted by philosophies, ideologies and narratives, Russell was forced throughout his life to navigate between different power groups when positioning his theories and interventions. While in his essays and in the Tribunal he aligned himself with the political left and even with Ho Chi Minh, in earlier stages of his career he worked alongside the political right and the anti-communists—for instance closely working with the CIA-funded Congress for Cultural Freedom, a propaganda machine created by the United States in 1950 to combat communism in the ideological arena. These shifts were especially poignant regarding the interplay between science, technology and politics, which is at the core of our book's investigation. In 1949, Russell supported propagandistic attacks against Soviet science which used the communist party's official support of Lysenko one year earlier to denounce "The Destruction of Science in the USSR" (Wolfe 2018, 64). In the 1960s, on the contrary, Russell's target was American science, which in his view had been corrupted and put at the service of American imperialism, recast as the devil itself. In this epic battle played in Russell's imagination between the forces of good and evil, the Vietnam War played the part of the Judgement Day: the imminent conflict where humankind's final fate would be decided once and for all. The urgency of stopping the war did not lie in saving Vietnamese lives, but in preventing universal evil to cast its shadows over all human existence.

NOTE

1. In Alexander's words: "During the traumas of the late 1960s, American television news brought evocative images of terrible civilian suffering from the Vietnam War into the living rooms of American citizens. These images were seized on by antiwar critics. The conservative American politician, vice-president Spiro Agnew, initiated virulent attacks against the "liberal" and "Jewish-dominated" media for their insistence that the Vietnamese civilian population was being traumatized by the American-dominated war" (Alexander 2003, 100).

Conclusion

The History of Humankind and the Rashomon Effect

Bertrand Russell: British Lord, logician, mathematician, metaphysician, epistemologist, moralist, cultural critic. Who was Russell and what was his main historical and cultural role in the 20th century? And what can the analysis on Russell tell us today? Dramaturgically speaking, Russell held so many masks and performed on so many stages, that these questions cannot be answered easily. Nevertheless, in this book we have done much more than a collage of Russell's main views on metaphysics, epistemology, ethics, society, and politics. We have invested our best efforts in providing a new analysis on Russell taking as backbone the relationships between Russell's ideas on the techno-scientific sphere and the final fate of humankind.

Through many of his most notorious performances, Russell became a cultural living totem; a sort of messianic figure that delivers humankind from evil. In the general scenography of his life, Russell accepted such a salvific role. And not only in a dramatic way; also, and more specifically, in a tragic one. This could be summarized by this powerful Russell's quote:

> Like Cassandra, I am doomed to prophesy evil and not be believed. Her prophecies came true. I desperately hope that mine will not. Sometimes one is tempted to take refuge in cheerful fantasies and to imagine that perhaps in Mars or Venus happier and saner forms of life exist, but our frantic skill is making this a vain dream. Before long, if we do not destroy ourselves, our destructive strife will have spread to those planets. (Russell 1962)

Returning to this general idea, a few years later, at 95, Russell wrote one of his last essays, soberly titled "1967".[1] In it, Russell posed a reflexive question which he had also tried to answer in "A Free Man's Worship" and in the prologue to his *Autobiography*: whether his life had had a real purpose.

"Unfortunately," Russell responded to his own question, "no answer is possible for anyone who does not know the future" (Russell 2010[1975]). The answer in his *Autobiography* is, though, more direct and optimistic: he had written both abstract and concrete books which had been able to affect many people's thoughts. "To this extent," he concluded, "I have succeeded" (Russell 2010[1975], 701). But was this relative success of Russell's published work a sufficient criteria to gauge his entire life?

Russell had written what would become the first volume of his *Autobiography* in the 1930s and most of what would be the second volume in the 1950s. He wrote the last of the three volumes published from 1967 to 1969 with a great deal of help from Edith and in a rush to obtain funds for the Bertrand Russell Peace Foundation (Monk 2001, 470). In all of these and other autobiographical texts, Russell boast a personal happiness that contradicts many of the stories he himself goes on to narrate, and certainly what we now know about his tragic personal and family life. But personal happiness was also not the criteria Russell was looking for in "1967". The real question of that text was, in Russell's own words, what he had "personally contributed" in the face of "the magnitude of evil". Russell's measuring stick for success or failure was no less than stopping apocalypse. If others were to follow his own ideas and example, there was still room for hope:

> Consider for a moment what our planet is and what it might be. At present, for most, there is toil and hunger, constant danger, more hatred than love. There could be a happy world, where co-operation was more in evidence than competition, and monotonous work is done by machines, where what is lovely in nature is not destroyed to make room for hideous machines whose sole business is to kill, and where to promote joy is more respected than to produce mountains of corpses. Do not say this is impossible: it is not. It waits only for men to desire it more than the infliction of torture. There is an artist imprisoned in each one of us. Let him loose to spread joy everywhere. (Russell 1967)

Nuclear doom and the US universal empire of evil were open doors to hell: a "magnitude of evil" greater than the Nazis that humankind was facing in all its brutality for the first time. It might seem that an individual could do little against those baneful destructive forces, but it was not the first time that Russell took upon himself humanity's final fate. It is because of this that, through the years, he repeatedly claimed that his public role was more urgent and more important than his facet of analytic philosopher. With insight, we are perhaps in a better position than Russell himself to gauge the real meaning of his public political interventions in historical processes like the two world wars, the nuclear age (including in particular the Cuban missile crisis), and Vietnam. But what interest us here are the very ideas of utopia and apocalypse that, as our book argues, structure Russell's thoughts and actions in general, and regarding science and technology in particular.

We have approached Russell's recurring rhetoric of utopia and apocalypse through three main theses grounded on cultural sociology and cultural history of science: that events do not overdetermine interpretations, that cultural interpretations draw on ancient structures of meaning, and that Russell as a public intellectual was expected to engage with those structures of meaning. For Russell, wicked leaders and irrational peoples (consciously or unconsciously) announced the coming Judgment Day. But they did so on the shoulders of science and its technology, which enabled universal doom. The combination of modern science and human nature seemed to be a secure formula for unprecedented global sorrow. After World War I, science retained for Russell its status as the almighty ruler of human progress and happiness. But this crown coexisted with a much darker one which turned science into a terrible king guiding humanity's destiny towards annihilation. The duality between utopia and apocalypse accompanied Russell's thinking of science from the 1920s onwards. But, despite glimpses here and there of possible hope for the future of humankind, pessimism was perhaps more and more dominant as the years passed by and presented new political, social, and technological challenges. And yet, we have insisted throughout the book, the intrinsic impact of historical events underdetermines their cultural interpretation and symbolic attribution.

NECESSITY AND CONTINGENCY IN HUMAN ACTION

Regarding Russell's changing views of the relationships between science and human progress and decadence, we have emphasized a complex interplay between necessity and contingency in the cultural construction of views of the present and the future in general, and utopian and apocalyptic narratives specifically. Necessity, for instance, concerns the minimal factors for dramatic intellectuals to become socially successful, such as the *need* to have access to influential symbolic means of production or to create powerful emotional attachment in their audiences through binaries around sacred-good and profane-evil. Contingency, on the other hand, is given both by individual interventions and by changing social and cultural environments, from cultural symbols and narratives to material factors and social structures.

Material factors (such as geography, ecology, and demography) do not predetermine social structure (such as family types and workplace organization). Social structure, in turn, does not predetermine cultural structures (such as language, religion, and aesthetics). Furthermore, cultural structures (although always through the actions of factual individuals), have a powerful impact in shaping, changing, and even destroying social structures and material factors—think for instance of consumerism and the Anthropocene.

People of flesh and blood are much more than empty shells through which either the material background, social structure, or cultural structures (or all of them at the same time!) resonate. For starters, one has to add biological factors into this already baroque picture—C. Wright Mills's traditional concept of "sociological imagination" was thus reductionistic in leaving biology out of the picture. And one must do that without descending into the dangerous traps of biological determinism, which in any case is already avoided by non-reductionist biologists themselves through concepts such as epigenetic changes, neuroplasticity, and the Baldwin effect.

But it is not just a matter of adding factors to account for action. Individuals are, in Aristotelian terms, greater than the sum of their parts. The ontological convergence of multiple courses of reality often produces emergent dimensions. Human freedom or agency is one of these arising realities. Recognizing its existence does not equate to embracing idealism or mystical spiritualism; it simply means to emphasize the relative independence of the multiple dimensions that constitute human beings and their societies and cultures, including their dreams and worst nightmares.

Avoiding the spell of the biological, structural or cultural *moirai* (the Greek goddesses of fate) does not necessarily lead to embracing contingentism and radical discontinuism; but it does require to take seriously the dialectical imbroglio of contingency and necessity, starting with overcoming its more simplistic binary forms. Natural, social, and biosocial scientists who talk about the human pretending to ignore ontological and epistemological considerations are just deceiving themselves.

When emphasizing relative contingency, it is not just that political systems, values, public discourses and narratives are not natural and could have been different from what they have been, like post-Marxist author Ernesto Laclau and others have argued against determinism (Butler, Laclau, and Žižek 2011). After all, even the most reductionistic Marxists could say that culture is contingent—as long as social structure and material factors *do* change. The ontological and epistemological peculiarities of contingency run deeper. Take, for instance, the ideological packages, packs or set-menus we mentioned in the Introduction and in Chapter 2 (Russell's anti-war sentiment included as an extra fundamental change in his views on socialism and, later on science). These *packs* structure collective identities by gathering themes and narratives which lack internal logical connections between them.

Moreover, what comes in each pack varies with the cultural landscapes. In one of *Pulp Fiction's* most celebrated conversations, two gangsters are surprised that in France you can order a beer with a Big Mac. Similarly, in Communist countries the political left presented abortion, homosexuality and sex outside the wedlock as polluting social threats while in other places these themes formed part of the backbone of the leftist political position. A current example is provided by right-wing approaches to the centralized state power, which is fought against by conservative groups in the US and defended by similar groups in Spain.

The specific contents of ideological packs thus depend on the historical and cultural conditions behind their construction and maintenance. And yet, once they are functioning, these menus provide a significant degree of predictability of a person's ideological nebula just by attending to one or a couple of isolated ideological items. For instance, if an American citizen is against gun control, it is very likely that he or she is also against abortion, the power of the federal government, secularism, policies against climate change, and so on. This is despite the lack of a logical connection, in its traditional sense, between guns, abortion and global warming.

Nevertheless, there is variance and hierarchies within these packages. Some themes are bestowed of more symbolic power than others. Thus, a member of a social group might be allowed to disagree on one or two non-fundamental themes. Similarly, dramatic intellectuals targeting a particular audience may not need to just repeat the whole menu. But they will need at least to connect theoretically and emotionally with their audience's most sacred symbols and totems. Audiences are therefore never passive in the process of what Alexander and others call *fusion*—the moment in a social performance when the various elements click together and the (never passive) audience identifies with the actors and their script (Taylor 2021).

Intellectuals, even the most powerful ones, have a limited symbolic range of motion if they want to preserve their audiences. Baert claims that "certain types of positioning prosper in particular settings and (. . .) societal shifts can precipitate both their decline and the emergence of new types of positioning" (Baert 2015, 189). One wrong step, and they can fall from grace. We agree with this stance as long as it recognizes the relative independence of culture: i.e., as we defended in the Introduction of this book, changes in the structure of society do not necessarily reflect on cultural changes and vice versa.

At a cultural level, social groups usually change opinion not because they are really convinced by the logical force of the arguments of their opposite enemies. Rather, there are other cultural factors at work, such as the changes of position of the public charismatic figures that those social groups have already bestowed legitimacy. But sacred cows can also be sacrificed and canceled if they step too far into fields which their audiences are convinced to be inherently evil or polluted. Intellectual positioning is like walking on thin ice. Symbolic attributions can cut deeper than swords. And remaining a successful public intellectual over time is truly an art in which conscious, unconscious, strategic and random factors come into play. Specifically in times of cultural turmoil. Russell was only partially aware of this in his *Autobiography*:

> The longing has often been strong enough to lead me into self-deception. I have imagined myself in turn a Liberal, a Socialist, or a Pacifist, but I have never been any of these things, in any profound sense. Always the sceptical intellect, when I have most wished it silent, has whispered doubts to me, has cut me off from the facile enthusiasms of others, and has transported me into a desolate solitude. (Russell 2010[1975], 246)

Though Russell was by no means so prudent as he here claims, it is true that he did never entirely fit into any of the ideological packs he mentions. And this even in the occasions when he tried hard to publicly fit into one of them (recall the Russell Tribunal on Vietnam!). Throughout his life, Russell navigated intellectual rigor and the desire to act in the world by connecting to public opinion. This tortuous dialectic can often be observed in the tensions and even contradictions between dramatic intellectuals' most sophisticated works and their most successful social performances in front of larger audiences. This phenomenon can be clearly seen in the gap between Russell's metaphysical and epistemological works and his political and social works. For instance, in his epistemological works Russell repeatedly defended that there were no real rational arguments against subjective idealism beyond belief, filling many pages about the problem of the inference of the external world from our private perceptions. By contrast, in political works such as *Power*, Russell held that "the existence of the external world (. . .) can only be denied by a madman" (Russell 2004[1938], 212).

An even more shocking tension exists between Russell's more abstract ethical and political books and many of his public social performances in a context in which he considered his activism to be urgent and decisive. In the latter case, Russell's positionings could be surprisingly simplistic and Manichean. But these oversimplifications often had powerful symbolic effects. Radical binaries can be more powerful than nuclear bombs; if this sounds too strong, allow us to recognize that at least they can be the condition of possibility of such a monstrous thing as a nuclear bomb—rather, per our Chapter 4, of a monstruous interpretation of some bombs and not of others.

Under the strong influence of Moore's moral philosophy, in "The Elements of Ethics" (1910) Russell defended an ethical cognitivism, i.e., the stance according to which ethical statements (such as "X is good") express propositions that have truth-value. That means that they are either true or false independent of our contingent opinions and emotions. Nevertheless, his reading of Santayana's book *Winds of Doctrine* (1913) made Russell change his mind on ethical issues until the end of his life, converting to an ethical non-cognitivism according to which ethical statements do not have truth-value. In Russell's ethical theory, ethical statements might seem fact-stating when expressed in indicative mood, but they are always optative or desire expressing (Russell 1935). The contradictions between this philosophical stance and Russell's incendiary rhetoric about for instance the United States as a "universal empire of evil" are obvious. Russell positioned his public stances on universal evil (whether it was embodied by the pro-war politicians, the Soviet Union, the Nazis, or the United States) as objective and even absolute undeniable truths; truths that only a mad or a wicked person would deny. And such persons are the bringers of apocalypse.

INTELLECTUAL CONTRADICTIONS AND CULTURAL LOGIC

Lack of logical coherence might seem surprising when discussing one of the most eminent philosophers of the 20th century. But this surprise is in turn the result of a distorted view on the relationships between reason and culture. "Outside the realm of Kantian philosophy and Habermasian pragmatics," Jeffrey Alexander stated in a recent interview, "logical rationality has little effect on the meanings of social life. Modernity, despite its extraordinary scientific and technological achievements, is more meaningful than logical" (Alexander and Pérez-Jara 2021). Russell provides just one more example of the ideological schizophrenia that simplistic binary logic leads to.

But there might be, after all, some kind of logic behind the contradictions entailed by binary *logic*. Studying the logical contradictions that pervade pre-state societies, cultural anthropologist Lucien Lévy-Bruhl (2015[1910]) famously characterized the "prelogical" nature of the "primitive mind" by its violations of the traditional logical laws of identity, contradiction, and excluded middle. He showed that logical contradictions are not threatening for natives' worldviews. Other authors have since extended this view to "civilized" societies, even for allegedly disenchanted modern societies discussed in our book's Introduction. George Orwell sarcastically dubbed "doublethink" the simultaneous acceptance of arguments based on completely opposite principles and standards to favor group interests. But this is not only present in nightmarish totalitarian regimes; it is a feature of most ideological formations, however harmless. The cultural logic operating in simplistic binaries, as well as in seemingly contradictory symbolic conceptualizations, is mainly concerned with preserving the group's glue.

The rules of traditional logic are so often sacrificed on the altar of a collective identity opposed to competing identities. Psychologists analyze cognitive biases and subconscious defense mechanisms as many philosophers analyze logical fallacies and sophisms. All these important studies are concerned (let's say) with individual or group sacrifices of a coherent logical picture of reality. But what we want to emphasize is the cultural dimension of these phenomena. Coherence and contradiction are also meanings of cultural life. Authors like Judith Shklar have attempted to explain the social limits of "reason" by pointing to psychological biases and their role in the success of ideologies (Shklar 1966). This psychological approach, however, tends to overlook the power of cultural structures. While those structures are intertwined with the psychological dimension of social actors, they are unable to be reduced to them.

For a cultural-sociological analysis focusing on the importance of the categories of *meaning* and *meaningfulness* in cultural life, the logical contradictions that populate cultural life are as essential to it like proteins are for biological life. Public intellectuals often detect and denounce some of these contradictions, but time and again they do so only to find themselves supporting other logical contradictions in their narratives that give them access to certain audiences. Think for instance of the current examples of those right-wing intellectuals who demonize feminism against the political left but encourage it against Islam. Or of the left-wing opinion-leaders who claim that political nations are outdated institutions that should disappear in a world without borders, but at the same time encourage the creation of new political nations with their borders in "disputed" places such as Catalonia, the Basque Country, Tibet, or Hong Kong.

The cultural logic operating in these and other examples has to do with the systematic negation of any position held by an ideological opponent (which, in turn, can perform a similar maneuver, escalating the cultural conflict in Zoroastrian ways). Behind these strong ideological denials there are usually powerful unconscious or invisible cultural processes and emotional attachments. In this view, the value of traditional logic emerges as a tool helpful for social analysis even when, or precisely when, it is absent from the actor's narratives: it is useful in locating contradictions in social discourses which in turn force the analyst to find alternative mechanisms to account for how discourses and symbolic attributions are formed. For instance, if an ideological package defies traditional logic, then we know that its seemingly unbreakable unity ought to be explained by other sociocultural mechanisms and factors. These other mechanisms and factors, we want to emphasize, can also be understood as logical, but in a broad cultural sense; a muddy *logos* from the point of view of the transparent and pure reason of Western traditional epistemology.² In contrast to the *micrologic* of traditional Ancient Greek "rules of logic," the *macrologic* of cultural life feeds on meanings intertwined with prejudices, unconscious biases, and contradictions. Embracing traditional reason can be irrational for a given group if it means the dissolution of its social ties.

IDEOLOGY IN SOCIAL ANALYSIS

Different approaches to ideologies are available within the social sciences. In the turn of the 19th century, Antoine Destutt de Tracy coined the term "ideology" as the name for his new "science of ideas." But it was Karl Marx who gave the term the sense that has evolved into modern usages of the word: as a system of ideas rooted in a social group against others. For Marx, the ideas of ideologies always imply a significant degree of distortion of reality, since they are linked to interests of domination, and therefore to social structure. Within the Marxist tradition, authors like Louis Althusser (1970) defended that ideologies are the products of social practices, not the reverse. Ideologies are always embodied in actions, which are inserted into practices. Ideologies, therefore, have a material existence, and they represent "the imaginary relationship of individuals to their real conditions of existence". The dominant class takes advantage of such cultural formations to justify and legitimate their power and status. Interestingly enough for our approach, Althusser recognized the relative independence of the "superstructure" of society (including here culture and its ideological formations) from the material, techno-economic "base"—which would be determinant only in the "last instance" (Althusser 1970). The problem is that this "last instance" becomes some sort of *deus ex machina* of reductionistic materialism, sabotaging Althusser's theoretical building from our cultural-sociological perspective.

Social analysts who study ideologies are of course themselves living within ideologized groups and mobilizing ideological tools. Karl Mannheim (1991[1923]) famously defended this thesis. He proposed to broaden the Marxist concept of ideology to include within it the ideas and beliefs of every socialized person—including Marx. That gave rise to the so-called "Mannheim's Paradox", according to which social theorists are subject to the same kind of prejudices, biases and cultural structures that they study.³ This necessarily introduces a significant degree of distortion in their investigations. The positivist dream of detached ideological purity assumed that social theorists spoke from a watchtower free from the contamination of social dogmas, biases, and the like. Once the assumption is removed, the problem of relativism presents itself with all its strength.

Within Mannheim's broad understanding of ideologies, Clifford Geertz (1964) held that ideologies are cultural systems composed of symbols that aim at representing reality like maps that shrink a space to make it more understandable. But ideologies are more than filtered low-resolution pictures of reality: as any map, ideologies have an essential practical side in orienting humans in an obscure social world that they can only try to decipher symbolically. By dismissing the traditional Marxist conception of ideology as the expression of class struggle linked to false consciousness, Geertz was implicitly placing Marxism itself in the broad realm of ideologies. Nevertheless, Geertz also wanted to stop any form of imperialism or hubris of ideologies. Specifically, he proposed to overcome Mannheim's Paradox by distinguishing science from ideology as "related" but "different enterprises": "where, if anywhere, ideology leaves off and science begins has been the Sphinx's Riddle of much of modern sociological thought and the rustles weapon of its enemies" (Geertz 2006[1973], 194). In Geertz's view, "the social function of science *vis-a-vis* ideologies is first to understand them in what they are, how they work, what gives rise to them, and second to criticize them, to force them to come to terms with (but not necessarily to surrender to) reality" (Geertz 2006[1973], 232).

Not very differently, Talcott Parsons (1959) had before proposed to overcome Mannheim's Paradox by focusing on how "deviations from [social scientific objectivity] emerge as the essential criteria of an ideology". As if ideology were a notorious mistress, very few social theorists wished to be seen in its company in public. Which means that the shadow of Marx's original connotation of "ideology" as a polluted way of representing the world is large. In this view, *science* would have the power of exorcising the subjectivist and distorting demons of *ideology*. But what if, as authors like Jurgen Habermas (1969) in his famous essay "Technology and Science as Ideology" held, modern "science" has become a form of ideology? From this perspective (which we do not share), if we cannot have access to reality as it really is that means that we are condemned to live in a "postmetaphysical thinking" alien to the inner contents, structure, and mechanisms of reality (Habermas 1994). This would render *ideological* the very distinction between science and ideology.

Philosophical critiques of naïve realism have put into question the relationships between our maps of reality and reality itself. Such critiques have become a part of the ontological and epistemological assumptions of the most important 20th-century social theories (Baert 2005). Focusing on ideologies' practical side, Michael Freeden (2003) has defended, in the name of cultural diversity, that it is incorrect to ask whether ideologies are true or false. In line with Richard Rorty (2017[1979]) and other thinkers, ideologies are not, and cannot be, mirrors or pictures of absolute reality. Ideologies are indicative of the way people socially construct the world around them—which, according to Nietzsche and Foucault, always has a dimension related to *power*.

Other authors have inferred that, if ideologies are not representative of an absolute reality, and they are just linked to polluted political and social struggles, they ought to disappear. Daniel Bell's famously prophesied the end of ideologies (Bell 2000[1960]). Technocratic governments and social systems proved that ideologies, as Marx understood them, had been exhausted. New systems of ideas would emerge, but they would not be class-generated ideologies. The heated ideological wars of the 1960s and 1970s proved their prophecies to be mere wishful thinking. And yet, the prophecies came back in the postmodernists' thesis on the death of Modernity's great metanarratives and in Francis Fukuyama's (1992) theory of the "end of history". The idea of a post-ideological world is the definitive ideological fantasy in the same way that the dream of the death of metanarratives is itself a humongous metanarrative (Zizek 2009; Bueno 2016). Delving into Mannheim's Paradox, Freeden (2003) observes the also paradoxical behavior of those social theorists who deny objective truth and at the same support one ideology over its competitors.

Is there a criterion for the analyst to choose between ideologies and ideological packages or is the search for objective truth incompatible with any ideological commitment? For instance, with today's insight we can strongly disagree with Russell's positions on women, blacks, and homosexuals, or with his trivializing of the mass killing of Japanese and South Vietnamese civilians. Moreover, many current ideological changes regarding race, gender, or environmentalism are something to celebrate. And yet, it would be very hard to argue that these ideological shifts result from an alleged internal social or historical law guiding social opinion towards progress and good. Ideological transformations are more likely the product of contingent cultural processes and factors, many of them invisible to most actors who participate in them. In this sense, our study of Russell's public thought on science and technology also aims to contribute to discerning the cultural mechanisms operating behind the ideologies of social commentators.

UTOPIA, APOCALYPSE, AND REALITY'S MUZZLE

"Bertrand Russell" is not what it used to be. Russell continues to be one of the most important philosophers and activists of the 20th century, but that does not make him famous *today*. While Russell's fame has significantly faded, the views on salvation and apocalypse which he shared and help spread are today as alive as they were in Russell's times. They have been alive and well for millennia, although of course adopting very different historical configurations in different places and times. As we discussed in this book's Introduction, ancient binaries structure much of today's public debates on issues like politics, morality, the environment, or the COVID-19 pandemic. Between those who announce doomsday and those who preach paradise, the idea that nothing really changes that much is often presented as reasonable middle-ground.

But there is no reason to accept the false trilemma between global progress, global decadence, and some kind of "iron constant".[4] From an ontologically pluralist point of view that emphasizes a complex interplay of continuities and discontinuities in reality, it does not make much sense to think of a universal direction towards decadence or progress. Some key social and economic indicators obviously point towards a worldwide decline of absolute poverty, war, violent crime, and disease with a corresponding increase of life expectancy, literacy rates, and civil rights. However, there is also a global increase of natural disasters linked to pollution and other human activities. Progress in some fronts seems to have brought decline in others. In the industrialized world, for instance, increasing wealth has gone in many occasions hand in hand with rising loneliness and social isolation, from depressed teenagers with serious socializing problems to elderly people who live and die alone. New addictions have also appeared, with their associated health conditions. It is no wonder that, depending on which data people choose to focus, they will perceive an ever-brighter future or long for an imagined golden past.

Kurosawa's famous film *Rashomon* has come to exemplify the different readings the same events can get from divergent points of views, recollections, and interests. Similar competing processes of coding are at play for almost every specific lapse of human history. Russell's 20th century is a perfect example. In many of his most relevant cultural products, war butchers emerge as heroes and apotropaic totems of justice and freedom; non-violent and hard-working citizens appear as sub-humans or evil oppressors; the mass destruction of cities full of civilians in air raids are presented as something either laudable or forgettable in comparison with a dared all-annihilating bomb. The schemes of utopia and apocalypse serve to extend this process of constant interpretation and reclassification from specific events to the history of humanity as a whole. Finding a direction in history, however, requires shocking levels of symbolic plasticity in which history becomes a giant Rorschach test.

This is not a call for relativism. It is a description of an empirical analysis which refutes the naturalistic fallacy. There is an essential hiatus between what ontologically is and what symbolically "should be". It seems scientifically well-proven that we are born with certain innate tendencies that biologists call "preparedness". But the symbolic plasticity of culture can be so powerful that, through the appropriate sociocultural processes, what is extremely awful and unbearable in one culture can be presented as pure and sacred in another. Philosophers of history, for instance, have discussed isolated tribes as either savage and irrational or closer to a paradisiac golden age. The subculture of drugs, crime, social instability, and de-industrialized poor infrastructures is hailed by some as liberating and inspiring and abhorred by others as dangerous and dehumanizing. The symbolic flexibility of the concepts of good-pure-sacred and evil-polluted-profane is astonishing.

Nevertheless, the critique of the naturalistic fallacy does not mean drawing an insurmountable line between absolute reality and cultural perceptions. Throughout this book, and together with cultural sociologists, we have distanced ourselves from both reductionist materialism and spiritual idealism by emphasizing that culture independence from reality is always *relative*. The same or very similar material contexts and social structures allow for different cultural values, symbols, and narratives. But many of our current values, symbols and narratives would be unimaginable in societies with technologies or social structures very different from ours. Maintaining a healthy middle ground between radical historicism and structuralism, we have also stressed the relative continuity of millennial structures of meaning. Without denying the emergence of novelty and historical specificity, it is still possible to study the symbolic similarities between pre-state and current ways of structuring social narratives. Despite this relative independence of culture from reality, there is still some room for (non-naïve) realism. For instance, some cultural systems of meaning might be taken to be about *representation* of reality in certain limited realms. This is, we think, the case for scientific and philosophical statements under certain conditions.

There is a strong sense in which ideologies and reality drift apart. In the realm of values, the links between absolute reality and coding are faintest or non-existent. Non-zoological reality is meaningless. Rather than being a dimension of absolute reality, axiological meaningfulness only emerges through complex interactions between animals and their environments. Things are not pregnant of values, waiting for us to unveil them like the hidden toys of Kinder Eggs. In our cultural life, "justice", "good", "evil", and "beauty" look *as real* as the stars, mountains, or atoms. And they have *become real*, but only in relation to our cultural lives. Upon certain conditions and contexts, values come to be embraced by certain social groups as something objective. Change those conditions, and values might crack and shatter. As culturally constructed realities, values would fade away without us. And the "us" of humans is always fragmented, contextualized, and morphing. It is therefore pointless to search for convergences or correspondences between ethical, artistic or political values and absolute reality. Within certain evolutionary and social limits, social constructionism is here on point.

Because every ideology incorporates a powerful axiological dimension, ideologies are in no way representative of reality. But ideologies cannot be completely oblivious to reality. Absolute reality is indifferent to the symbolic attributions that humans unconsciously project upon it. This means that, at the end of the day, reality invisibly imposes its ontological contents, structures, and mechanisms upon human symbolic worlds. This is what we called *reality's muzzle* in our Introduction—in truth, because reality is plural, this muzzle is made of many muzzles: among others, physio-muzzles, chemo-muzzles, bio-muzzles, and socio-muzzles. Take for instance death, which every human society has untiringly to face. Regardless of our beliefs, all of us are finite and will die. Similarly, a poison remains a poison even if presented as pure and sacred. And if rulers were to command their subjects to take the poisonous substance on the grounds of its alleged virtues, they would find themselves with no subjects to rule over. Back to more familiar Russellian grounds: air raids on civilian population might be narrated as heroic and good but their fire burned the flesh of hundreds of thousands of civilians, nonetheless.

And yet, death can be perceived as an illusion, poison can be taken to be curative and bombing civilians can be seen as a necessary lesser evil or even as a glorious divine task. For all the current talk on post-truth and fake news, culture's symbolic plasticity has always worked as a powerful *wrapper* of reality's muzzle. Here we call for strengthening the ties between philosophical analysis and sociological theorizing. Further philosophical analysis is needed to explore the tension between reality's muzzle and culture's symbolic plasticity with the theoretical depth it deserves. This tension should not be interpreted in any simplistic binary sense. The point is not to divide reality into two realms with well-defined borders: absolute reality and human symbolism. Both realms belong to the same general reality, and at the same time their relative incommensurability forces us to reinterpret reality as plural and tension filled.

One of the most pressing questions in this regard is again the paradoxical place of the analyst who claims that there is a divide between reality and discourse. And yet, we would like to think that we can only *touch* reality's muzzle if we interpret (micro)logical and rigorous reasoning as sacred and pure, rather than as profane and polluted (Alexander and Pérez-Jara 2021). This has been a main motivation for our book. In working around Russell's role in the cultural construction of utopia and apocalypse in relation to science and its technology, we wanted to think, and invite others to think, about the role of science in human progress and decadence in our current epoch.

NOTES

1. Russell's last hand-written manuscript represents a very peculiar exception: Unlike the majority of Russell's papers, this manuscript did not go either to the Russell Archives in McMaster University set up in 1968, nor to "Second Russell Archives", also set up in McMaster after Russell's death. Fortunately, Ray Monk published it first in *The Independent* of London on the 25th anniversary of the Russell Archives. Russell continued to write and publish letters until just a few days before his death. But he often just put his signature on what were writings by his wife Edith or his secretary, Ralph Schoenman. "1967", on the contrary, is hand-written by Russell himself.

2. For millennia, philosophers in the Western tradition have emphasized the necessity of broadening the traditional concept of logic, from Heraclitus's Logos structuring particular logical contradictions, Nicholas of Cusa's contradictory (but real) God, to Hegelian logic, modern paraconsistent logics, and Graham Priest's and other's dialetheism. We also call for non-reductionist understanding of logic that includes cultural logic as distinct from a traditional one.

3. Authors like Giovanni Sartori have opposed Mannheim's inflationist concept of ideology and have argued that not every symbolic formation is ideological. But this does not challenge the pertinence of "Mannheim's Paradox".

4. In reference to Hesiod's Iron Age.

Bibliography

Ackerman, R. 2002. *The Myth and Ritual School: J. G. Frazer and the Cambridge Ritualists*. New York: Routledge.
Adams, R. J. Q. 2013. *Balfour: The Last Grandee*. London: Thistle Publishing.
Adamson, M., Camprubí, L., and Turchetti, S. 2014. "From the Ground Up: Uranium Surveillance and Atomic Energy in Western Europe". In S. Turchetti and P. Roberts (Eds.), *The Surveillance Imperative*. New York: Springer.
Alexander, J., and Mast, J. 2016. *Politics of Meaning/Meaning of Politics. Cultural Sociology of the 2016 U.S. Presidential Election*. New York: Palgrave Macmillan.
Alexander, J. and Pérez-Jara, J. 2021. "Mito y rito en el corona-drama internacional. Jeffrey Alexander en diálogo con Javier Pérez Jara". In Juan del Llano y Lino Camprubí (Eds.), *Sociedad Entre Pandemias*. Madrid: Gaspar Casal Foundation. English version "Ritual and Myth in the International Corona-Drama. A Conversation with Jeffrey Alexander". Available at https://ccs.yale.edu/news/interview-jeff-alexander-ritual-and-myth-international-corona-drama).
Alexander, J. C. 2001. "Toward a Theory of Cultural Trauma". In J. Alexander et al. (Eds.), *Cultural Trauma and Collective Identity*. California: University of California Press, pp. 1–30.
Alexander, J. C. 2003. *The Meanings of Social Life: A Cultural Sociology*. Oxford: Oxford University Press.
Alexander, J. C. 2004. "Cultural Pragmatics: Social Performance between Ritual and Strategy." *Sociological Theory*, 22. Malden: John Wiley & Sons Inc on behalf of the American Sociological Association: 527–573.
Alexander, J. C. 2005. "Why Cultural Sociology Is Not 'Idealist': A Reply to McClennan." *Theory, Culture & Society*, 22, 6.
Alexander, J. C. 2006a. *The Civil Sphere*. Oxford: Oxford University Press.
Alexander, J. C. (Ed.). 2006b. *Social Performance: Symbolic Action, Cultural Pragmatics, and Ritual*. Cambridge: Cambridge University Press.
Alexander, J. C. 2008. *The Civil Sphere*. Oxford: Oxford University Press.
Alexander, J. C. 2011. *Performance and Power*. Cambridge: Polity Press.

Alexander, J. C. 2013. *The Dark Side of Modernity*. Cambridge: Polity.
Alexander, J. C. 2016. "Dramatic Intellectuals". *International Journal of Politics, Culture and Society* 29, 4: pp. 341–358.
Alexander, S. 1910. "On Sensations and Images". *Proceedings of the Aristotelian Society*, X: 156–178.
Allan, R. 1988. *Bertrand Russell: a Political Life*. London: Penguin Press.
Althusser, L. 1970. "Idéologie et appareils idéologiques d'État (Notes pour une recherche)". *La Pensée* 151.
Andersson, S. (Ed.). 2017. *Revisiting the Vietnam War and International Law*. Cambridge: Cambridge University Press.
Apostolova, I. 2010. *Sensation, Memory and Imagination in Bertrand Russell's Philosophy 1910–1926*. Ottawa: University of Ottawa.
Asay, J. 2013. *The Primitivist Theory of Truth*. Cambridge: Cambridge University Press.
Austin, J. L. 1976[1962]. *How to Do Things with Words: Second Edition*. Oxford: Oxford University Press.
Baert, B. and Morgan, M. 2017. "A Performative Framework for the Study of Intellectuals" *European Journal of Social Theory*.
Baert, P. 2005. *Philosophy of the Social Sciences: Towards Pragmatism*. Cambridge: Polity.
Baert, P. 2011a. "Jean-Paul Sartre's positioning in Anti-Semite and Jew." *Journal of Classical Sociology* 11, 4: 378–397.
Baert, P. 2011b. "The sudden rise of French existentialism: A case-study in the sociology of intellectual life". *Theory and Society* 40, 5: (pp. 619–644). New York: Springer.
Baert, P. 2012. "Positioning theory and intellectual interventions". *Journal for the Theory of Social Behaviour* 42, 3: 304–325.
Baert, P. 2015. *The Existentialist Moment: the Rise of Sartre as a Public Intellectual*. Cambridge: Polity.
Baert, P. and Booth J. 2012. "Tensions within the public intellectual: political interventions from Dreyfus to the new social media". *International Journal of Politics, Culture, and Society* 25, 4: 111–126.
Baert, P. and Shipman, A. 2012. "Transforming the intellectual." In F. Dominguez Rubio and P. Baert (Eds.), *The Politics of Knowledge*. London: Routledge, pp. 179–204.
Barnes, A. C. 1944. *The Case of Bertrand Russell Versus Democracy and Education*. Merion: A.C. Barnes.
Baumesiter, R. F. 1999. *Evil: Inside Human Violence and Cruelty*. New York: Henry Holt.
Bell, Daniel. 2000[1960]. *The End of Ideology: On the Exhaustion of Political Ideas in the Fifties*. Cambridge: Harvard University Press.
Bell, J. (Ed.). 1935. *We Did Not Fight: 1914–18; Experiences of War Resister*. London: Cobden-Sanderson.
Bergson, H. 2010. *Matter and Memory*. USA: CreateSpace, 2010.

Bikson, T. H. 1967. *The Logical Atomism of Bertrand Russell: A Critical Evaluation.* Columbia: University of Missouri.

Blackbourne, D. 2007. *The Conquest of Nature: Water, Landscape, and the Making of Modern Germany.* New York: Norton.

Blaser, A. W. 1992. "How to Advance Human Rights without Really Trying: An Analisis of Nongovernmental Tribunals". *Human Rights Quarterly* 14, 3: 339–370.

Blitz, D. 1999. "Russell and the Boer War: From Imperialist to Anti-Imperialist". In *The Journal of Bertrand Russell Studies* 19, 2.

Blitz, D. 2002a. "Reply to Ray Perkins on Russell's Conditional Threat of War". *Russell*, n.s. 22: 166–172.

Blitz, D. 2002b. "Did Russell Advocate Preventive Atomic War against the USSR?" *Russell*, n.s. 22: 5–45.

Bourdeau, M., Pickering, M., and Schmaus, W. (Eds.). 2018. *Love, Order and Progress. The Science, Philosophy & Politics of Auguste Comte.* Pittsburgh: University of Pittsburgh Press.

Bowler, P. J. 2001. *Reconciling Science and Religion: The Debate in Early 20th Century Britain.* Chicago: The University of Chicago Press.

Bowler, P. J. 2017. *A History of the Future. Prophets of Progress from H. G. Wells to Isaac Newton.* Cambridge: Cambridge University Press.

Bridger, S. 2015. *Scientists at War. The Ethics of Cold War Weapons Research.* Cambridge: Harvard University Press.

Broncano, F. 2015. *Bertrand Russell. Conocimiento y felicidad.* Batiscafo.

Brown, D. G. 1974. *Bertrand Russell's Earlier Views on the Nature of Mind and Matter 1911–1919.* Canada: McMaster University.

Bud, R. 2014. "Biological Warfare Warriors, Secrecy and Pure Science in the Cold War: How to Understand Dialogue and the Classifications of Science". *Medicina nei Secoli Arte e Scienza* 26, 2: 451–468.

Bud, R. 2018. "Modernity and the ambivalent significance of applied science: motors, wireless telephones and poison gas." In R. Bud, P. Greenhalgh, F. James and M. Shiach (Eds.), *Being Modern. The Cultural Impact of Science in the Early Twentieth Century.* London: University College London: 95–129.

Bud, R. et al. (Ed.). 2018. *Being Modern. The Cultural Impact of Science in the Early Twentieth Century.* London: UCL Press.

Bueno, G. 1972. *Ensayos Materialistas.* Madrid: Taurus.

Bueno, G. 1991. *Primer ensayo sobre las categorías de las 'ciencias políticas'.* Logroño: Biblioteca Riojana.

Bueno, G. 1992. *Teoría del Cierre Categorial.* 5 vols. Oviedo: Pentalfa.

Bueno, G. 2003. *El Mito de la Izquierda.* Barcelona: Ediciones B.

Bueno, G. 2010. Cuatro modos de conceptualizar las "crisis institucionales" (o "crisis de valores"): anarquía, anomia, oligarquía y poliarquía. *El Catoblepas* 104, 2.

Bueno, G. 2014. Ensayo sobre el fundamentalismo y los fundamentalismos. *El Basilisco*, 44: 4–60.

Bueno, G. 2016. *El mito de la cultura.* Oviedo: Pentalfa.

Bunge, M. 2010. *Mind and Matter: A Philosophical Inquiry.* New York: Springer.

Burke, K. 1974[1941]. *The Philosophy of Literary Form.* London: University of California Press.

Buronson and Hara, Tetsuo. 1983 to 1988. *Fist of the North Star.* Tokyo: Weekly Shōnen Jump.

Butcher, S. I. 2005. "The Origins of the Russell-Einstein Manifesto". *Pugwash History Series*, 1: 1–35.

Butler, Judith, Laclau, Ernesto, and Žižek, Slavoj. 2011. *Contingency, Hegemony, Universality: Contemporary Dialogues on the Left.* London: Verso.

Camic, C. and Gross, N. 2001. "The New Sociology of Ideas." In J. Blau (Ed.), *The Blackwell Companion to Sociology.* Oxford: Blackwell, pp. 236–250.

Camprubí, L. 2020. "Engineering as Cultural Hegemony: What a Gramscian Interpretation of Francoism Teaches about Gramsci". In M. Badino and P. D. Omodeo (Eds.), *Cultural Hegemony in a Scientific World.* Vol. 2. *Civil Society and Scientific Culture.* Leiden: Koninklijke Brill, 2020: 258–273.

Carr, E. H. and Cox, Michael. 2001[1939]. *The Twenty Years' Crisis 1919–1939: An Introduction to the Study of International Relations.* New York: Palgrave Macmillan.

Carroll, S. J. 2010. *Fill the Jails: Identity, Structure and Method in the Committee of 100, 1960– 1968.* Sussex: University of Sussex.

Casey, S. 2010. *Selling the Korean War: Propaganda, Politics, and Public Opinion in the United States, 1950–1953.* Oxford: Oxford University Press.

Cassin, C. E. 1968. *The Origin And Development of Bertrand Russell's Theory of Descriptions.* Tallahassee: Florida State University Press.

Chomsky, N. 1971. "Foreword to the War Crimes Tribunal on Vietnam". In *Bertrand Russell War Crimes Tribunal on Vietnam.* (http://www.chomsky.info/articles/1971----.htm).

Ciguere, J. A. 1970. *Bertrand Russell's Theory of Empiricism: An Analysis of His Later Works.* Wisconsin: University of Marquette.

Clack, R. J. 1964. *Analysis and Ontology: a Study of Reconstructionism in the Early Philosophy of Bertrand Russell.* The University of North Carolina at Chapel Hill.

Claeys, G. 2010. *Imperial Sceptics. British Critics of Empire, 1850–1920.* Cambridge: Cambridge University Press.

Clark, R. 1975. *The Life of Bertrand Russell.* London: Jonathan Cape/Weidenfeld & Nicolson.

Clifford, N. R. 2001. "The Long March of 'Orientalism': Western Travelers in Modern China". *New England Review* 22, No. 2: 128–140.

Coates, K. (Ed.). 1971. *Prevent the Crime of Silence: Reports from the Sessions of the International War Crimes Tribunal.* London: Allen Lane.

Cohen, D. 2007. *Equations from God. Pure Mathematics and Victorian Faith.* Baltimore: John Hopkins University Press.

Collini, S. 2002. "'Every Fruit-Juice Drinker, Nudist, Sandal-wearer. . .': Intellectuals as Other People". In H. Small (Ed.), *The Public Intellectual.* Oxford: Blackwell: 203–223.

Comte, A. 1830–1842. *Cours de philosophie positive*, 6 vols. Paris: Bachelier.

Connelly, J. 2021. *Wittgenstein's Critique of Russell's Multiple Relation Theory of Judgement.* Anthem Press.

Copleston, F. 1994. *A History of Philosophy.* Vol. 7. *Modern Philosophy, Empiricism, Idealism, and Pragmatism in Britain and America.* New York: Image Books Doubleday.

Crim, B. E. 2018. *Our Germans. Project Paperclip and the National Security State.* Baltimore: Johns Hopkins University Press.

Cushing, M. P. 2004. *Baron D'holbach. A Study Of Eighteenth Century Radicalism.* Whitefish: Kessinger Pub. Co.

Darlington, E. 1978. *Bertrand Russell's Causal Theories.* Canada: University of McMaster.

Daston, L. 2012. "When Was Modernity, and Why Do We Care?" In C. Pichler and S. Neuburger (Eds.), *The Moderns.* Wien: Springer Verlag, 143–159.

Daston, Lorraine. 2006. "The History of Science as European Self-Portraiture". *European Review* 14, 4: 523–536.

Daston, Lorraine. 2016. "When Science Went Modern". *Hedgehog Review* 18: 18–32.

Davis, J. H. 1984. *The Kennedys: Dynasty and Disaster.* New York: S. P. Books, 437.

Davis, M. 2000. *Late Victorian Holocaust. El Niño Famines and the Making of the Third World.* London: Verso.

Denton, P. H. 2001. *The A B C of Armageddon: Bertrand Russell on Science, Religion, and the Next War, 1919–1938.*

Dewey, J. 1941. *The Bertrand Russell Case.* New York: Viking Press.

Douglas, M. 1966. *Purity and Danger: An Analysis of Concepts of Pollution and Taboo.* London: Routledge.

Dronamraju, K. R. (Ed.). 1995. *Haldane's Daedalus Revisited.* New York: Oxford University Press.

Duffett, J. 1968. *Against the Crime of Silence: Proceedings of The Russell International War Crimes Tribunal.* New York: O'Hare Books.

Durkheim, E. 1995[1912]. *The Elementary Forms of Religious Life.* New York: The Free Press.

Durkheim, E. 2008[1912]. *The Elementary Forms of the Religious Life.* Oxford: Oxford University Press.

Durkheim, E. and Mauss, E. 2010[1903]. *Primitive Classification.* London: Routledge.

Eames, E. R. 1969. *Bertrand Russell's Theory of Knowledge.* London: George Allen and Unwin.

Edgerton, D. 2006. *The Shock of the Old.* Cambridge, Mass.: The MIT Press.

Edgerton, D. 2006. *Warfare State: Britain, 1920–1970.* Cambridge: Cambridge University Press.

Editors, *Law Review*. 1940. "The Bertrand Russell Litigation". *The University of Chicago Law Review. The University of Chicago* 8, 2: 316–325. Retrieved 17 November 2017.

Edmunds, J. and Turner, B. S. 2002. *Generations, Culture and Society.* Buckingham: Open University Press.

Effron, M. and Johnson, B. 2017. *The Function of Evil across Disciplinary Contexts.* Lanham: Lexington Books.

Elkind, L. and Landini, G. (Eds.). 2018. *The Philosophy of Logical Atomism: A Centenary Reappraisal.* Cham: Palgrave Macmillan.

Ellison, H. 2016[1969]. *A Boy and His Dog*. Open Road Media Sci-Fi & Fantasy.
Elshakry, M. 2007. "The Gospel of Science and American Evangelism in Late Ottoman Beirut", *Past & Present* 196: 173–214.
Epple, Moritz. 2011. "Between Timelessness and Historiality on the Dynamics of the Epistemic Objects of Mathematics". *Isis* 102: 481–493.
Erickson et al. 2013. *How Reason Almost Lost Its Mind. The Strange Career of Cold War Rationality*. Chicago: The University of Chicago Press.
Eyerman, R. 1994. *Between Culture and Politics: Intellectuals in Modern Society*. Cambridge: Polity.
Eyerman, R. 2001. *Cultural Trauma, Slavery and the Formation of African American Identity*. Cambridge: Cambridge University Press.
Eyerman, R., Alexander J. C., and Breese, E. B. 2013. *Narrating Trauma: On the Impact of Collective Suffering*. Boulder: Paradigm Publishers.
Falk, R. A. 1968. *The Six Legal Dimensions of the Vietnam War*. Princeton: Princeton University Press.
Falk, R. A. and Hanrieder, W. F. (Eds.). 1968. *The Vietnam War and International Law*. Philadelphia: J. B. Lippincott & Co.
Falk, R. A. and Melman, S. (Eds.). 1968. *In the Name of America—The Conduct of the War in Vietnam by the Armed Forces of the U.S.* New York: E. P. Dutton.
Farrell, J. 2017. *The Battle for Yellowstone: Morality and the Sacred Roots of Environmental Conflict*. Princeton: Princeton University Press.
Feinberg, B. and Kasrils, R. 2013. *Bertrand Russell's America: His Transatlantic Travels and Writings, 1896–1945*, Vol. 1 New York: Routledge.
Ferreirós, J. 2007a. "*Ho theos arithmetidsei*. The Rise of Arithmetic as Pure Mathematics with Gauss". In C. Goldstein, N. Schappacher and J. Schwermer (Eds.), *The Shaping of Arithmetic after C.F. Gauss's Disquisitiones Arithmeticae*. Berlin: Springer: 234–268.
Ferreirós, J. 2007b. *Labyrinth of Thought. A History of Set Theory and Its Role in Modern Mathmeatics*. Second revised edition. Basel: Birkhäuser.
Ferreirós, J. 2008. "The Crisis in the Foundations of Mathematics". In T. Gowers (Ed.). *The Princeton Companion to Mathematics*. New Jersey: Princeton University Press: 142–156.
Ferreirós, J. 2009. Hilbert, Logicism, and Mathematical Existence. *Synthese* 170: 33–70.
Ferreirós, J. 2016. *Mathematical Knowledge and the Interplay of Practices*. New Jersey: Princeton University Press.
Ferreirós, J. 2020. "Gauss and the Mathematical Background to Standardisation". *HoST-Journal of History of Science and Technology* 14, 1: 32–51.
Frank, P. 1959. *Alas, Babylon*. Philadelphia: J. B. Lippincott & Co.
Frascolla, P. 1997. "The Tractatus System of Arithmetic". *Synthese* 112: 353–378.
Frascolla, P. 2017. "Wittgenstein's Early Philosophy of Mathematics". In Hans-Johann Glock and Freeden, M. 2003. *A Very Short Introduction to Ideology*. Oxford: Oxford, Oxford University Press.
Fukuyama, F. 1992. *The End of History and the Last Man*. New York: Free Press.

Galuagher, J. 2013. *Russell's Philosophy of Logical Analysis, 1897–1905*. London: Palgrave MacMillan.
Gandon, S. 2012. *Russell's Unknown Logicism. A Study in the History and Philosophy of Mathematics*. New York: Palgrave Macmillan.
Geertz, C. 1964. "Ideology as a Cultural System". In In David Apter (Ed.), *Ideology and Discontent*. New York: The Free Press of Glencoe.
Geertz, C. 1973. *The Interpretation of Cultures*. New York: Basic Books.
Geertz, C. 2006[1973]. *The Interpretation of Cultures*. New York: Basic Books.
Gerassi, J. 1968. *North Vietnam: A Documentary*. Crows Nest: George Allen & Unwin.
Ghamari-Tabrizi, S. 2005. *The World of Herman Kahn. The Intuitive Science of Thermonuclear War*. Cambridge, Mass.: Harvard University Press.
Girard, M. 2008. *A Strange and Formidable Weapon: British Responses to World War I Poison Gas*. University of Nebraska Press.
Goethe, N. B. 2007. "How did Bertrand Russell make Leibniz into a 'fellow spirit'?" In P. Phemister and S. Brown (Eds.). *Leibniz and the English-Speaking World*. Springer: 195–205.
Gordin, M. 2007. *Five Days in August. How World War II Became a Nuclear War*. Princeton: Princeton University Press.
Gramsci, A. 2011. *Prison Notebooks*, vols. 1, 2, and 3. New York: Columbia University Press.
Gray, Jeremy J. 2006. "Modern Mathematics as a Cultural Phenomenon". In J. Ferreirós and J. J. Gray (Eds.). *The Architecture of Modern Mathematics. Essays in History and Philosophy*. Oxford: Oxford University Press: 371–395.
Griffin, N. 1991. *Russell's Idealist Apprenticeship*. New York, Oxford University Press; Claredon Press.
Griffin, N. 1992. *The Selected Letters of Bertrand Russell*. New York. Routledge.
Griffin, N. 2003. *The Cambridge Companion to Bertrand Russell*. Cambridge: Cambridge University Press.
Griffin, N. 2003. "Russell's Philosophical Background". In Nicholas Griffin (Ed.), *The Cambridge Companion to Russell*, 84–107. Cambridge: Cambridge University Press.
Gruender, D. 1953. *On a Theory of Knowledge of Bertrand Russell*. Chicago: University of Chicago Press.
Habermas, J. 1968. "Technology and Science as 'Ideology'". In *Toward a Rational Society*. Boston: Beacon Press.
Habermas, J. 1969. *Toward A Rational Society*. Boston: Beacon Press.
Habermas, J. 1994. *Postmetaphysical Thinking*. Cambridge: The MIT Press.
Haldane, J. B. S. 1925. *Daedalus: Or Science and the Future*. Dutton: E. P. Dutton & Company.
Hamblin, J. 2013. *Arming Mother Nature. The Birth of Catastrophic Environmentalism*. Oxford: Oxford University Press.
Harding, D. J., Dobson, C.C., Wyse, J. J. B., and Morenoff, J.D. 2016. "Narrative change, narrative stability, and structural constraint: The case of prisoner reentry narratives." *American Journal of Cultural Sociology* 5, 1: 261–304.

Hardy, G. H. 1970. *Bertrand Russel and Trinity*. Cambridge: Cambridge University Press.
Harré, R. 1993. *Social Being*. Oxford: Blackwell.
Harrison, Peter. 2015. *The Territories of Science and Religion*. Chicago: University of Chicago Press.
Harrison, R. 1989. "Russell's Politics; Review of Alan Ryan, *Bertrand Russell: a Political Life*". *Russell: the Journal of Bertrand Russell Studies* 9, 1: 64–71.
Hecht, G. 2009. *The Radiance of France: Nuclear Power and National Identity after World War II*. Cambridge, Mass.: The MIT Press.
Hegel, G. W. F. 1977[1807]. *Phenomenology of Spirit*. Oxford: Oxford University Press.
Hegel, G. W. F. 1998[1831]. *Hegel's Science of Logic*. New York: Humanity Books.
Heidegger, M. 2010[1927]. *Being and Time*. New York: State University of New York Press.
Heins, V. M., and Langenohl, A. 2011. A Fire That Doesn't Burn? The Allied Bombing of Germany and the Cultural Politics of Trauma. In R. Eyerman, J. Alexander, E. B. Breese (Eds.), *Narrating Trauma: On the Impact of Collective Suffering*. Yale Cultural Sociology Series. New York: Paradigm Publishers/Routledge.
Heis, Jeremy. 2020. "'If numbers are to be anything at all, they must be intrinsically something': Bertrand Russell and mathematical structuralism". In E. H. Reck and G. Schiemer (Eds.), *The Prehistory of Mathematical Structuralism*. Oxford: Oxford University Press: 303–328.
Hesseling, Dennis. 2003. *Gnomes in the Fog. The Reception of Brouwer's Intuitionism in the 1920s*. Basel: Springer.
Hochschild, A. 2011. *To End All Wars: A Story of Loyalty and Rebellion, 1914–1918*. Boston: Houghton Mifflin Harcourt.
Horkheimer, M. & Adorno, Th. W. 2002. *Dialectic of Enlightenment*. Stanford: Stanford University Press.
Horowitz, D. 1998. *Radical Son: A Generational Odyssey*. New York: Touchstone.
Hume D. 1978[1739]. *A Treatise of Human Nature*. Oxford: Clarendon Press.
Hunt, A. E. 1999. *The Turning: A History of Vietnam Veterans against the War*. New York: New York University Press.
Huxley, A. 1948. *Ape and Essence*. New York: Harper & Brothers.
Huxley, A. 1980[1932]. *A Brave New World*. New York: Harper Perennial Modern Classics.
Hyman, J. (Ed.). *A Companion to Wittgenstein: Blackwell Companions to Philosophy*. Malden: Wiley-Blackwell.
Jasanoff, S. and Kim, S. H. (Eds.). 2015. *Dreamscapes of Modernity. Sociotechnical Imaginaries and the Fabrication of Power*. Chicago: Chicago University Press.
Josephson-Storm, J. 2017. *The Myth of Disenchantment*. Chicago: Chicago University Press.
Kahn, H. 1965. *On Escalation: Metaphors and Scenarios*. New York: Frederick A. Praeger.
Kendrick, O. 2012. *To Touch the Face of God: The Sacred, the Profane, and the American Space Program, 1957–1975*. Baltimore: Johns Hopkins University Press.

Kennedy, W. B. and White Jr., W. R. 1941. "The Bertrand Russell Case Again". *Fordham Law Review*. Fordham University. 10, 2: 196–218. Retrieved 17 November 2017.

Kerry, J. et al. 1971. *The New Soldier*. New York: Collier Books.

Kline, R. 1995. "Construing 'Technology' as 'Applied Science'. Public Rhetoric of Scientists and Engineers in the United States, 1880–1945". *Isis* 86, 2: 19–221.

Kluge, E.-H. W. 1980. *The Metaphysics of Gottlob Frege. An Essay in Ontological Reconstruction*. Dordrecht: Springer.

Korhonen, A. 2013. *Logic as Universal Science Russell's Early Logicism and Its Philosophical Context*. New York: Palgrave MacMillan.

Kwon, H. 2010. *The Other Cold War*. New York: Columbia University Press.

Lackey, D. P. 1996. "Reply to Perkins on 'Conditional Preventive War'". *Russell*, n.s.: 85–88.

Landes, D. 1969. *The Unbound Prometheus: Technological Change and Industrial Development in Western Europe from 1750 to the Present*. Cambridge University Press.

Lebens, S. 2017. *Bertrand Russell and the Nature of Propositions: A History and Defense of the Multiple Relation Theory of Judgement*. New York: Routledge.

Leithauser, G. G. 1997. *Principles and Perplexities: Studies of Dualism in Selected Essays and Fiction of Bertrand Russell*, Wayne State University, Detroit, Michigan, USA, 1977.

Levi-Strauss, C. 1974. *Structural Anthropology*. New York: Basic Books.

Levi-Strauss, C. 1975. *Myth and Meaning: Cracking the Code of Culture*. Toronto: University of Toronto Press.

Levi-Strauss, C. 1983. *The Raw and the Cooked*. Chicago: University of Chicago Press.

Lévy-Bruhl, L. 2015[1910]. *How Natives Think*. Eastford: Martino Fine Books.

Lewy, G. 1978. *America in Vietnam*. Oxford: Oxford University Press.

Locke, J. 1979[1695]. *An Essay concerning Human Understanding*. New York: Oxford University Press.

Lynd, S. 1967. "The War Crimes Tribunal: A Dissent", *Liberation* (December 1967).

MacLeod, R. 1993. "The Chemists Go to War: The Mobilization of Civilian Chemists and the British War Effort, 1914–1918", *Annals of Science* 50, 5: 455–481.

Madigan, T. 2003. "Monk's 'Patography'", *Russell: The Journal of Bertrand Russell Studies* 23, 1: 77–82.

Maloney, S. M. 2020. *Deconstructing Dr. Strangelove. The Secret History of Nuclear War Films*. University of Nebraska Press.

Mancosu, P. 1999. "Between Russell and Hilbert: Behmann on the Foundations of Mathematics". *The Bulletin of Symbolic Logic* 5, 3: 303–330.

Mannheim, K. 1952. *Essays in the Sociology of Knowledge*. London: Routledge & Kegan Paul.

Mannheim, K. 1991[1923]. *Ideology and Utopia*. London: Routledge.

Marcuse, H. 1991[1964]. *One-Dimensional Man: Studies in the Ideology of Advanced Industrial Society*. Boston: Beacon Press.

Marx, K. 1963a[1867]. *Capital*, vol. 1. Moscow: Foreign Languages Publishing House.
Marx, K. 1963b. "Economic and Philosophical Manuscripts". In Karl Marx, *Early Writings*. New York: McGraw-Hill.
Mast, J. 2012. *The Performative Presidency: Crisis and Resurrection during the Clinton Years*. Cambridge: Cambridge University Press.
Mays, W. 1967. "Recollections of Wittgenstein". In K. T. Fann (Ed.), *Ludwig Wittgenstein: The Man and His Philosophy*. N.J.: Atlantic Highlands. Humanities Press.
Mazower, M. 2004. "The Strange Triumph of Human Rights, 1933–1950". *Historical Journal* 47, 2: 379–398. Cambridge: Cambridge University Press.
McKeever, P. 1973. *Acquanitance and Description in the Writings of David Hume and Bertrand Russell*. Halifax: Dalhausie University.
Merrill, D. D. 1990. *Augustus de Morgan and the Logic of Relations*. Dordrecht: Kluwer Academic Publishers.
Miller, A. 2015. "Bertrand Russell". In *The International Encyclopedia of the First World War*. https://encyclopedia.1914-1918-online.net/article/russell_bertrand.
Monk, R. 2001. *Bertrand Russell. The Ghost of Madness, 1921–1970*, vol. 2. New York: Free Press.
Monk, R. 2016. *Bertrand Russell. The Spirit of Solitude 1872–1921*, vol. 1. New York: The Free Press.
Moore, G. E. 1914. "Symposium: The Status of Sense-Data". *Proceedings of the Aristotelian Society* 14: 335–380.
Moore, K. 2008. *Disrupting Science: Social Movements, American Scientists, and the Politics of the Military, 1945–1975*. Princeton, N.J.: Princeton University Press.
Moorehead, C. 1992. *Bertrand Russell: A Life*. New York: Viking.
Moreno Márquez, C. A. 2000. *Fenomenologia y filosofia existencial. Enclaves fundamentales*. Madrid: Síntesis.
Moreno Márquez, C. A. 2000. *Fenomenologia y filosofia existencial II. Entusiasmos y disidencias*. Madrid: Síntesis.
Nakano, A. 2021. "On Ramsey's Reason to Amend *Principia Mathematica* and Wittgenstein's Reaction". *Synthese* 199: 2629–2646.
Nakazato, N. 2016. *Neonationalist Mythology in Postwar Japan: Pal's Dissenting Judgment at the Tokyo War Crimes Tribunal*. London: Lexington Books.
Nasim, O. W. 2007. *Constructing the World: Russell and the Edwardian Philosophers*. Toronto: University of Toronto.
Nasim, O. W. 2008. *Bertrand Russell and the Edwardian Philosophers: Constructing the World*. Basingstoke: Palgrave Macmillan.
Navarra Ordoño, A. 2014. *1914. Aliadófilos y germanófilos en la cultura española*. Madrid: Cátedra.
Navarro, J. 2017. "Promising Redemption: Science at the service of secular and religious agendas." *Centaurus* 59: 173–188.
Nunn, T. P. 1910. "Symposium: Are Secondary Qualities Independent of Perception?" *Proceedings of the Aristotelian Society* 10: 191–218.
Orwell, G. 1998. *Facing Unpleasant Facts, 1937–1939*. London: Secker & Warburg.
Orwell, G. 2014[1948]. *1984*. New York: Harper Perennial.

Otomo, K. 1982–1990. *Akira*. Tokyo: Young Magazine.
Pais, A. 1994. *Einstein lived here*. Oxford: Oxford University Press.
Park, J. 2013[1963]. *Bertrand Russell on Education*. London: Routledge.
Parsons, T. 1959. "An Approach to the Sociology of Knowledge". In *Transactions of the Fourth World Congress of Sociology*. Milan and Stressa, pp. 25–49.
Pears, D. F. 1972. *Bertrand Russell and the British Tradition in Philosophy*. Michigan: Fontana.
Peñalver, P. 1989. *Del espíritu al tiempo. Lecturas de «El Ser y el Tiempo» de Heidegger*. Barcelona: Anthropos.
Pérez-Jara, J. 2014. *La filosofía de Bertrand Russell*. Oviedo: Pentalfa.
Pérez-Jara, J. 2015. "Ritual and Myth in the Russell War Crimes Tribunal on Vietnam". *University of Cambridge's Centre of Governance & Human Rights Working Paper Series*, 11.
Pérez-Jara, J. 2022. "Discontinuous Materialism". In E. G. Romero, J. Pérez-Jara. and L. Camprubí (Eds.). *Contemporary Materialism: Its Ontology and Epistemology*. New York: Springer.
Perkins, R. (Ed.). 2001. *Yours Faithfully, Bertrand Russell: Letters to the Editor 1904–1969*. Chicago: Open Court.
Perkins, R. 1996. "Response to Lackey on 'Conditional Preventive War'". *Russell*, n.s. 16: 169–170.
Perkins, R. 2002. "Bertrand Russell and Preventive War". In Alan Schwerin (Ed.), *Bertrand Russell on Nuclear War, Peace, and Language: Critical and Historical Essays*. London: Praeger.
Perkins, R. 2002. "Russell and Preventive War: a Reply to David Blitz." *Russell*, n.s. 22: 161–165.
Perkins, R. K. 1973. *Meaning and Acquaintance in the Early Philosophy of Bertrand Russell*. Durham: Duke University Press.
Pickering, A. 1995. *The Mangle of Practice: Time, Agency and Science*. Chicago: University of Chicago Press.
Podhoretz, J. 2006. "Oh, Yeah, Bertrand Russell Was a Great Man. . . ." New York: National Review (July 13).
Podhoretz, N. 2004. *The Norman Podhoretz Reader: A Selection of His Writings from the 1950s through the 1990s*. New York: The Free Press.
Pool, Ithiel de Sola. 1983. *Technologies of Freedom*. Cambridge: Belknap.
Popper, K. & Eccles, J. 1984[1977]. *The Self and Its Brain: and Argument for Interactionism*. New York: Routledge.
Popper, K. 2000[1994]. *Knowledge and the Body-Mind Problem. In Defence of Interaction*. New York: Routledge.
Porter, T. 2009. "How Science Became Technical", *Isis* 100: 292–309.
Porter, T. 2012. "Thin Description: Surface and Depth in Science and Science Studies", *Osiris* 27, 1: 209–226.
Pulido, M. 2009. "The Place of Saying and Showing in Wittgenstein's Tractatus and Some Later Works". *Aporia* 19, 2.
Rees, A. and Morus, I. R. 2019. "Presenting Futures Past: Science Fiction and the History of Science", *Osiris* 34: Introduction to special issue.

Reid, T. 2005. *Del Poder*—translation, prologue and notes by Francisco Rodriguez Valls. Madrid: Encuentro.
Rempel, Richard A. (Ed.). 2003. *The Collected Papers of Bertrand Russell*. New York: Routledge.
Rhodes, R. 1986. *The Making of the Atomic Bomb*. New York: Simon & Schuster.
Richards, Joan. 2011. "God, Truth and Mathematics in Nineteenth-Century England", *Theology and Science* 9: 1, 53–74.
Rodríguez-Consuegra, Francisco A. 1991. *The Mathematical Philosophy of Bertrand Russell: Origins and Development*. Basel: Birkhäuser.
Romero, E. G., Pérez-Jara, J. and Camprubí, L. 2022. *Contemporary Materialism: Its Ontology and Epistemology*. New York: Springer.
Romero, G. E. 2018. *Scientific Philosophy*. New York: Springer.
Rorty, Richard. 2017[1979]. *Philosophy and the Mirror of Nature*. Princeton: Princeton University Press.
Ross, William T. 1994. "Bertrand Russell and the Colonialist Assumption". *The Centennial Review* 38, 2: 387–399.
Rotblat, J. 1982. *Proceedings of the First Pugwash Conference on Science and World Affairs*. London: Pugwash Council.
Russell, B. 1901. "Recent Work on the Principles of Mathematics". *The International Monthly* 4 (Jul 1901), pp. 83–101 (Repr. as "Mathematics and the Metaphysicians" in B. Russell. *Mysticism and Logic and Other Essays*. London: Longmans, Green, and Co., 1918, pp. 74–96).
Russell, B. 1903. *The Principles of Mathematics*. Cambridge: Cambridge University Press (2nd edition 1937).
Russell, B. 1905. "On Denoting". *Mind*, vol. 14.
Russell, B. 1910. "The Study of Mathematics," *The New Quarterly* 1 (Nov 1907) Repr. *Philosophical Essays*, Longmans, Green, and Co.
Russell, B. 1914. "The Relation of Sense-Data to Physics". *Scientia* 16: 1–27; reprinted in *Mysticism and Logic and Other Essays*. New York, London: Longmans, Green & Co., 1918, 145–179; also appearing in *Collected Papers*, volume 8.
Russell, B. 1916a. *Principles of Social Reconstruction*. London: George Allen & Unwin.
Russell, B. 1916b. *Why Men Fight*. New York: The Century Co.
Russell, B. 1916c. *The Policy of the Entente, 1904–1914: A Reply to Professor Gilbert Murray*. Manchester: The National Labour Press.
Russell, B. 1917a. *Mysticism and Logic*. Watford: Taylor Garnett Evans & Co.
Russell, B. 1917b. *Justice in War-time*. Chicago: Open Court.
Russell, B. 1917c. *Political Ideals*. New York: The Century Co.
Russell, B. 1918. *Mysticism and Logic and Other Essays*. London: Longmans, Green, and Co.
Russell, B. 1919. *Introduction to Mathematical Philosophy*. London: Allen & Unwin.
Russell, B. 1922. *Free Thought and Official Propaganda* (lectured delivered and published at South Place Institute).
Russell, B. 1922. *The Problem of China*. London: George Allen & Unwin.
Russell, B. 1923. *The ABC of Atoms*. New York: E.P. Dutton & Company.

Russell, B. 1923. *The Prospects of Industrial Civilization*. London: George Allen & Unwin.
Russell, B. 1925. *The ABC of Relativity*. London: Kegan Paul, Trench, Trubner.
Russell, B. 1928. "Eastern and Western Ideals of Happiness,"
Russell, B. 1935. *Religion and Science*. Oxford: Oxford University Press.
Russell, B. 1936. *Which Way To Peace?* London: Michael Joseph.
Russell, B. 1938. [First published 1903]. *Principles of Mathematics* (2nd ed.). W. W. Norton & Company.
Russell, B. 1938. *Power: A New Social Analysis*. London: Allen & Unwin.
Russell, B. 1945. "The Bomb and Civilization". *Glasgow Forward* 39, 33: 1, 3 (18 August 1945).
Russell. B. 1948. "Speech at Royal Empire Society". *United Empire* 39, Feb. 1948: 18–21.
Russell, B. 1949. "The Philosophy of Logical Atomism". Minneapolis: Department of Philosophy, University of Minnesota (reprinted as *Russell's Logical Atomism*, D. F. Pears [Ed.]. Oxford: Fontana/Collins, 1972).
Russell, B. 1949. *Authority and the Individual*. London: George Allen & Unwin.
Russell, B. 1950. *Unpopular Essays*. London: George Allen & Unwin.
Russell, B. 1953a. *Satan in the Suburbs and Other Stories*. London: George Allen & Unwin.
Russell, B. 1953b. *Why I Am Not a Christian and Other Essays on Religion and Related Subjects*. New York: Rouben Mamoulian Collection (Library of Congress).
Russell, B. 1954a. Letter published in *Saturday Review* on 16 October 1954.
Russell, B. 1954b. *Human Society in Ethics and Politics*. London: George Allen & Unwin.
Russell, B. 1956. *Logic and Knowledge*. London: Allen & Unwin.
Russell, B. 1959. "Bertrand Russell BBC Interview on 4 March 1959". *The Listener* 61 (19 March 1959): 505.
Russell, B. 1961a. "Civil Disobedience". *New Statesman*, 17 February 1961 (available electronically at https://www.newstatesman.com/2013/11/civil-disobedience).
Russell, B. 1961b. *Has Man a Future?* London: George Allen & Unwin.
Russell, B. 1963a. *Unarmed Victory*. New York: Simon & Schuster.
Russell, B. 1963b. Interview in *Playboy* 10, 3: 42, (March 1963).
Russell, B. 1967. *War Crimes in Vietnam*. New York: George Allen & Unwin.
Russell, B. 1967[1945]. *A History of Western Philosophy*. New York: Simon & Schuster.
Russell, B. 1967[1957]. *Why I Am Not a Christian and Other Essays on Religion and Related Subjects*. New York: Simon & Schuster.
Russell, B. 1968[1952]. *The Impact of Science on Society*. New York: AMS Press.
Russell, B. 1975[1959]. *My Philosophical Development*. London: George Allen & Unwin Ltd.
Russell, B. 1984. *The Collected Papers of Bertrand Russell. Theory of Knowledge. The 1913 Manuscript*, vol. 7. New York: Routledge.
Russell, B. 1990[1968]. *The Art of Philosophizing, and Other Essays*. New York: Philosophical Library.

Russell, B. 1992[1927]. *The Analysis of Matter*. London: Routledge.
Russell, B. 1993. *The Collected Papers of Bertrand Russell towards the "Princples of Mathematics"*, vol. 3 *1900–1902*. Edited by Gregory H. Moore. London: Routledge.
Russell, B. 1993[1945]. *A History of Western Philosophy*. New York: Routledge.
Russell, B. 1995[1917]. "A Summer of Hope". In *Pacifism and Revolution*. New York: Routledge.
Russell, B. 1997[1935]. *Religion and Science*. Oxford: Oxford University Press.
Russell, B. 1997[1940]. *An Inquiry into Meaning and Truth*. New York: Routledge.
Russell, B. 1998[1967–1969]. *The Autobiography of Bertrand Russell* [one single volume with an introduction by Michael Foot]. New York: George Allen & Unwin.
Russell, B. 1998[1967–1969]. *The Autobiography of Bertrand Russell*. New York: George Allen & Unwin.
Russell, B. 2000[1922]. *Uncertain Paths to Freedom: Russia and China, 1919–22*. New York: Routledge.
Russell, B. 2001[1912]. *The Problems of Philosophy*. Oxford: Oxford University Press.
Russell, B. 2003. *The Collected Papers of Bertrand Russell: Man's Peril, 1954–55*. London: Routledge.
Russell, B. 2004[1925]. *What I Believe*. New York: Routledge.
Russell, B. 2004[1938]. *Power: A New Social Analysis*. London: Routledge.
Russell, B. 2005[1921]. *The Analysis of Mind*. London: Routledge.
Russell, B. 2005[1924]. *Icarus: Or the Future of Science*. Nottingham: Spokesman Books.
Russell, B. 2009[1914]. *Our Knowledge of the External World as a Field for Scientific Method in Philosophy*. London: Taylor & Francis.
Russell, B. 2009[1918]. *Mysticism and Logic and Other Essays*. Ithaca: Cornell University Library.
Russell, B. 2009[1948]. *Human Knowledge: Its Scope and Limits*. New York: Routledge.
Russell, B. 2010[1975]. *Autobiography*. London: Routledge.
Russell, B. 2011. "1967." *The Independent* (Sunday 23 October 2011). https://www.independent.co.uk/life-style/the-last-testament-of-bertrand-russell-published-for-the-first-time-his-final-word-on-the-state-of-the-world-and-his-own-achievements-and-failures-introduced-by-ray-monk-1506341.html.
Russell, B. 2011[1960]. *Bertrand Russell Speaks His Mind*. Whitefish: Literary Licensing.
Russell, B. 2011[1966]. *War Crimes in Vietnam*. New York: Monthly Review Press.
Russell, B. 2013[1930]. *The Conquest of Happiness*. New York: Liveright.
Russell, B. 2013[1959]. *Common Sense and Nuclear Warfare*. New York: Routledge.
Russell, B. 2014. "Bertrand Russell On Zionism". Archived from the original on 4 March 2016. Retrieved 13 September 2014.
Russell, B. 2019[1951]. *New Hopes for a Changing World*. London: George Allen & Unwin.

Russell. B. 2009[1956]. *The Basic Writings of Bertrand Russell*. New York: Routledge.
Ryan, A. 1988. *Bertrand Russell: A Political Life*. London: Allen Lane.
Salema, A. G. 1971. *Bertrand Russell and the Theory of Sense-Data*. Montreal: McGill University.
Santayana, G. 2016[1913]. *Winds of Doctrine*. Scotts Valley: CreateSpace Independent.
Schatzberg, Eric. 2018. *Technology. Critical History of a Concept.* Chicago: The University of Chicago Press.
Schmidt, J. 2004. "In Praise of Kenneth Burke: His 'The Rhetoric of Hitler's "Battle"' Revisited". *Rhetor*, vol. 1. Ottawa: Canadian Society for the Study of Rhetoric.
Schroeder-Gudehus, Briggitte. 2016. "Probing the Master Narrative of Scientific Internationalism: Nationals and Neutrals in the 1920s". In Lettevall et al., *Neutrality in Twentieth Century Europe.* Routledge: 19–45.
Schwerin, A. (Ed.). 2002. *Bertrand Russell on Nuclear War, Peace, and Language: Critical and Historical Essays*. London: Praeger.
Scott, K. A. 2013. *Reining in the State: Civil Society and Congress in the Vietnam and Watergate Eras.* Lawrence: University Press of Kansas.
Seckel, Al. 1984. "Russell and the Cuban Missile Crisis". *Russell: the Journal of Bertrand Russell Studies*. McMaster University, vol. 4 (1984), issue 2, Winter 1984–85, pp. 253–261.
Seed, D. 2013. *Under the Shadow: The Atomic Bomb and Cold War Narratives.* Kent: The Kent State University Press.
Shapin, S. 2008. *The Scientific Life. A Moral History of a Late Modern Profession.* Chicago: The University of Chicago Press.
Sheehan, T. 2009. *Heidegger: The Man and the Thinker*. New Jersey: Transaction Publishers.
Sheehan, T. 2014. *Making Sense of Heidegger: A Paradigm Shift*. Lanham: Rowman and Littlefield.
Shelley, D. 1965. "Influx or Exodus? Anarchists and the Committee of 100," Anarchy, no. 50, April 1965.
Shindler, C. 2007. *What Do Zionists Believe?* London: Granta.
Shklar, J. 1966. *Political Theory and Ideology*. New York: Macmillan.
Singh, A. 1987. *The Political Philosophy of Bertrand Russell*. Delhi: Mittal Publications.
Sledd, A. E. 1994. "Pigs, Squeals and Cow Manure; Or Power, Language and Multicultural Democracy" JAC. Archived from the original on 20 November 2008. Retrieved 7 February 2009.
Slot, L. 2008. *Consistency and Change in Bertrand Russell's Attitude towards War.* Leiden: Sidestone Press.
Smith, P. 2005. *Why War? The Cultural Logic of Iraq, the Gulf War, and Suez*. Chicago: University of Chicago Press.
Somsen, G. 2020. "The Philosopher and the Rooster: Henri Bergson' French Diplomatic Missions, 1914–1925", *Historical Studies in the Natural Sciences* 50, 4: 364–383.

Somsen, G. J. 2008. "A History of Universalism: Conceptions of the Internationality of Science from the Enlightenment to the Cold War", *Minerva* 46: 361–379.

Stevens, G. 2005. *The Russellian Origins of Analytic Philosophy: Bertrand Russell and the Unity of the Proposition*. New York: Routledge.

Stevens, G. 2018. "Wittgenstein and Russell". In *A Companion to Wittgenstein* (Blackwell Companions to Philosophy). Hans-Johann Glock and John Hyman (Eds.). Malden: Wiley-Blackwell.

Stewart, B. D. 1961. *The Role of Analysis in the Philosophy of Bertrand Russell*. London: The University of Western Ontario.

Stewart, L. J. 2018. "Too Loud to Rise Above the Silence: The United States vs. the International War Crimes Tribunal, 1966–1967". *The Sixties: A Journal of History, Politics and Culture*, 11: 17–45.

Stone, I. F. 1981. "Bertrand Russell as a Moral Force in World Politics". *Russell*, n.s. 1: 7–26.

Stout, G. F. 1914. "Symposium: The Status of Sense-Data". *Proceedings of the Aristotelian Society* 14: 381–406.

Taylor, A. 2021. "Audience Agency in Social Performance". *Cultural Sociology*, vol. 16, 1.

Taylor, R. 1988. *Against the Bomb. The British Peace Movement 1958–1965*. Oxford: Oxford University Press.

Torell, D. 2015. "Remember the Russell Tribunal?" In Reading, A. and Katriel, T. (Eds.), *Cultural Memories of Nonviolent Struggles*. London: Palgrave Macmillan.

Totten, S. and Parsons, W. S. 2013. *Centuries of Genocide: Essays and Eyewitness Accounts*. New York: Routledge.

Turchetti et al. 2020. "Introduction: Just Needham to Nixon? On Writing the History of "Science Diplomacy". *Historical Studies in the Natural Sciences* 50, 44: 323–339

Vartanian, A. (Ed.). 1960. *La Mettrie's L'homme machine. A Study in the Origins of an Idea*. Princeton: Princeton: Princeton University Press.

Vélez-Vélez, R. 2016. "Sixty years before the homicide: The Vieques movement and trauma resolution". *American Journal of Cultural Sociology* 4, 1: 46–67.

Vellacott, Jo. 1980. *Bertrand Russell and the Pacifists in the First World War*. Brighton: Harvester Press.

Wagar, W. W. 2004. *H.G. Wells: Traversing Time*. Middletown: Wesleyan University Press.

Walsh, Lynda. 2013. *Scientists as Prophets: A Rhetorical Genealogy*. Oxford University Press.

Warwick, A. 2003. *Masters of Theory. Cambridge and the Rise of Mathematical Physics* (Chicago: Chicago University Press).

Weber, Max. 1993. *The Sociology of Religion*. Boston: Beacon Press.

Wells, H. G. 1914. *The World Set Free*. New York: Macmillan Publishers.

Wiener, N. 1953. *Ex-Prodigy: My Childhood and Youth*. Cambridge: MIT Press.

Willbanks, James H. and Wert, Hal Elliott. 2017. *Vietnam War Propaganda: Analyzing the Art of Persuasion during Wartime*. Santa Barbara: ABC-CLIO.

Wise, Norton M. 2016. "Agency", *Isis* 107, 4: 781–784.

Wittgenstein, L. 2001[1921]. *Tractatus Logico-Philosophicus*. New York: Routledge.
Wittner, Lawrence S. 1984. *Rebels against War: The American Peace Movement, 1933–1983*. Philadelphia: Temple University Press.
Wittner, Lawrence S. 1993. *One World or None: A History of the World Nuclear Disarmament Movement through 1953*. Stanford: Stanford University Press.
Wolfe, A. J. 2018. *Freedom's Laboratory. The Cold War Struggle for the Soul of Sciences*. Baltimore: John Hopkins.
Woodhouse, H. R. 1980. *The Concept of the Individual in Bertrand Russell's Educational Thought*. Canada: University of Toronto.
Zizek, S. 2009. *The Sublime Object of Ideology*. London: Verso.
Zunino, M. 2016. "Subversive Justice: The Russell Vietnam War Crimes Tribunal and Transitional Justice". *The International Journal of Transitional Justice* 10, 2: 211–229.

Index

9/11 Attacks, 85
a priori, 15, 16, 28, 35, 39, 46
Abrahamic gods, 15
Activism, 66, 68, 72–75, 77, 134, 149, 153, 155, 158, 162, 163, 190
   anti-nuclear, 158
   anti-war / antiwar, 66, 72, 73, 77
   nuclear, 149, 153
   pacifist, 75
   political, 134, 164, 166
   public, 66
   Russell's, 68, 75
Actor-Network Theory, 7
Air raids, 127–28, 157, 158, 160, 164, 196, 198
Aldermaston marches, 154
Alexander, Jeffrey, ix, 8, 19, 108, 183, 191, 201
Alexander, Samuel, 94
Allan, Ryan, 3
Allies, the, 70, 128, 162, 168
Althusser, Louis, 193
American Civil Liberties Union, 132
Anarchism, 70
Ancient, 7, 11, 12, 14, 15, 39, 40, 42, 49, 71, 82, 115, 134, 137, 169, 174, 187, 193, 196
   myths, 42
   binaries, 15, 174, 196

   binary, 40, 137
   codes of thought, 11
   cultural structures, 15
   deity, 14
   Empires, 82,
   epistemological problem, 7
   Greece, 49, 71
   Greek "rules of logic",
   Minotaur, 115
   mythical qualities, 12
   mythical structures, 174
   radical binaries, 169
   Romans, 14
   sinful schism, 12
   structures of meaning, 187
Anti-Americanism, 143, 156
Anti-Christian, 129, 130
Anti-nuclear movement, 149, 152, 155, 156, 159, 160
Anti-Sovietism, 143
Antinomies, 33, 36, 39
Apocalypse, i, iii, 1, 4–6, 14, 17–19, 61, 62, 78, 82, 84, 85, 116, 120, 121, 125, 134, 139, 145, 148–50, 157, 159, 160, 165, 167, 169, 183, 186, 187, 191, 195, 196, 198
   avoid the, 150
   harbingers of, 139, 148
   Imminent, 14, 149

nuclear, 85, 157, 159, 160
prophet of, 120
techno-scientifically produced, 167
world, 165,
Apocalyptic, 14, 15, 19, 20, 22–24, 32, 61, 67, 75, 84, 85, 113, 119, 124, 157–60, 163, 166, 171, 175, 187
account of the 20th century, 160
annihilation, 119
dilemmas, 20
evil, 166
flip, 75
imaginaries, 61
interpretation of science, 67
language, 24
narratives, 158, 187
nature of the techno-scientific sphere, 85
rhetoric, 175
threats, 23
view of the times to come, 24, 84
world, 113
Apotropaic, 34, 159, 196
Arcadia, 19
Ariadne's thread, 4, 89
Ariadne's threads, 2, 3
Aristotelian, 33, 37, 188, 202, 210, 211, 216
Aristotle, 19, 57, 219
Arithmetic, 27, 28, 35, 38–40, 43, 44, 46–47, 58, 206, 207
Astrophysics, 94
Atomic, 52–56, 103, 119, 120, 134–136, 138, 140, 142, 176, 201, 203, 212, 216
bomb, 119, 120, 134–36, 138, 140, 176, 212, 216
element, 53
energy, 135, 140, 142, 201
fact, 53–55
power, 120
race, 140
theories, 135
theory, 103
war, 203

warfare, 56
Atomism, 2, 20, 32, 34, 37, 49, 50–59, 92, 93, 96, 100, 101, 203, 206, 213
logical, 2, 20, 32, 34, 37, 50–59, 92, 93, 96, 100, 101, 203, 206, 213
role of, 55
Atoms (logical), 51, 53
Audience(s), 9, 17, 18, 20, 22, 32, 49, 66, 71, 72, 79, 84, 87, 103, 121, 122, 127, 140, 145, 146, 151, 157–60, 165, 169, 173, 176, 177, 179, 187, 189, 190, 192, 216
Ayer, A. J., 3, 30, 177

Baert, Patrick, 4, 9, 18, 21, 22, 189, 194, 202
Baldwin effect, 188
Balfour, Arthur, 74, 201
Barnes, Albert C., 132, 133, 202
Baron d'Holbach, 12, 205
BBC, 141, 142, 214
Behaviorism, 89, 91, 110, 112,
Behmann, Heinrich, 46, 210
Belief, 4, 5, 27, 29, 56, 82, 83, 95, 100, 105, 110, 111, 112, 116, 117, 146, 177, 190, 193, 198
Bell, Daniel, 195, 203,
Bergson, Henri, 23, 114, 203, 216
Berkeley, George, 94, 98, 110, 113–115
Bertrand Russell Case, 120, 128, 131, 133, 205, 209
Bertrand Russell Peace Foundation, 1, 155, 163, 169, 170, 176, 178, 186
Bertrand Russell Society of Japan, 163
Bible, 95
Binary, 6–8, 11, 12, 14, 15, 18, 20, 30, 40, 54, 58–61, 67, 71, 75, 76, 111, 114, 124, 126, 137, 145, 157, 162, 163, 176, 177, 183, 188, 191, 198
between China and Japan, 162
between sacred-good and profane-evil, 15,
between total ontological transparency and total ontological opacity, 7

Index

between West and East
categories, 11,
code(s), 6, 15, 75, 76, 176, 183
distinction, 71,
forms, 188
logic, 75, 145, 157, 176, 177, 191
opposition between utopia and apocalypse, 6
opposition(s), 6, 12, 18, 67,
oppositions structuring civil discourse, 18
positioning, 183
recollection(s), 30
saying/showing, 54
sense, 198
simplistic, 7, 60, 61, 76, 124, 157, 183, 188, 191, 198
strong, 59, 177
structure(s), 8, 124, 177
between the sacred and the profane, 14
Bio-muzzles, 198
Blake, Dora, 73, 78, 87, 113, 128
Bolshevik, 73
Bolyai, Farkas, 35
Bolzano, Bernard, 37, 40
Boole, George, 39, 43
Bourdieu, Pierre, 8, 15
Bradley, Francis Herbert, 33–35, 37, 50, 58
Brain, 90, 107–9, 116, 212
British, iv, 22, 23, 28, 32–34, 37, 39, 54, 60, 66, 68, 70–74, 77, 79, 84–86, 93, 111, 120–23, 126, 127, 132, 137, 139–41, 144, 145, 149–51, 153, 154, 156, 160, 162, 171, 185, 204, 207, 210, 211, 216
actions, 127
anti-Japanese propaganda, 137
anti-nuclear movement, 149
audience(s)
authorities, 171,
bomb, 150
civil sphere, 70
defeat, 126
disarmament, 150
Empire, 68, 71, 85, 122, 127
empire, 68, 71, 85, 122, 127,
establishment, 141
ethics, 127
expansionism, 123
government, 72, 73, 84, 141
handling of the Indians, 127
idealism, 37, 39, 60
idealist(s), 28, 33, 34, 37, 111
imperialism, 66, 69
imperialist(s), 66
intellectuals, 77
Labour Party, 154
left, 162
liberalism, 66
mainstream newspapers, 86
military, 145
narratives, 79
neutrality, 66, 151
New Left Movement, 154
pacifist activists, 79
pacifist movement, 70
partners in the Western block, 141
people opposed the war, 68
political establishment, 127
public opinion, 121
society, 120
triumphant narratives, 139
Brixton Prison, 74, 155
Broad, C. D., 4
Buddhism, 110, 117
Bueno, Gustavo, ix, 7, 16, 22, 76, 176, 195, 203, 204

Cambridge, ix, 22, 28, 30, 33, 34, 37, 41, 66, 68, 69, 72–74, 80, 86, 87, 98, 133, 141, 201–4, 206–8, 210–12, 217, 219
Cambridge University, 33, 69, 201–204, 206–10, 212
Camelot, 19
Campaign for Nuclear Disarmament (CND), 150, 153–55
Cantor, Georg, 36, 38–40, 42, 43–45, 49

Carnap, Rudolf, 48, 55, 56, 129
Cassandra, 185
Castro, Fidel, 153, 167
Causal, 8, 92, 98, 102, 105, 108, 115, 117, 205
  chains, 115
  connection, 117
  laws, 98, 105
  power, 8
  relationships/relations, 102, 105
  theory, 92, 108
Causality, 95, 102, 105, 106, 117
Charismatic, 18, 21, 189
Chemo-muzzles, 198
China, 78, 82, 87, 137, 144, 149, 162, 166, 169, 172, 176, 193, 204, 213, 214, 219
Chinese, 137, 144
  border, 144
  communist revolution, 144
Chomsky, Noam, 14, 172, 177, 179, 181, 204
Christian, 12, 28, 39, 67, 113, 129, 130, 133, 150, 161, 178, 213, 214
  climate, 130
  conservationism, 133
  conservatives, 130, 133
  critics, 130
  eschatology, 12
  faith, 28
  lobbies, 130
  positioning, 129
  Quaker, 178
  values, 130
Christianity, 34, 145, 160
CIA, 22, 141, 183
Citizens Commissions of Inquiry (CCI), 176
City College of New York, 130, 131
Civil, 9, 16, 18, 70, 123, 130, 132, 148, 154, 159, 159, 160, 164, 181, 182, 196, 201, 202, 204, 214, 215
  discourse, 18
  disobedience, 154, 155, 159, 214
  Liberties Union, 132,
  opposition of the American intervention in Vietnam, 182
  rights movement(s), 160, 181
  sphere, 9, 70, 130, 148, 159, 160, 201, 202
Civilization, 18, 22–24, 68, 71, 78–80, 83, 86, 112, 120, 121, 134, 136–38, 157, 213
  collapse of our, 83
  European, 71
  human, 23, 24, 157
  industrial, 18, 78, 83, 213
  machinic, 79
  Western, 121
Coates, Ken, 172, 173, 175, 177, 180, 205
Coding, 9, 10, 17, 167, 175, 177, 180, 196, 197
Cohen, Morris Raphael, 131
Committee of 100, 154–56, 159, 204, 216
Communism/communist, 74, 125, 128, 139–41, 144–48, 150, 158, 167, 168–171, 176–83, 189
Comte, August, 11–13, 57, 111, 203, 205
Condemnation, 62, 121, 128, 144
Congress for Cultural Freedom, 141, 183
Consciousness, 76, 92, 96, 97, 110–12
Conservatives, 79, 130, 131, 133, 154
Contingency, 7, 9, 15, 17, 53, 102, 115, 187, 188, 204
Contingentism, 100, 188
Conventionalism, 28, 30, 36, 61
Correlationism, 115, 117
Cortázar, Julio, 177
COVID-19 pandemic, 196
Critical theory, 13
Cuba, 152, 153, 171
Cuban Missile Crisis, 1, 152, 186, 215
Cultural, iii, ix, x, 1, 6, 8–11, 14–19, 21, 23–25, 31, 41, 59, 65, 69–71, 75, 81, 83–86, 114, 119, 123, 124, 127, 130, 131, 137, 141, 145, 152, 155,

157–59, 165–69, 171, 173, 177, 178, 180–82, 185, 187–99, 201–4, 206–8, 216, 217, 219
-sociological, 1, 6, 21, 31, 114, 119, 124, 127, 158, 192, 193
analysis of ideology, 25
attribution, 85
categories of "good" and "evil", 9
circumstances, 10, 169
classification, 13, 85, 86
codification, 8
conflict, 192
construction of evil, 166, 168
construction(s), 17, 159, 166, 168, 187, 198
context, 10, 59, 70, 177
devices, 168
environments, 187
factor(s), 59, 159, 166, 189
feedback, 157, 168
formation(s), 193
idealism, 8
impact, 159, 180–82, 203
Influence, 71, 169
interpretation of the Great War, 24
Kantianism, 15
landscapes, 188
level, 189
life, 168, 192, 193, 197
logic, 191, 192, 199, 216
mechanism(s), 192, 195
paradox(es), 130, 158
perception, x, 23, 158, 165, 182, 197
Phenomenon, 17, 207
power, 168
pragmatics, 167, 201
process(es), 9, 10, 18, 75, 85, 165, 166, 192, 195, 197
product, 10, 196
production, 171
progress, 14
realism, 8
reconstruction, 85
references, 157
relevance, 181

repercussion, 171
representation, 166
responsibility
riverbeds, 83
role, 167, 181, 185
sense, 10, 192
sociology, iii, ix, 6, 11, 85, 180, 187, 201, 202, 208, 216, 217, 219
sphere(s), 9, 11, 23, 173, 182
structures, 11, 15, 19, 187, 188, 192, 193
success, 127, 166
symbol(s), 8, 9, 17, 187
system(s), 194, 197, 207
theorizing, 8
tradition, 41
trauma(s), 24, 85, 127, 152, 157, 158, 169, 180, 182, 201, 206
turmoil, 190
values, 197
wars, 131
weight of evil, 11
Culture, 8, 9, 13, 15, 20, 59, 71, 76, 158, 160, 166, 188, 189, 191, 193, 197, 201, 202, 204, 206, 209, 216
's symbolic plasticity, 10, 198
absolute independence of, 8
relative independence of, 15, 158, 189, 197

Daedalus, 5, 80, 81, 115, 205, 208
Darwin, Charles/Darwinian 21
De Morgan, Augustus, 40, 57, 210
Dedekind, Richard, 38, 42, 44, 48–50
Defence of the Realm Act (DORA), 73
Democracy, 71, 72, 120, 123, 125, 129, 133, 139, 145, 160, 177, 202, 216
Denmark, 172
Descartes, René, 95, 111
Destutt de Tracy, Antoine, 193
Determinism, 8, 123, 188
  biological, 188
  economic, 123,
  technological, 8
Deus ex machina, 193

Dewey, John, 131–133, 205
Dialectical, 28, 33, 36, 37, 49, 62, 171, 177, 188,
   materialism, 161, 177
   metaphysics, 28, 33, 36, 37
   method, 33, 62
   philosophy, 36
   understanding of logic, 28
Dialektik der Aufklärung, 13
Diplomacy, 141, 148, 151, 181, 217
Discontinuism, 188
Donnellan, Keith, 51,
Doomsday, 145, 151, 196
Dramatic, 5, 6, 16–20, 35, 84, 85, 134, 167, 173, 180, 185, 187, 189, 190, 202
   actor(s), 17, 173
   intellectual(s), 6, 16, 84, 85, 167
   opposition, 5
   rhetoric, 84
Dramaturgy, 18, 21, 87
Dresden, 128
Dreyfusan, 17
Dualism, 66, 89, 90, 114, 115, 209
Durkheim, Emile, 11, 75, 205

Economics, 9, 158, 160
Eddington, Arthur, 27, 108, 113
Education, 1, 2, 5, 21, 28, 34, 41, 68, 76, 79, 82, 91, 112, 113, 116, 124, 125, 130, 132, 133, 202, 211, 217
   cambridge, 41
   higher, 21, 130, 132
   liberal, 5, 76, 91, 112
   mathematical, 28, 34
   scientific, 91
Einstein-Russell Manifesto, 1, 156
Einstein, Albert, 1, 22, 104, 131, 133, 141, 147–49, 156, 159, 162, 204, 211
Eisenhower, Dwight D., 146, 149, 176
Elliot, Thomas, 84
Emotional attachments, 9, 16, 18, 20, 157, 192

Empiricism, 5, 23, 31, 38, 48, 50, 55–57, 90, 92, 94–100, 109, 114, 204, 205
   analytical, 50
   pure, 99, 100
   radical, 95, 99
   Russell's, 90
   traditional, 94
End of history, 195, 207
Enlightenment, 11, 13, 23, 76, 133, 208, 216
Entente, 70, 71, 213
Epigenetic changes, 188
Epistemology, 2, 3, 20, 24, 28, 29, 33, 43, 47, 51–54, 56, 57, 59, 60, 62, 84, 91, 93, 99, 104, 132, 185, 192, 211, 212, 219
   epistemologically optimistic movements, 14
   Russell's, 24, 43, 47, 91, 93, 100, 114
   self-contradictory, 7
   traditional, 192
Ethics, 2, 20, 67, 72, 75, 81, 84, 87, 123, 127, 130, 143, 146, 147, 150, 185, 190, 203, 213
Euclid, 35
Euclidean, 34–36, 46
Eugenics, 82, 117,
Evil, 5, 6, 9–11, 18, 28, 45, 61, 62, 65–67, 69, 75–77, 83–85, 120–22, 126, 131, 133, 139, 144, 145, 156, 158, 160, 163, 165–70, 174, 175, 177, 178, 180, 181, 183, 185–187, 189, 191, 196198, 202, 206
   "embodying", 75
   absolute, 9, 10, 18, 77, 174
   apocalyptic, 166
   communist propaganda, 180
   cultural construction of, 166, 168
   Gordian knot, 10
   Imminent, 22
   lesser, 10, 69, 120, 122, 145, 156, 158, 169, 198

ontological views of, 166
oppressors, 196
problem of, 10
radical, 174
scale of, 174
techno-scientifically produced universal, 67
universal empire of, 10, 165, 167, 174, 186, 191
Universal, 67, 174, 183, 191
weighting, forces of, 66, 69, 139, 166, 183
world, 167, 169
Experience, 9, 10, 46, 47, 54–56, 59, 62, 78, 80, 93, 95–97, 100, 105, 110, 113, 117, 120, 128, 134, 173
bodily, 47
mystical, 54
of evil, 9
sensed, 55
sensory, 93
subjective, 113
world of, 117
worldly, 62
Extra-mental, 94
Eyerman, Ron, 10, 69, 180, 206, 208

Fact(s), 9, 30, 39, 42, 44, 50, 53–55, 77, 78, 81, 85, 91, 105, 109, 110, 116, 129–31, 138, 154, 166, 170, 179, 182, 191, 211
atomic, 53–55
painful, 30
pure, 109
structural *factum*, 115
Factors, 4, 6, 8, 9, 22, 24, 59, 159, 166, 171, 187–90, 192, 195
biological, 188
cultural, 4, 9, 24, 59, 159, 166, 189
material, 6, 8, 187, 188
psychological, 9
random, 190
sociocultural, 4, 9, 24
Falk, Richard A., 173, 181, 206
Fat man, 135

Feminism, 192
Finch, Edith, 144, 171
First World War, 9, 120, 127, 157, 159, 210, 217
Formalism, 46, 48, 62
Forman, Paul, 59
Foucault, Michel, 15, 161, 195
Frankfurt School, 13
Freeden, Michael, 194, 195, 207
Freedom, 9, 13, 70, 74, 77–79, 84, 85, 87, 117, 131, 137, 139, 141, 160, 164, 166, 171, 173, 174, 180, 183, 188, 196, 212, 214, 217
Frege, Gottlob, 30, 43, 45, 47, 50, 209
Friedrich Gauss, Carl, 35, 206, 207
Fukuyama, Francis, 195, 207
Fundamentalism, 76

Gandhi, Mahatma, 127, 161
Gas, 78, 79, 174, 203, 207
Geertz, Clifford, 8, 194, 207
Geometry, 28, 34–36, 38–40, 43, 45–48, 61
Euclidean, 34
Kantian view of, 28
non-Euclidean, 34
principles of, 43
Germany, 12, 35, 71, 76, 112, 120–22, 125, 127, 129, 144, 147, 150, 156–58, 162, 181, 203, 208
declaration of war to, 112
destruction of, 86
Nazi, 121, 122, 125, 127, 181
God, 13, 14, 35, 36, 62, 65, 95, 106, 113, 124, 131, 140, 161, 199, 205, 209, 212
Gödel, Kurt, 57, 62, 133, 161
Golden Age, 14, 24, 44, 80, 84, 85, 197
Gordin, Michael, 120, 135, 136, 139, 207
Government(s), 5, 11, 66, 69–74, 78, 80–85, 87, 121, 125, 135, 138, 140, 141, 144–46, 148, 150, 153, 154, 159, 160, 166, 167, 169, 172, 174, 176–78, 181–83, 189, 195

American, 74, 153, 166, 169, 176, 181, 183
Asquith's Coalition, 74,
British, 72, 73, 84, 141
central, 82, 145
centralized, 81
civilized, 66
coalition, 74
communist, 177
despotic, 80, 82
federal, 189
global, 121
labour, 141
Mao's, 144
North Vietnamese, 172
of New York City, 131
powerful, 148
single, 140
soviet, 140
tyrannical, 160
United States/US, 174, 181
wicked, 82
world, 69, 78, 80, 83, 121, 125, 127, 135, 138, 140, 141, 145, 148, 153, 158, 160, 167
Gray, Jeremy, 59, 207
Great Britain, 12, 66, 70, 122, 141, 149, 150, 156
Great War, ix, 5, 24, 62, 66, 69, 77, 80, 83–85, 124,
Group identities, 17
Guevarist years
of Bertrand Russell, 167

H-bombs, 145, 153
Habermas, Jürgen, 10, 13, 191, 194, 208,
Habermasian, 191
Haldane, John Burdon Sanderson, 5, 80, 81, 87, 205, 208
Han, Byung-Chul, 14,
Harper's Magazine, 170
Harré, Rom, 21, 183, 208
Harris, Sam, 14
Harrison, Peter, 12, 16, 208

Harvard University, 132, 203, 207
Hegel, 32, 33, 36, 38, 39, 50, 58, 91, 208
Hegelian/neo-Hegelian, 5, 23, 28, 32–39, 42, 49, 55, 60, 62, 65, 90, 93, 100, 110, 199
arguments, 38,
dialectical method, 33, 62
dialectics, 60
idealism, 55, 93, 100
interpretation of mathematics, 38
logic, 199
metaphysics
notion of logic, 35
philosophy, 34
program, 36
rejection of the objective
independence of mathematical truths, 28
speculations, 37
view, 37
worldview, 23,
youth, 90, 110
Heidegger, Martin, 13, 115, 208, 211, 216
Hero(es), 14, 44, 196,
Hesiod, 77, 199
Hesseling, Dennis, 48, 59, 208
Hilbert, David, 46, 57, 207, 210
Hiroshima, 120, 134–36, 138, 139
Historical developments, 14
Historicism, 15, 197
Hitler, Adolf, 120, 122, 125, 126, 156, 161, 215
Ho Chi Minh, 22, 172, 183,
Hölderlin, Friedrich, 13
Holism, 6, 17, 20, 32, 37, 49, 50, 59
Holistic, 28, 33, 33, 126
Holocaust, 152, 157, 158, 160, 174, 205
Nuclear, 152, 157, 158, 160
Victorian, 205
Horkheimer, Max, 13, 208
Horowitz, David, 178, 179, 181, 208
Hubble, Edwin, 104
Hubris of the psyche, 33

Human, ix, 1, 2, 5–7, 13, 14, 19, 23–25, 29, 32–35, 37, 40, 41, 43, 47, 49, 50, 55, 56, 58, 61, 62, 65, 67, 69, 71–73, 75, 76, 78, 80–82, 84–87, 91–93, 99, 100, 101, 106–109, 111–13, 116, 120–23, 127, 134, 135, 137, 145, 146, 151, 152, 154, 157–60, 162, 173, 174, 177, 181, 183, 187, 188, 196, 198, 202, 203, 209–11, 213, 215
   impulses, 58, 71
   race, 5, 69, 76, 78, 82, 86, 134, 135, 160, 162
Humankind, vii, 5, 9, 14, 23, 77, 84, 120, 121, 127, 135, 141, 144, 145, 158–60, 183, 185–87
Hume, David, 9, 33, 50, 56, 92, 95, 98, 101, 102, 105, 110, 111, 115–17, 209, 210
Husserl, Edmund, 114, 117, 96
Huxley, Aldous, 80, 113, 163, 209
Huxley, Henry, 12

Ibáñez, Blasco, 70,
Icarus, vii, 1, 23, 42, 68, 80–82, 84, 113, 115, 117, 124, 145, 146, 214
Icon, 65, 23, 155
Idealism, 5, 7, 8, 15, 24, 33, 37–39, 50, 55, 56, 58, 60, 90, 92–96, 98, 100, 101, 106, 107, 110, 114, 115, 117, 188, 190, 197, 205
   absolute, 33
   Berkeley's, 98
   Berkeleyan, 114
   British, 37, 39, 60
   cultural, 8
   Neo-Hegelian, 55, 93, 100
   objective, 92, 106
   phenomenal, 117
   Russell post-1898 rejection of, 115
   spiritual, 197
   subjective, 58, 92, 96, 101, 107, 190, the demon of, 107, 115
Ideological, 7, 18, 60, 69, 70, 72, 79, 127, 167–69, 173, 174, 176, 177, 181–83, 188–95, 199,
   arena, 183
   battle around Vietnam, 167
   changes, 195
   context, 176
   denials, 192
   formations, 191, 193
   interests, 7
   interests, 7
   justifications, 72
   labels, 177
   landscape, 127
   layer, 176
   monopoly, 181
   opponent, 192
   packages/packs/set-menus, 18, 79, 188–90, 192, 195,
   polarizations, 70
   purity, 193
   resources, 60
   schizophrenia, 191
   seeds, 182
   shifts, 195
   spectrum, 176, 181
   struggles, 183
   tools, 193
   transformations, 195
   transformations, 195
   void, 69
   wars, 195
   world, 195
Ideology, 13, 25, 72, 144, 193–95, 198, 199, 203, 207, 208, 210, 216, 217
If-thenism, 46, 60, 62, 63
Illiberalism, 143
Illusion, 7, 9, 34, 101, 115, 198,
Imperialism, 18, 66, 69, 86, 137, 143, 148, 153, 156, 167, 171, 183, 194
   British, 66, 69
Incendiary bombs, 158
Independent Labour Party, 72
Individuals, 4, 6, 17, 46, 93, 101, 111, 117, 136, 137, 172, 188, 193
Indochina, 166, 169, 172, 176,

Industry/industrial, 12, 18, 22, 65, 74, 78, 79, 81, 83, 135, 137, 162, 176, 178, 209, 210, 213
Inference(s), 46, 57, 95, 98, 99, 100, 102, 103, 107, 110, 115, 190
Infinity, 38, 39, 44, 45
Intellectual, 1, 2, 4–6, 9, 14, 16–22, 29, 31–34, 41, 54, 60, 61, 65, 66, 69, 70, 72, 74–77, 80, 83–85, 87, 89, 112, 119, 121, 124, 129, 131, 139, 141, 145, 157–59, 163, 165, 167–69, 171, 174, 177, 182, 187, 189–92, 202, 205, 206
   arena, 84
   career, 6, 29, 33, 61, 83, 89, 145
   contexts, 171
   contradictions, 191
   diplomacy, 141
   dramatic, 6, 17–20, 84, 85, 167, 187, 189, 190, 202
   limitations, 169
   performances, 174
   positioning, 21, 189
   prestige, 72,
   product(s), 4, 21, 163,
   progressive, 70
   public, 4, 17, 19–22, 65, 66, 74, 119, 121, 149, 141, 158, 168, 187, 190, 202, 205
   rigor, 190
   virtues, 61, 76
Intuitionism, 43, 46–48, 62, 208
Iron Age, 199
Italy, 43, 125

James, William, 90, 96, 111, 114,
Janus god, 14,
Japan, 121, 135–39, 156–59, 161–63, 211,
Jassonoff, Sheila, 8
Johnson, Lyndon (President), 168, 172, 174
Joliot-Curie, Frédéric, 147, 148, 162
Judgment Day, vii, 165, 187

Kahn, Herman, 151, 152, 159, 162, 207, 209
Kant, Immanuel, 33, 35, 37, 39, 40, 95
Kantian, 5, 28, 35, 39, 43, 61, 62, 90, 94, 99, 117, 191
Kennedy, John F., 152, 156
Kent Massacre/Kent State Massacre, 166, 182
Kent State University, 166, 216
Khrushchev, Nikita, 149, 152, 153
Knowledge, 2–5, 7, 23, 24, 32, 35, 39, 48–56, 58, 60, 66, 67, 78, 79, 89–100, 102, 103, 105, 107, 108, 111, 113–16, 161, 202, 205, 207, 208, 210–15
   by description, 51
   direct/by acquaintance, 51, 93
   entire edifice of, 98
   epistemological foundations of, 4
   human, 7, 32, 50, 55, 56, 67, 93, 99, 100, 215,
   inferred, 92, 97
   metaphysical, 100
   necessary, 102
   of the universe, 5, 24
   philosophical, 23, 51, 91
   pre-scientific, 100
   private, 95
   probabilistic or statistical, 102
   pure, 35, 79
   scientific, 7, 23, 24, 53, 91, 99, 100, 111, 114
   search for, 3
   tautological, 99
   theory of, 2, 51, 52, 94, 96, 99, 108, 116, 205, 208, 214
   true, 56
Korean War, 143, 146, 165, 166, 204
Kripke, Saul, 51

Laclau, Ernesto, 188, 204
Lamarckian, 2, 21, 183
   ecology, 183

Language, 2, 6, 21, 24, 25, 31, 32, 37, 39, 42, 43, 45, 50–57, 62, 71, 75, 92, 93, 102, 103, 124, 187, 211, 215, 216
Latin America, 153, 171
Latour, Bruno, 7, 14
Laurence, William L., 136
Law of Three Stages, 12
Lawrence, David Herbert, 69, 70
Laws of logic, 40, 58
League of Nations, 78, 138
Left, 17, 18, 35, 38, 40, 54, 97, 103, 127, 140, 144, 154, 155, 162, 166, 170, 176, 177, 179, 183, 189, 192, 204
  -wing bias, 177
  Leftist, 69, 70, 162, 167, 189
  political, 18, 176, 183, 189, 192
Left/right, 176, 177
  divide, 177
  political distinction, 176
Leibniz, Gottfried Wilhelm, 37, 43, 50, 207
Lévy-Bruhl, Lucien, 191, 209
Lévy-Strauss, Claude, 11
Liberal, 5, 71, 72, 76, 79, 86, 87, 91, 112, 120, 129, 132, 134, 150, 171, 178, 183, 190
  American magazine, 150
  association, 87
  defense of individual freedoms, 171
  democracies, 120, 134
  ideas, 71
  imperialists, 79
  newspaper
  Party, 71, 87
Liberalism, 66, 72, 81
  British, 66
  political, 81
Little Boy, 135
Locke, John, 33, 95, 98, 99, 110, 114, 115, 117, 209,
Logic, vii, 1, 2, 15, 19–21, 23, 27–33, 35–43, 46, 48–53, 55–61, 67, 75, 77, 91, 99, 106, 114, 130, 145, 157, 176, 177, 191–93, 199, 208–210, 212, 213, 215, 216
  binary, 75, 145, 157, 176, 177, 191
  Boolean, 57
  cultural, 191, 192, 199, 216
  pure, 37, 48, 67, 99
  symbolic, 31, 37, 40, 42, 57, 58, 210
  traditional, 37, 192
Logical, 2, 9, 12, 14, 18–20, 28, 30–34, 37, 38, 40, 43, 45, 47, 48, 50–61, 92–94, 96–98, 100–102, 104, 106, 108, 114, 115, 121, 169, 171, 188, 189, 191, 192, 198, 199, 203, 206, 207, 213
  analysis, 32, 50, 53, 55, 56, 60, 61, 101, 207
  atomism, 2, 20, 32, 34, 37, 51–59, 92, 93, 96, 100, 101, 203, 206, 213
  contradictions, 191, 192, 199
  deductive/demonstrative
  holism, 20, 37, 50, 59
  justification, 72, 100, 168, 174
  mathematical, 51
  structure, 30, 51, 53, 97
Logicism, 2, 24, 28–32, 41, 43, 45–49, 55, 57, 60–62, 207, 209
London, 129, 154, 160, 172, 199, 201–5, 207, 210–16
Los Angeles, 129
Lynd, Staughton, 178, 210

MacArthur, General Douglas, 144
Mach, Ernst, 90, 96, 114
Macmillan, Harold, 156
Macrologic, 193
Mad Tea-Party of Trinity, 33
Manhattan Project, 147
Manichean, 11, 18, 20, 31, 45, 66, 75, 127, 179, 190
  approach to the war, 179
  binaries, 18
  categories, 66
  ideological landscape, 127
  language
  rhetoric, 45

structures, 31
tradition, 11
Mannheim, Karl, 193–95, 199, 210,
  Mannheim's Paradox, 193–95, 199
Manning, Dr. William Thomas, 130, 132
Mao, Zedong, 144
Marseille, Walter W. 140–42
Marx, Karl, 12, 17, 79, 177, 193, 195, 210
Marxism/Marxist, 72, 177, 188, 193, 194,
Mass-destruction, 68
Master stories, 18
Materialism, 8, 106, 107, 114, 161, 177, 193, 197, 211, 212, 219
  19th century, 106
  dialectical, 161, 177
  reductionist/reductionistic, 8, 193, 197
  simplistic, 8
Mathematical, 2–4, 6, 23, 27–32, 34–40, 43, 46–49, 51, 57, 60–63, 74, 89, 91, 92, 99, 102–4, 106, 108, 114, 115, 151, 207, 208, 212, 213, 217
  abstractness, 104
  analysis, 35, 47
  aspects, 151
  axioms, 35, 43
  characters, 106
  construct, 48
  developments, 35
  education, 28, 34
  entities, 27, 29, 30, 35, 36, 39, 40, 60, 62
  equations, 4
  equivalence, 108
  essences, 89
  fallacies, 36
  logic, 2, 23, 36, 57, 99, 106, 114
  necessity, 40
  objects, 35, 61–63
  philosophy, 3, 32, 46, 49, 74
  practices, 6
  principles, 34
  problems, 48

properties, 106
propositions, 30, 102
relations, 28, 37, 61
science, 36
signs, 46
structure of physical objects, 49
training, 35
truths, 28, 29
Mathematics, vii, x, 1, 23, 27–50, 52, 55, 56, 59–62, 66, 67, 73, 90, 93, 106, 130, 205–7, 210, 212, 213
  applied, 34, 41, 46, 67
  axioms of, 43
  foundational, 59
  foundations of, 28, 206, 210
  Kantian interpretation of, 35
  logic as foundational of, 31
  nature of, 30, 37
  philosophy of, 23, 31, 36, 42, 44, 46, 47, 130, 207
  Platonic interpretation of, 27
  principles of, 38, 42–45, 47–50, 66, 212, 213
  pure, 32, 34–37, 39–42, 44, 46, 49, 50, 52, 55, 59, 67, 205, 206
  study of, 40, 45, 46, 212
  Wittgenstein's characterization of, 30
Matter, iv, ix, 14, 24, 31, 34, 38, 41, 42, 44, 47, 48, 53, 69, 72, 78, 89, 90, 92–95, 97–110, 114–117, 203, 204, 214
McCarthy, Joseph R., 144, 134
McTaggart, John M. Ellis, 33–37, 62
Meaning, 6, 11, 15, 17, 19, 23, 27, 30, 41, 43, 47, 51, 52, 55, 57, 58, 83, 92, 96, 97, 111, 120, 124, 132, 168, 186, 187, 192, 197, 202, 209, 211
Meaningfulness, 192, 197
Means of symbolic production, 17, 157, 165, 182
Mechanics, mechanism, 8, 15, 34, 48, 78, 89, 94, 102–6, 112, 114, 119, 192, 194, 195, 198
Media, 17, 20, 22, 70, 157, 167, 169, 175, 176, 181–83, 202, 206

Meta-adversaries, 18
Meta-characters, 18, 20
Metanarratives, 195
Metaphysics, 10, 12, 13, 20, 23, 27, 28, 32–34, 36, 37, 43, 50, 53, 54, 56, 58, 77, 89, 94, 103, 105, 110, 111, 114, 130, 185, 209
  Berkeley's, 94
  consummation of, 13
  developmental, 33
  dialectical, 28, 33, 36, 37
  ego-centered, 111
  Frege's, 43
  pluralist, 23, 32
  substance, 105, 114
  theological, 10, 77
  traditional, 110
Methodology, 8, 110
Micrologic, 193
Middle ground, 6, 8, 15, 16, 58, 196, 197
Military-industrial complex, 176
Mind, vii, ix, 24, 34–39, 41, 47, 48, 74, 76, 81–83, 89–94, 96–98, 100, 103, 106–16, 122, 126, 127, 141, 143, 146, 151, 156, 165, 176, 179, 191, 203, 204, 206, 212, 214, 215
Modernism, 59, 62
Modernity, 11, 13, 14, 111, 191, 195, 202, 203, 205, 209
Moirai, 188
Molecular, 52
Monism, 4, 24, 28, 32–34, 49, 51, 57, 90–92, 94, 96–99, 103, 107, 108, 114–16
  absolute, 34
  Hegelian, 32
  holistic, 28
  neutral, 24, 32, 51, 57, 90–92, 94, 96–99, 103, 107, 108, 114–16
  radical form of, 33
Monist/Monistic, 28, 33, 37, 98
  believes, 37
  doctrine, 37
  synthesis, 28

Monk, Ray, 3, 10, 19, 29, 36, 45, 60, 62, 68–73, 78, 79, 99, 108, 113, 117, 119, 120, 122, 126, 129–31, 133, 134, 140–44, 146, 148, 153, 154, 156, 161–63, 167, 170–72, 186, 199, 210, 215
Moore, G. E., 4, 9, 33, 34, 36, 37, 50, 56, 62, 75, 94, 101, 176, 190, 210, 214
Moral, 1–3, 5, 9, 11, 29, 41, 66, 68, 78, 112, 113, 123, 124, 134, 139, 147, 153, 165, 167, 173, 179–81, 190, 216
  authority, 167, 173
  codes, 11
  codification of science, 68
  doctrines, 124
  failures, 134
  force, 41, 216
  ideas, 3
  issues, 1
  landscape, 1
  legislator, 139
  legitimacy, 153
  obligation, 179
  philosophers, 2
  philosophy, 190
  political choices, 112
  power, 123
  prestige, 165
  progress, 9, 29
  reform, 5
  restitution, 180
  Training, 113
  virtues, 78
Morris, Charles W., 129
Multidisciplinary approach, 10
Mussolini, Benito, 125, 161
Mutual Assured Destruction (MAD), 151
My Lai Massacre, 176
Mysticism, 20, 38, 42, 58, 59, 67, 113, 212, 213, 215
Myth, 7, 12, 13, 138, 168, 171, 174, 201, 209, 211
Mythology, 13, 77, 177, 211

Nagasaki, 120, 135, 136, 138,
Napalm, 157, 160, 169
Narration, 8, 9, 24, 65, 75, 124, 166
National Veterans Inquiry, 176, 182
Nationalism, 78, 141, 145, 153, 163, 167
Nationalist, 69, 73, 167
Naturalistic fallacy, 9, 85, 196, 197
Navarro, Jaume, 12, 211
Nazi, 19, 121, 122, 125–27, 143, 170, 175, 181
  crimes, 175
  cruelty, 122
  domination, 119, 122
  Germany, 121, 122, 125, 181
  ruling, 126
Networks of meaning, 23
Neuroplasticity, 188
New Statesman, 76, 126, 149, 154, 214
New York Times, 136, 156, 169, 170, 177, 182
Newman, M. H., 108
Nietzsche, Friedrich, 7, 109, 195
No-Conscription Fellowship (NCF), 72
Nobel Prize, 141, 147, 156, 158, 162
Non-Marxist, 72
North Korea, 144
Nuclear, vii, ix, 2, 7, 24, 67, 83, 85, 119–21, 128, 134–36, 138–44, 146–60, 163–65, 168, 175, 186, 190, 207, 208, 210, 211, 215, 217
  activism, 149, 153, 158
  Age, 157, 186
  annihilation, 139, 144, 149, 175
  apocalypse, 85, 157, 159, 160
  apocalypse, 85, 157, 159, 160
  apocalyptic narratives, 158
  Armageddon, 143
  arms race, 165
  attack on the Soviet Union, 83
  attack, 83, 142, 143, 144, 151, 153, 156, 168
  bases, 153
  blast, 138
  bombing of Hiroshima and Nagasaki, 120, 135
  bombings, 136
  bombs, 120, 136, 143, 156, 158, 190
  capability, 135
  catastrophe, 146
  catastrophists, 140
  club, 149, 151
  dangers, 158
  death(s), vii, 119, 156
  destruction, 149
  devices, 149, 150, 159
  disarmament, 150, 153–55, 217
  energy, 135, 147
  equipped submarines, 149
  era, 138
  escalation, 139, 144, 146, 149, 152
  fallout, 147
  holocaust, 152, 157, 158, 160
  international authority, 150
  missiles in Cuba, 152
  missiles, 152
  movement, 149, 152, 154–56, 159, 160
  myth, 138
  order, 156
  plans, 140
  powers, 146, 147
  preventative war against the Soviet Union, 119
  preventive attack, 141
  programs, 148
  strategist, 151
  strategy, 149
  subjects, 147
  thought, 146
  threat, 140
  utopias, 134
  war, 2, 121, 128, 138, 139, 142–44, 146, 152, 155, 156, 160, 207, 210, 211, 215
  warfare, 143, 150, 152, 215
  weaponry, 151, 158
  weapons, ix, 24, 67, 85, 119, 120, 134, 135, 136, 138–40, 146, 148–51, 154, 157–60, 164
  World War, 151
  world, 151, 163

Numbers, 24, 27, 36, 38, 44, 46, 47, 69, 93, 107, 108, 159, 164, 208
  as classes, 93
  Cantor's transfinite, 36
  fictional character of, 46
  infinitesimals
  irrational, 38
  natural, 44, 47
  new definitions of, 44
  Platonism of, 108
  rational, 38
  real, 38
  true nature of, 47
Nunn, T. P., 94, 211
Nuremberg Trials, 128

Oakes, John B., 170
Object-language, 55, 57
Ontological, 2, 4–9, 13, 20, 31–34, 43, 50, 53, 56, 57, 60–62, 89–91, 93, 95, 97, 100–103, 106–8, 110, 114, 116, 117, 124, 166, 188, 194, 198, 209
  assumptions of the most important 20th century social theories, 194
  atomism, 93,
  contents, 198
  contingentism, 100
  convergence of multiple courses of reality, 188
  critique to traditional concepts of the mind,
  development of Russell's thought, 57
  differences, 93
  dimension, 13, 102
  discontinuities in reality, 33
  elements, 53
  fabric of social reality, 124
  framework, 57
  import of Russell's logical analysis, 32
  investigations, 100
  meaning of Russell's logicism, 43
  mutability, 100
  necessity for the existence of the external world, 95
  nihilism, 117
  optimism, 61
  peculiarities of contingency, 188
  pluralism, 4, 5, 101, 114
  pluralist, 34
  plurality and contingency, 53
  plurality, 53, 100
  premises, 103
  principle "natura non facit saltus", 33
  principles of logical atomism, 56
  principles, 56, 101
  privilege over logical constructions, 93
  reality, 114
  status of physical laws, 106
  studies of mind and matter/ approaches to mind and matter, 89
  take on matter, 102
  thought, 89, 91
  transparent realities, 48
  unity, 101
  views of evil, 166
Ontology, 2, 3, 20, 24, 28, 33, 37, 47, 48, 50, 54, 56, 59, 60, 62, 84, 91, 93, 99, 102, 104, 114, 204, 211, 212
  bundle and event, 114
  general, 93
  of matter, 104
  of mind and matter, 24, 47
  pluralist/pluralistic, 37, 102
  Russell's, 28
  science-based, 60
Optimism, 45, 60, 61, 67, 73, 77, 78, 167
Orwell, George, 124, 125, 211,
Ottoline, Lady, 72, 86
Oxford, 33, 66, 71, 73, 201, 202, 204, 205, 207–9, 211, 213, 214, 216, 217

Pacifism, 1, 10, 65, 70, 72, 87, 119–22, 126, 128, 134, 138, 214,
Parsons, Talcott, 11, 194, 211, 217
Particulars, 52, 53, 93, 97, 98, 101, 102, 109, 111

Peace, 1, 5, 9, 66, 69, 71, 72, 74, 79, 84, 121, 122, 126, 135, 138, 139, 143, 145, 147–50, 153, 155, 157, 159, 162, 163, 166, 169, 170, 171, 173, 176, 178, 186, 211, 213, 215–17
Peace Act, 155
Peano, Giuseppe, 43, 44, 49
Perception, x, 10, 23, 24, 28, 35, 51, 90–96, 98, 99, 101, 104, 105, 107–10, 114, 115, 120, 157, 158, 165, 168, 176, 182, 190, 197, 211
Percepts, 91, 96, 98–100, 105
Performance(s), 1, 4, 8, 9, 15–17, 19, 20, 21, 84, 87, 127, 133, 153, 158–60, 168, 170, 174, 182, 185, 189, 190, 201, 202, 216,
  civil, 16
  counter-, 21, 84
  dramaturgical, 9, 158
  individuals', 4
  intellectual, 174
  notorious, 185
  public, 20, 182
  Russell's, 20, 170
  social, 1, 8, 15, 127, 133, 153, 159, 160, 168, 189, 190, 201, 216
  symbolic, 16
  theatrical, 84, 160
Performativity
Pessimism, 60, 77, 113, 124, 187
Phenomenology, 14, 96, 208
Philosophical, 1–7, 16, 18–20, 23, 24, 28, 29, 31, 32, 34–39, 41, 42, 45, 47–49, 51, 52, 54–57, 60, 62, 67, 83, 87, 89–92, 94, 97, 104, 106, 110, 111, 114, 119, 163, 169, 170, 180, 191, 194, 197, 198, 204, 207, 209, 210, 212, 214
  analysis, 51, 198
  anthropology, 163
  antinomies, 36
  approaches to psychoanalysis, 111
  assumptions, 6, 16
  career, 5, 24, 55
  complexity/complexities, 18, 20
  convictions, 170
  critiques of naïve realism, 194
  debate, 94
  depth, 169
  development, 4, 6, 29, 31, 45, 67, 83, 87, 90, 97, 114, 214
  difference between geometry and arithmetic, 47
  difficulties, 114
  disputes, 38
  figure, 2
  framework, 114
  idea, 54
  ideas, 6
  insights, 51
  interpretation(s), 104, 114
  knowledge, 23, 51, 91
  language(s), 54
  logic, 1, 39, 41, 42, 48
  positions, 106
  problem, 52, 56, 62, 92,
  project, 28
  propositions, 54, 56
  questions, 32, 67
  reform, 5
  rigor, 19
  stance, 191
  subjects, 87
  testament, 67
  themes, 114
  theories, 114
  theory of mind, 110
  theses, 5
  thinking, 49, 119
  tool, 57, 60
  tribulations, 90
  truths, 34
  understanding of language, 51
  works, 19, 180
  works, 19, 180
  worldview, 37, 90
  writing, 19
Philosophy, x 1–4, 6, 7, 12, 15, 19, 20, 23, 24, 31–37, 39, 42, 44, 46–52, 55–59, 61, 62, 66, 67, 69, 70, 74–76,

84, 89–94, 97, 98, 100, 102, 104, 106–8, 111, 112, 114, 116, 117, 119, 123, 124, 130–33, 147, 171, 190, 191, 202–7, 209–16, 219
  academic, 69, 119
  analytic, 1, 3, 15, 55, 216
  British, 33
  continental, 2
  current, 39
  Dewey's, 131
  dialectical, 36
  empiricist, 90, 92
  historians of, 31
  history of, 20, 58, 205
  Hume's, 117
  Kantian, 191
  Marx's, 123
  mathematical, 3, 32, 46, 49, 74, 212, 213
  natural, 12
  neo-Hegelian, 34
  non-scientific, 67
  of absolute contingency, 102
  of language, 2, 32, 37, 50–52, 55, 93
  of matter and physics, 100
  of mind and psychology, 108
  political, 70, 84, 124, 147, 216
  popularization of, 3
  problems of, 51, 67, 93, 97, 214
  profane, 130
  pure, 20, 42, 91
  Russell's, 2, 3, 24, 32, 47, 51, 57, 90, 92, 94, 98, 123, 202, 207
  scientific, 20, 23, 67, 75, 89, 100, 212
  skeptical, 117
  strict, 2, 3
  theological, 106
  value of, 116
  Western, 20, 59, 133, 214
  William James's, 111
  Wittgenstein's, 19, 55
Physics, 1, 2, 24, 27, 34, 36, 48, 57, 59, 81, 91, 92, 97–110, 114, 115, 117, 175, 176, 213, 217

Physio-muzzles, 198
Physiologist's paradox, 107
Physiology, 2, 5, 24, 91, 92, 98, 100, 107, 108, 114
Pinker, Steven, 14
Platonic, 4, 27–29, 32, 36, 38, 41, 42, 45–49, 60, 61, 92, 110
Platonism, 4, 20, 24, 28–31, 36, 38, 40, 43, 46–49, 51, 60–62, 106, 108
Plotinus, 10
Pluralism, 4, 5, 28, 32, 36, 37, 50, 57, 101, 102, 114
Pluralistic, 37
Podhoretz, Norman, 178, 181, 212
Poincaré, Henri, 36, 47, 61
Polarization, 69, 70 169
Politics, 2, 3, 19, 20, 22, 24, 29, 67, 91, 121, 128, 136, 141, 146, 147, 150, 153, 155, 158, 183, 185, 196, 202–4, 206, 208, 210, 213, 216
Polluted, 12, 14, 15, 32, 37, 40, 47, 58, 60, 76, 84, 117, 124, 145, 162, 175, 189, 194, 195, 197, 198
Polluting, 79, 121, 123, 126, 131, 133, 189
  "autocracies", 126
  force of evil, 121
  force of intolerance and fanaticism, 133
  influences in the United States, 131
  social behaviors, 123
  social threats, 189
Positioning, 4, 9, 20–22, 69, 75, 79, 80, 84, 120, 121, 129, 133, 134, 141–44, 158, 167, 183, 189, 190, 202
  about the loss of Soviet lives, 143
  binary, 183
  intellectual, 21, 189
  orthodox, 141
  political, 121, 183
  regarding German and Japanese loss of civilians lives, 143
  theory, 21, 202
Positivism, 11, 14, 56, 76, 111
  Logical, 14, 56

Simonean and Comtean, 11
  Comte's 19th century, 111
Positivists, 55–57, 69
Postmetaphysical thinking, 194, 208
Postmodernists, 195
Power, 5, 6, 8, 9, 15–17, 20, 21, 23, 24,
    29, 34, 48, 49, 55, 60, 71, 73, 78,
    80–83, 90, 112, 120, 122–30, 134,
    136, 138, 139, 141, 145, 146, 149,
    150, 153, 154, 157, 158, 161, 165,
    167, 168, 173, 175, 181–83, 189,
    190, 192–95, 202, 208, 209, 213,
    214, 216
  American, 129
  atomic, 120
  balance of, 150
  characters' 173
  cultural, 168
  definition of, 15, 123
  destructive, 139, 153
  forms of, 123, 124
  Hitler's ascend to, 122
  laws of, 123
  limitation of, 165
  moral, 123
  of cultural structures, 192
  of destruction of the War, 128
  of science and technology, 23, 124
  performative, 16, 173
  physical, 173
  ritualistic, 173
  Russell's theory of, 124
  sacred/pure, 124
  soft-, 141
  state's, 146
  symbolic, 15, 16, 21, 133, 136,
    189
  Weberian notion of, 173
Prelogical, 191
Primitive mind, 191
Probability, 56, 90, 95, 115, 151
Profane, 6, 11–15, 17–19, 25, 40, 61,
    76, 79, 84, 124, 130, 131, 167, 169,
    177, 187, 197, 198, 209
Profane-evil, 15, 18, 187

Progress, 4, 5, 9, 11, 12, 14, 29, 41, 61,
    65, 66, 73, 75–77, 79–81, 83–85, 87,
    116, 145, 187, 195, 196, 198, 203
Prometheus, 77, 137, 209
Propositions, 30, 37, 48, 50, 52, 54–56,
    58, 61, 102, 111, 190, 209
Pseudo-problem, 115
Psycho-analysis/Psychoanalysis, 89, 91,
    110–12, 114,
Psychologism, 41, 90, 114
Psychology, 1, 2, 24, 36, 57, 80, 82, 91,
    92, 97–101, 107–15, 117, 123, 158
  analysis of, 115
  behavioral, 112
  hubris of, 92, 98
  preeminence of psychology over
    physics, 99
Public, 1–4, 8, 9, 14–17, 19–22, 24, 31,
    32, 40, 45, 56, 60, 65–67, 70–72,
    74, 75, 80, 83–85, 87, 119, 121, 124,
    126, 129, 131–34, 136, 141–44, 146,
    150, 153–155, 158, 159, 165–69,
    172, 174, 176, 177, 179, 181, 182,
    186–92, 194–96, 202, 204, 205, 209
  anti-nuclear campaigning, 121
  Awareness, 166
  awareness, 166
  charismatic figures, 189
  demonstration, 150
  discourses, 188
  fame, 129
  identity, 142
  impact, 150
  intellectual(s), 1, 4, 9, 17, 19–22, 65,
    66, 74, 83, 119, 121, 129, 141, 158,
    159, 165, 168, 187, 190, 192, 202,
    205
  lectures, 141, 142
  life, 22, 119
  opinion makers, 136
  opinion, 1, 16, 70, 72, 121, 136, 153,
    154, 168, 176, 181, 190, 204
  persona, 22, 45, 60, 143
  political interventions, 186
  role, 31, 186

scandal, 132
social performances, 190
stances on universal evil, 191
statements, 67, 146, 167
support that Russell received from Dewey, 133
support, 133, 174, 176
utterances, 4, 144, 177
Pugwash Conferences, 148, 149

Quantum mechanics, 15, 89, 94, 103–6, 114

Racism, 130, 175
Ramsay, William, 135
Rashomon Effect, vii, 185
Realism, 4, 5, 7–9, 32, 36, 37, 46, 47, 50, 55, 61, 90, 92, 94, 108, 114, 115, 194
  anthropic, 7
  complex, 53
  constructed, 197
  cultural, 8
  epistemological, 114
  external, 98, 100, 115
  forms of, 9
  Inferred, 47, 93, 94
  naïve, 7, 8, 94, 108, 194, 197
  non-naïve, 197
  of propositions, 50
  ontologically transparent, 48
  physical, 7
  Platonic, 32, 46
  political, 7
  Russell's conception of, 94
  sociocultural, 7
  structural, 115
Realities, 7, 15, 47, 48, 53, 93, 94, 98, 100, 115, 188, 197
Reality, 7, 9, 10, 13, 14, 24, 28, 32–34, 36–38, 42, 49, 50, 52, 53, 55, 57, 58, 89, 90, 91–97, 99, 102, 103, 105–11, 114, 115, 117, 124, 163, 188, 192–98,

absolute, 32, 46, 49, 58, 92, 99, 107, 115, 195, 197, 198
coherent logical picture of, 192
contents, structure, and mechanisms of, 194
discontinuities in, 33, 196
distortion of, 193
external, 95, 97, 103, 107, 115,
intrinsic relations of, 102
low-resolution pictures of, 194
maps of, 194
material, 105
neutral / (neutral), 89, 94, 97, 108, 109
non-zoological, 197
objective, 28, 95
ontological convergence of multiple courses of, 188
ontological dimensions of, 13
ontological, 114
plural, 108
prior, 96
reality's muzzle, 7, 10, 195, 198
representation of, 197
social, 124
structural properties of, 115
structure of, 33, 53
ultimate intrinsic nature of, 106
unitary, 36
Reduction ad Hitlerum, 175
Reductionist/reductionistic, 6, 8, 15, 56, 57, 62, 109, 188, 193, 197, 199,
  biologists, 188
  definition of power, 15
  impulses, 109
  Marxists, 188
  materialism, 8, 193, 197
  mechanism, 8
  non-, 6, 188, 199
  turn, 62
  understanding of logic, 199
  view of philosophy, 56
Reid, Thomas, 95, 212
Relation(s)/relationship(s), 4, 5, 7, 8, 16, 17, 28, 32, 34, 37, 40, 43, 50–53,

55, 57, 60, 61, 73, 75, 87, 90–92,
94, 96–102, 104, 105, 109, 114, 117,
121, 132, 145, 155, 162, 185, 187,
191, 193, 194, 197, 198, 204, 205,
209, 210, 213
all kinds of, 52
between phenomena and noumena, 117
between physics and psychology, 109
between reason and culture), 191
between Russell's ideas on the techno-scientific sphere and the final fate of humankind, 185
between science and human progress and decadence, 187
between science and politics, 121
between sense data and matter, 94
between the redshifts of the galaxies and their, 104
causal, 102, 105
cognitive, 51
constitutive, 34
external, 32, 37, 50, 100
foreign, 73
internal, 37
intrinsic, 102
logic of, 40, 210
logical, 60
mathematical, 28, 37, 61
multiple-relation theory of judgement, 51
necessary, 102
of an individual to the State, 155
of the British left and the CND to the military industrial, 162
perceptions and percepts, 91
plural, 34
plurality of, 34
power of science in relation to society, 90
reality of, 34
relational structures, 29, 37, 47
Russell's relationship to Wittgenstein's philosophy of language, 55

science and society, 91
science of relational structures, 29, 37
simple, 53
simultaneous, 101
specific, 53
theory of, 37
to the British military, 145
top-down, 16
with epistemological realism, 114
complex, 162
treatment of relations introduced in modern logic, 57
Relative independence of culture, 15, 158, 189, 197
Relativity, 89, 92, 103, 104, 106, 213
General, 104
principle, 104
theories, 92
theory of, 89, 106
Religion(s), 5, 6, 9, 12, 13, 17, 20, 42, 58, 59, 67, 75, 76, 113, 168, 187, 203, 205, 208, 213, 214, 217
conflict between science and religion, 12
criticism of, 5
Eddington's attempt to fuse science with religion, 113
Enlightenment's attacks to, 13
ideas of, 12
religion and ethics, 67
religion and magic, 168
science versus religion, 20
Religious, 5, 6, 11–13, 16, 18, 29, 32, 39, 40, 65, 73, 75, 76, 79, 85, 137, 205, 211
aspects of formal logic, 40
background, 11
categories, 12
codes, 85
conversion, 65
cultural structures, 11
envelop, 40
fundamentalism, 76
historical and social phenomena, 5

language, 6, 32
leaders, 18
movements in Britain, 79
persecution, 73
philosopher, 40
religious belief in a Platonic eternal world, 29
religious-inspired categories, 11
rhetoric of salvation and doom, 6
rulers, 16
system of the Shogun and the Mikado, 137
thinking, 11
thought, 75
Renaissance, 77
Riemann, Bernhard, 35
Right, 15, 28, 56, 71, 84, 101, 108, 110, 113, 127, 131, 146, 152–54, 159, 170, 176–78, 182, 183, 189, 192
political, 183
Ritual(s), 15, 87 168, 171, 174, 201, 211
Rorty, Richard, 194, 212
Rotblat, Joseph, 147, 148, 162, 163, 212
Rules of logic, 39, 193
Russell Tribunal/Russell-Sartre Tribunal, 1, 165, 168, 169, 173, 178, 180–83, 190, 217,
Russell–Einstein Manifesto, 143, 147–49, 159, 162, 204
Russell, Dora, 73, 78, 113, 128
Russia, 74, 78, 87, 119, 125, 136, 140, 142–44, 146, 214
Rutherford, Ernest, 135
Ryan, Alan, 3, 6, 66, 71, 73, 119, 121, 122, 142–44, 147, 150, 154, 167, 172, 173, 178, 208, 215

Sacred/Sacred-good, vii, 6, 11–15, 17–19, 25, 27–29, 40, 60–62, 76, 79, 84, 85, 90, 112, 121,124, 125, 133, 145, 159, 160, 166, 169, 173, 174, 177, 180, 187, 189, 197, 198, 206, 209
Saint Augustine, 10
Salvation, 6, 14, 17, 19, 62, 84, 148, 160, 169, 195

Santayana, George, 75, 191, 215
Sartori, Giovanni, 199
Sartre, Jean-Paul, 165, 172, 173, 177, 178, 179, 182, 202
Schelling, F. W. J., 33, 117
Schelling, Thomas, 152
Schiller, Friedrich, 11, 13
Schoenman, Ralph, 153–56, 163, 167, 169, 170–72, 199
Schopenhauer, Arthur, 117
Science, I, ii, vii, 1, 2, 4–6, 8, 9, 11–15, 20, 22–25, 27–29, 31, 32, 34–37, 41, 42, 46, 48, 52, 5762, 65–68, 75–85, 89–92, 98–100, 102–10, 112–16, 119, 121, 124, 130, 133, 134, 136, 137, 144–146, 148, 157, 159, 167, 175, 176, 183, 187, 188, 193–95, 198, 203, 205–14, 216, 217
American, 183
combination of modern science and human nature, 187
cultural history of, 6, 187
destruction of science in the USSR, 183
distinction between science and ideology, 194
distinguishing science from ideology, 194
interplay between, 183
pure, 25, 203
relationships between science and human progress and decadence, 187
role of science in human progress and decadence, 198
role of science in society, 80, 114, 121, 157
Russell's public thought on, 195
Russell's thinking of science from the 1920s onwards, 187
science and technology as instruments for world evil, 167
science and technology as polluted, 175
social role of, 175
Soviet, 183

technology and politics, 183
technology and science as ideology, 13, 194
social, 25, 123, 124, 193, 202
Scientific. 1, 2, 5–9, 11–15, 20, 22–24, 28, 31, 34, 39, 41, 49, 51–61, 65–67, 75–82, 84, 85, 89, 91, 92, 94, 99–101, 103–5, 110–16, 119, 124, 125, 134, 136, 137, 141, 145–48, 168, 185, 191, 194, 197, 204, 212, 214–16
advances, 41, 81, 103
age, 119
and philosophical truths, 34
and political priorities, 8
and technological future imagined by Haldane, 80
and technological progress, 5
and technological tools, 85
betterment of the human race, 82
Cold War scientific and intellectual diplomacy, 141
constructivism, 14
disciplines, 57
discovery/discoveries, 5, 15, 80, 103, 104
education, 91
empirical, 53
fabric, 89
fundamentalism, 76
inferences, 100
innovation, 146
instruments, 7
internationalism, 148, 215
investigation, 53
kingdom, 61
knowledge, 7, 23, 24, 53, 91, 99, 100, 111, 114
languages, 54
logic, 57, 59
method in philosophy, 52, 66, 67, 214, 215
methods, 78
novelties, 39
outlook, 113, 124,

perspectives, 125
philosophizing, 94
philosophy, 20, 23, 67, 75, 89, 100, 212
point of view, 134
popularization, 104
postulates, 105
power, 134
problems, 22
progress, 9, 81
propositions, 55, 56, 58
psychological investigations, 112
psychology, 80, 82, 113
rationality, 11, 28, 49, 113
reason, 92
research, 76
results, 78, 110, 114
results, 78, 110, 114
rigor, 2, 103
scientifically driven present and future, 84
scientificity, 52
socialism, 12
stage, 12
successes, 134
temper, 78
theories and discoveries, 60
theories, 6, 60, 100
values, 116
World Federation of Scientific Workers, 147, 148
Scientism, 31
Sense-data, 51, 55, 57, 90–93, 96, 98, 210, 213, 215, 216
Set theory/Set-theory, 35, 42, 44, 45, 206
Signification, 9, 24, 65, 75, 166
Skeptical, 9, 34, 60, 82, 102, 108, 114, 117, 125
theory, 102, 108
Skepticism, 5, 20, 24, 31, 32, 41, 54, 57, 67, 90, 91, 98, 100
Social, 1, 2, 5–12, 14–22, 25, 31, 41, 50, 59, 61, 65, 66, 69–72, 74, 75, 79, 81, 82, 84–87, 92, 100, 112–14, 119,

121, 123–25, 127, 130, 133, 134, 137, 143, 153, 157, 159, 160, 163, 165–69, 171, 173–76, 178, 180–82, 187–98, 201, 202, 208, 210, 213, 214, 216
Action, 15, 18
actor(s), 10, 15, 17, 86, 87, 157, 166, 173, 192
life, 9, 16, 18, 20, 191, 201
trauma(s), 10, 143
Social wounds, 166, 169
Socialism/socialist, 12, 66, 68, 70, 72–74, 78, 125, 176, 177, 188, 190
party, 72
scientific, 12
Socialist(s)
anti-war activism, 22, 66, 68–70, 72, 73, 79, 126, 176, 177, 190
faith, 73
movements, 70, 176
Party, 72
Socio-muzzles, 198
Sociocultural, 4, 7, 9, 24, 75, 169, 183, 192, 197
factors, 4, 9, 24
point of view, 183
process(es), 75, 197
realities, 7
Sociology, iii, ix ,6, 11, 14, 15, 85, 109, 180, 187, 201, 202, 204, 208, 210, 211, 216, 217, 219
classical, 14, 202
cultural, ii, ix, 6, 11, 85, 180, 187, 201, 202, 208, 2016, 217, 219
political, 15
Soddy, Frederick, 135
Soviet, 74, 78, 83, 87, 119, 121, 125, 128, 135, 136, 138–45, 147–49, 152, 153, 156, 158, 168, 171, 174, 177, 180, 183, 191
ability for nuclear war, 143
aggressive move, 149
aircraft, 149
bomb, 143
Communism, 158

dominion, 143
expansionism, 143, 144
government, 140
interests, 148
lives, 143
nuclear threat, 140
Premier Nikita Khrushchev, 149
President, 153
propaganda machine, 135
propaganda, 135, 149
revolution, 87
Russia, 136, 142, 143
science, 183
sphere, 156
threat, 141
Union, 74, 78, 83, 119, 121, 125, 128, 135, 138, 139–143, 147, 149, 152, 153, 156, 168, 171, 174, 177, 180, 191
Spacetime, 99, 102
Spence, Marjorie Helen, 128
Spencer, Herbert, 12, 66
Sphere(s), 9, 11, 19, 21, 23, 59, 65, 70, 77, 85, 123, 124, 130, 137, 148, 156, 159, 160, 168, 173, 182, 185, 201, 202
civil, 9, 70, 130, 148, 159, 160, 201, 202
cultural, 9, 11, 23, 173, 182
economic, 123
intellectual, 9, 19, 21
of life, 59
political, 168
Soviet, 156
techno-scientific, 65, 77, 85, 124, 137, 168, 185
Sputnik, 150
Stalin, Joseph, 87, 125, 126, 140, 161
Stout, G. F., 94, 216
Strawson, P. F., 51
Structuralism, 15, 197, 208
Structure(s), 6, 8, 11, 15, 17, 19, 21, 23, 24, 28–31, 33, 35, 37, 45, 48–51, 53, 58, 60, 78, 83, 89, 92, 96, 97, 99, 101, 102, 106, 108, 115, 123,

124, 134, 174, 177, 187–89, 192–94, 196–98, 204
  Ancient mythical structures of good and evil, 174
  ancient structures of meaning, 187
  binary structures, 8, 124, 177
  cultural, 11, 15, 19, 187, 188, 192, 193
  of society, millennial structures of meaning, 197
  social, 8, 21, 187, 188, 193, 197
  structural conflict between intelligence and impulse, 147
  superstructure, 193
Subatomic, 98, 103, 105
  knowledge, 103
  level, 105
  matter, 103
  processes, 103
Substantialism, 110
Superpowers, 152
Superstructure, 193
Sweden, 172
Syndicalism, 70

Taboo of ego, 111
Tautologies, 4, 29–31, 48, 49, 54, 60, 61, 90, 106
Techno-scientific sphere, 65, 77, 85, 124, 137, 168, 184
Technologically-driven societies, 14
Technology, 1, 2, 4–6, 8, 11–14, 22–25, 31, 41, 60, 61, 65–68, 75–77, 79–81, 84, 91, 103, 124, 137, 138, 145, 149, 158, 161, 166–68, 175, 180, 183, 187, 194, 195, 198, 207–9, 215, 219
  mass destruction, 168
  military, 166, 180
  Modern, 145
  new, 161
Technoscientific expulsion of the sacred and the divine, 14
The New Republic, 150
The Observer, 149

The war to end all wars, 68, 69, 86
The Washington Post, 170
Theorem of Incompleteness, 62
Theory of judgement, 51, 205, 209
Thinking (techno-scientific), 13
Third Reich, 122
Thrasymachus, 8
Thunberg, Greta, 14
Tolstoy, Leo, 127
Totalitarian (regimes), 125, 191
Totem, 17, 21, 23, 159, 185, 189, 196
Trafalgar Square, 155
Trauma, 10, 69, 85, 127, 143, 152, 157, 158, 169, 180, 182, 201, 206, 208, 217
  cultural, 85, 127, 152, 157, 169, 182, 201, 206
  social, 10, 143
  sociologists, 69
Trinity College, 73, 75, 80, 133
Truman, Harry S. (President, Administration), 136, 140, 144
Truth, 17, 30, 34, 35, 40, 46, 52, 54–57, 67, 75, 91, 92, 97, 103, 109, 111, 117, 124, 132, 141, 143, 158, 161, 190, 191, 195, 198, 202, 212, 214
Tyndall, John, 12
Type theory

UCLA, 219, 229
UK, 71, 122, 147, 215
Union of Democratic Control, 71
United Kingdom, 70, 74, 133, 150, 172,
United States/US, 1, 10, 67, 70, 73, 74, 80, 83, 120, 121, 126, 128–31, 133–136, 138–40, 142–44, 146–49, 152, 153, 156, 160, 164–72, 174–83, 189, 191, 204, 209, 216
University of California, 129, 201, 204
Urbi et Orbi, 21
Utilitarian, 10, 33, 72
Utopia, 1, 4, 6, 19, 25, 62, 78, 82, 116, 121, 124, 125, 134, 186, 187, 195, 196, 198, 210

Valhalla, 19
Victorian, 39, 40, 68–70, 137, 205,
  Age, 40
  England, 39
  order, 68, 70
  orientalism, 137
  positivists and socialists, 69
Vienna Circle, 56
Viet Cong, 22, 169, 179, 183
Vietnam War, vii, ix, 1, 10, 22, 24, 83, 164–69, 173, 176–78, 181–83, 202, 206, 217
von Hartmann, K. R. E., 117

War, vii, ix, 1, 2, 5, 9, 10, 15, 22, 24, 29–31, 57, 59, 61, 62, 65–75, 77–87, 91, 109, 112, 116, 119–22, 124–30, 133–47, 150–53, 155–61, 163–83, 187, 188, 191, 196, 202–11, 213–17
  Cold War, 1, 9, 116, 121, 138, 141, 146, 150, 151, 157–59, 167, 169, 172, 173, 176, 179, 180, 203, 206, 209, 216, 217
  World War I/The Great War, vii, ix, 1, 5, 10, 22, 24, 29, 31, 59, 61, 62, 65–67, 69–72, 75, 77, 79, 80, 83–85, 91, 109, 112, 119, 124, 126, 127, 129, 134, 141, 167, 168, 177, 187, 207
  World War II, 10, 57, 69, 116, 129, 136, 143, 144, 166–68, 207, 208
Weber, Max, 8, 11, 13, 15, 217
Weierstrass, Karl, 38, 44, 49
Wells, H. G. 22, 69, 86, 135, 161, 203, 217
Whitehead, Alfred North, 4, 35, 43, 47, 66, 69
Wilson, Thomas Woodrow (President), 73
Wilsonian, 78
Winter Soldier Investigation, 176, 182
Wittgenstein, 19, 29, 30, 48, 51–55, 60, 111, 205, 207, 209, 210–212, 216, 217
World, vii, 1, 4–7, 9–14, 16, 20–24, 27–31, 35, 37–41, 46–48, 52, 54, 57–62, 65–73, 75, 77–80, 83–86, 90–93, 95–99, 101–10, 112–17, 119–22, 125–30, 132–41, 143–51, 153–55, 157–63, 165–71, 173–75, 177, 180, 183, 186, 187, 190, 192, 194–96, 204, 205, 207–12, 214–17, 219
  's greatest criminal, 169
  's ontological structure, 8
  abstract, 29
  actual, 29, 41, 46
  affairs, 129, 148, 212
  and prosperity, 5
  apocalypse, 165
  apocalyptic, 113
  authority, 138
  conflicts, 171
  control the, 60
  desacralization of the, 12
  description of the, 99
  disenchanted, 11
  disenchantment of the, 11, 13
  drama, 120
  empire, 119, 140
  empirical, 107, 109
  evil, 167, 169
  external, 24 52, 59, 90, 92, 93, 95–97, 99, 103, 105, 113–16, 190, 214, 215
  extramental, 95
  fabric of the, 113
  fame, 75, 158
  famous figures, 174
  First World War, 9, 120, 127, 157, 159, 110, 117
  full of evil and suffering, 28
  full of inevitable distortions, 23
  full-scale world war, 120
  fundamental furnishing of the, 91
  furniture of the, 24, 106
  Government, 69, 78, 80, 83, 121, 125, 127, 135, 138, 140, 141, 145, 148, 153, 158, 160, 167
  happier, 78
  happy, 186

history, 12
hope of the, 72
human, 13, 29
ideal, 27
industrialized, 196
leaders, 16, 22, 148, 153, 155, 171
logic of the, 30
material, 97, 102
menace to the, 77, 171
mental, 106
Microscopic, 107
modern, 113, 132, 161
news, 1
non-chaotic, 98
non-human, 29
objective image of the, 62
of abstractions, 29
of humans, 20
of love, 5
of our perceptions, 109
of perception, 104, 107
of physics, 104, 109
of Platonic essences, 38
of sense, 38
of shadows, 13
oppression, 180
outer, 40, 97, 110
outside, 109
peace and freedom, 84
peace, 84, 139, 143, 148–50, 157, 162, 173
physical, 106, 107
Platonic eternal, 29
politics, 128, 136, 150, 153, 155, 216
population, 154
populations, 86, 146
post-ideological, 195
power, 83
private, 98
problem of the external, 115

rationalization of the, 11
real, 61
saner, 68
save the, 73, 140, 143
savior, 149
sensible, 38
social, 6, 194
social, 6, 194
structure of the, 30, 31, 48
symbolic, 198
techno-scientific, 13
violence, 14
Western, 170
World Congress of Peace, 171
World Federation of Scientific Workers, 147, 148
World Wars, 10, 186
world-wide domination, 83
world-wide nuclear catastrophe, 146
worldly appearances, 49
worldly chaos, 28
worldly empirical appearances, 36
worldly experience, 62
worldly horrors, 29
worldly uncertainty, 34
worldview, 12, 23, 37, 53, 55, 57, 90, 96
worldwide decline of absolute poverty, 196
younger, 78
World Congress of Peace, 171
World War II, 10, 57, 69, 116, 129, 136, 143, 144, 166–168, 207, 208
Worldview, 12, 13, 23, 37, 53, 55, 57, 76, 90, 96, 191
Wright Mills, C., 188

Zeitgeist, 59
Zeno, 36, 39, 40, 44
Zoroastrian, 192